LIFE FORCE

The Creative Process in Man and in Nature

by

Charles R. Kelley

Cover and illustrations by Aschim Graphics, Vancouver, Washington

© Copyright 2004 Charles R. Kelley.
All rights reserved. No part of this publication may be reproduced, stored in a retrieval system, or transmitted, in any form or by any means, electronic, mechanical, photocopying, recording, or otherwise, without the written prior permission of the author.

Note for Librarians: a cataloguing record for this book that includes Dewey Decimal Classification and US Library of Congress numbers is available from the Library and Archives of Canada. The complete cataloguing record can be obtained from their online database at:
www.collectionscanada.ca/amicus/index-e.html
ISBN 1-4120-2338-6

TRAFFORD

Offices in Canada, USA, Ireland, UK and Spain

This book was published *on-demand* in cooperation with Trafford Publishing. On-demand publishing is a unique process and service of making a book available for retail sale to the public taking advantage of on-demand manufacturing and Internet marketing. On-demand publishing includes promotions, retail sales, manufacturing, order fulfilment, accounting and collecting royalties on behalf of the author.

Book sales for North America and international:
Trafford Publishing, 6E–2333 Government St.,
Victoria, BC v8t 4p4 CANADA
phone 250 383 6864 (toll-free 1 888 232 4444)
fax 250 383 6804; email to orders@trafford.com

Book sales in Europe:
Trafford Publishing (UK) Ltd., Enterprise House, Wistaston Road Business Centre,
Wistaston Road, Crewe, Cheshire cw2 7rp UNITED KINGDOM
phone 01270 251 396 (local rate 0845 230 9601)
facsimile 01270 254 983; orders.uk@trafford.com

Order online at:
www.trafford.com/robots/04-0166.html

10 9 8 7 6 5 4 3

Tree branches (leaves):
- autonomy
- radix process
- the quiet millions
- self and soul
- bioenergetics
- spiritual & scientific
- cosmic superimposition
- feeling and purpose
- what is dor?
- Big Bang?
- Ayn Rand
- Theodule Ribot
- heresy and cruelty
- steady-state cosmology
- character analysis
- radix block
- muscular armor
- Wilhelm Reich
- vitalism
- Freudian libido
- Karl Reichenbach
- odylic force
- Feng Shui
- Franz Mesmer

Tree roots:
- acupuncture
- astrology
- pantheism
- chi (ki)
- prahna
- primitive animism

ACKNOWLEDGEMENTS

I have been blessed with great teachers, colleagues, and friends. My intellectual debts are greatest to Wilhelm Reich, Ayn Rand, Hans Jonas and Thomas Szasz. They taught me extraordinary new and profound philosophical ideas. My professional debts are greatest to Margaret Corbett, the great vision teacher and teacher of teachers; William Thorburn, for nine years my steady and effective Reichian Therapist; and to Nathaniel Branden and Reuven Bar-Levav, the two most original and powerful group psychotherapists I have studied and worked with.

I have had many helpful suggestions on organizing and presenting the material of this book from advance readers that I recruited. I mention only a few major contributors. Alice Ladas, eminent sexologist and bioenergetic therapist, is a friend and colleague. She advised me on the presentation and contributed the preface to an early version of the manuscript. Lois Vincent, my sister, provided detailed thoughtful criticism of the entire manuscript. Allison Weicher, a professional editor and rewrite specialist, helped me make technical material more clear. Friend Jay Rubin, a former student and a longtime bodywork professional, provided many valuable technical suggestions about organizing the material.

At age 70 I asked my rheumatologist and primary care physician, Dr. Dejan Dordevich, if he could help me achieve ten or more years of clear mental functioning to wind up my work on the life force. This was in the face of my 40-year battle with rheumatoid arthritis and its many serious complications and strong drugs. My ten years are up, and here is their product. Thank you, my friend. Medical knowledge grows, and I even have hope of a few more mentally clear and emotionally satisfying years.

I must add one more name to those I have already acknowledged. My wife Erica has been my romantic partner and my professional colleague in virtually every important life enterprise I've engaged in for the thirty-six years we've been together. She has been editor-in-chief and producer of most of the volumes of material I write, and administrator of organizations we've created together. She was the first Radix apprentice/trainee, first teacher, first trainer of teachers, and Director of the European branch of Radix Personal Growth Work when it began spreading across America and Europe. All during these years together she has been, and remains, my best friend and the person whose company I most enjoy.

Thank you each and all. Your presence in my life has been my incredible good fortune.

Chuck Kelley
The Year 2004

TABLE OF CONTENTS

AUTHOR'S PREFACE xi

Chapter 1 INTRODUCING THE LIFE FORCE 1
    The Life Force: A Thumbnail History 3
    Chapter Notes 8

Chapter 2 SCIENCE AND RELIGION 11
    Dualism 13
    Science and the Rise of Scientism 15
    Spiritualistic Religion vs. Scientistic Science 16
    Scientism and Socialism 18
    Irrationality of Belief and the Cruelty Required to Sustain It ... 19
    The Quiet Millions 24
    Chapter Notes 28

Chapter 3 MUSCULAR ARMOR AND ORGONE ENERGY: 29
The Legacy of Wilhelm Reich 29
    Muscular Armor 32
    The Function of the Orgasm 33
    The Genital Character Myth 35
    Religion and the Reichians 38
    The Great Mystery: The Origin of Muscular Armor 40
    Hazards of Working with the Life Force 43
    The End of My Reichian Period 45
    Chapter Notes 46

Chapter 4 WHY HUMAN BEINGS ARE "ARMORED" 49
    Ayn Rand and the Armored Character 51
    Ribot and Voluntary Attention 55
    Armor as an Aid to Survival 58
    The Radix Block: The Positive Function of Muscular Armor ... 60
    Chapter Notes 62

Chapter 5 DE-ARMORING TO OPEN THE FEELINGS 65
    The Radix Block 70
    De-Armoring 72
    Chapter Notes 80

Chapter 6 PURPOSE 85
    Building the Radix Block..85
    Three Purposive Programs..88
    Purpose and Autonomy 102
    Chapter Notes 110

Chapter 7 THE RADIX DISCHARGE PROCESS 113
    The Orgasm Formula..114
    "Orgone Energy" and "Negative Entropy" 115
    Pulsation, Charge and Discharge 118
    Types or Forms of Respiratory Pulsation 120
    Radix Metabolism 121
    The Radix Process as Pulsation, Charge and Discharge................124
    The Second Discovery..126
    Creation and the First Two Laws of Thermodynamics 128
    Chapter Notes 130

Chapter 8 THE ALGEBRA OF RADIX DISCHARGE........................133
    Individuation..139
    The Radix Algebra of the Feelings 141
    "Venture" versus "Protect" Mode Emotions 144
    Applications of Radix Algebra 149
    Chapter Notes 151

Chapter 9 CENTERING, SOURCE, SELF AND SOUL.....................153
    Centering and Radix Source 155
    Radix Vision...161
    Self and Soul 166
    Chapter Notes 169

Chapter 10 SUPERIMPOSITION AND MATING.............................171
    Birth of a Cyclonic Storm..174
    About Superimposition 180
    Chapter Notes 182

Chapter 11 AUTONOMY..183
    Three Stages of Purpose 186
    The Individual Stage of Purpose 191
    The Autonomous Individual..195
    Autonomy and Selfishness 196
    Autonomy and Armor 197
    Autonomy and Government 199

The "Teaching" of Autonomy	201
Chapter Notes	202
Chapter 12 RADIX AND PHYSICAL SCIENCE	**203**
Before Radix Discharge	204
Radix Discharge	216
Energy and Antithesis	219
Motion and Time	220
Space and Radix Charge	223
Speculations About Space, Mass and Gravity	224
The "Weird" Science of the Life Force	229
Chapter Notes	235
APPENDIX A CLOUDBUSTING AND RAINMAKING	**241**
APPENDIX B CONVERGENT RADIX FORMS AND DEVICES: Pyramids, Cones, Funnels, Tubes and Spheres	**247**
APPENDIX C THE RADIX CHARGE OF LIVING PLACES	**249**
APPENDIX D DOR IN SPAIN	**255**
APPENDIX E DOR, DESERT, AND UNMATED RADIX CHARGE	**261**
APPENDIX F REICH'S ORGONE ACCUMULATOR (ORAC) and the Orgone Accumulator Paradox	**273**
APPENDIX G SHELDRAKE AND MORPHIC RESONANCE	**279**
APPENDIX H LANDMARKS IN THE EVOLUTION OF THE LIFE FORCE CONCEPT	**285**
BIBLIOGRAPHY	**295**
INDEX	**301**

AUTHOR'S PREFACE

This is a chronicle of adventures with the life force. New discoveries about the nature and properties of this force confirm what old civilizations like those of India and of China have taught for millennia. Other students have called the life force by various names, including *life energy, bioenergy, chi, spirit, soul*. Then there is Emerson's *oversoul*, my own *radix*, the pantheist's *god*, and the deist's God.

The life force can become the central concept in human knowledge. It sits astride the great divisions in knowledge that split mind and body in the individual, self and other in relationships, religion and science in human society. Knowing the nature and properties of the life force makes it possible to reconcile these divisions. First, however, long-cherished illusions of both religion and science must be given up. The greatest of these illusions is the belief that religion in itself or science in itself, one or the other, can provide an adequate explanation of the deeper nature of things.

The life force antedates biological life, which developed from it. My teacher, Wilhelm Reich, saw the life force as a "strictly physical" energy, the most basic form. In this belief he was in error, and in these pages I explain why.

We are now at a special, dangerous and wonderful turning point in the evolution of human knowledge. History shows us to be in a period in the spiraling growth of knowledge dominated by science, so the scientific branch of knowledge prevails in human institutions of knowledge today. A few brief centuries ago the exact opposite was the case, and orthodox religion claimed a monopoly on human knowledge. Now more and more people are also questioning science's claim to represent what is truly true in human knowledge. As I see it, throwing off religious claims of "truth" opened the possibility that scientific claims to truth were equally suspect, and that scientific authority, like religious authority, should be examined with skepticism. The point is then to keep looking and listening to both religious and scientific points of view, reserving the right to doubt either or both. From that standpoint one can continue looking as new ideas and discoveries, whether spiritual, scientific or embracing elements of both, are made known.

This book is born of this attitude. Over the years I have adopted the idea that the life force **is** what is called "God." That gradually triumphed in my mind over the idea that the life force was the agency through which "God" as a superintelligence has created and is creating the universe. I now experience myself, not as an agent but as an integral and inseparable part of God. God explores and learns to create the universe through me, and through you. At root we are all of us, whether we know it or not, only different parts of the same being. To know that being, don't look out to the external universe, but look inward toward the source.

I became a psychologist, not a clinical psychologist but a body-oriented applied experimental psychologist, with a focus on consciousness in its many forms. I had a strong interest in science and philosophy and became heavily schooled in sub-topics of psychology: perception, memory, emotion, the will, thinking, human performance, sexology, physiological psychology, character and personality, and personal growth. My primary area of expertise, individual human consciousness, involves the functioning of the life force in a person's body and its application to the various aspects of psychology. My hungry interest in physical science and the life force had to become secondary. It is concentrated into the last chapter and the Appendix. I hope that readers with a primary interest in the application of knowledge of the life force to physical science will study this last chapter and the Appendices carefully.

LIFE FORCE is a fascinating though incomplete story. I lift a phrase from the poet, Genevieve Taggard, as I say of my book, I have almost told you breathless things.

Chuck Kelley
Vancouver, WA
2004

Chapter 1

INTRODUCING THE LIFE FORCE

Before written history early humans saw all nature as alive, as having mind and soul and the power it brings. Sun moon and stars, atmosphere, oceans, rivers lakes and streams, storms winds and clouds, the earth itself, with its quakes and volcanoes, all were accorded their own forms or variety of consciousness. We modern humans can sometimes capture the mood of the primitive living close to nature. Think of the tension one feels before a storm, and the relief that comes when the storm arrives. If we are safe we can exult in the fury of the storm. It relieves the tension at the pit of the stomach. When it passes we breathe fully again. What if, like the primitive, we thought the storm had a kind of awareness, a subjective side of its nature, very different from our own?

Remember also softer times, like being outside on a peaceful summer evening at some special place in the mountains, on the desert, or sailing the ocean. The sun sinks over the western horizon, a disappearing yellow ball. The reds and yellows of sunset fade gradually to dim orange, then to the purples of twilight. The purples and blues of the sky slowly change to grays and blacks. A bright "star" appears in the west, the planet Venus. Dimmer true stars slowly follow. As night comes the heavens fill with stars.

Turning our back to the vanished glow of sunset and the now dark western sky, we face increasing light that was behind us. The moon is beginning to rise in the east. Soon it is big, round, quiet and beautiful, illuminating the eastern sky. Its light washes out nearby stars.

Away from the moon, the dark space between the stars takes up most of the area of the sky. It looks full and active, that space, not empty and dead. The sky forms a living ocean around earth, sun, moon and stars which are just highlights in a living universe into which we can blend. We too are highlights in this universe, highlights of a different kind. The universe nurtures many many forms and ways of being. Only one of them is ours.

The living ocean of sky in the heavens around us and within us is the subject of this book. This ocean is the cosmic medium, the life force, the substratum of existence from which all things, ourselves included, arise and will each return. There are secrets to be told about the cosmic force -- call it life force or radix -- and about the creative process by which people and things develop from it. It is an understatement to say that this process is not well understood. It involves central mysteries of existence: In reverse order these are: 1) the evolution of conscious intelligent self-aware and self-directed human beings and the knowledge they have produced; 2) the (prior) development of mind in its association with organic life; and, before that, 3) the creation of the "non-living" physical world, which may have forms with other kinds of consciousness than that of living animals, ourselves included.

The reverse order of these three areas of mystery has this reason. Experience has shown that in studying the life force the student should begin with the most alive and vivid in the here and now, present time experience of our lives. Then we can move gradually back as needed, and only as needed, to older earlier stages of consciousness from which today's experiences have evolved.

LIFE FORCE is a book about the present, with new discoveries that advance knowledge of the life force and open future possibilities for its students. With few exceptions, the material on these pages concerns events and discoveries that took place in my lifetime. In many of these I was an active participant and, when I was, I share my experience from a personal perspective.

The life force is an extraordinary topic, with ramifications in many directions. My teacher, Wilhelm Reich, used to refer to this as the "too muchness" of the subject matter. To help him keep on track in his writing and not go too far afield in the fascinating side topics and byways of the subject, he focused consciously on his unifying theme of "the function of the orgasm," which runs through all his work. By holding to this theme he became able to write about character analysis and psychotherapy, biology, biogenesis, biophysics and medicine, weather and atmospheric processes, cosmology and cosmogeny, etc. from the limited vantage point of his unifying theme. It kept him from getting lost in the many particulars of these topics and areas of application.[1]

My own work with the life force made me confront the same problem Reich had met. It went in too many directions, opened too many important avenues of inquiry, seemed to solve too many scientific problems. Yes, it was "too much." To keep my own work on track and within reasonable limits, I consciously chose the life force itself as my own unifying theme. I endeavor to make each chapter concerned with the life force, -- its nature, its properties and some of its present and potential applications.

The Life Force: A Thumbnail History[2]

The life force concept has been with us for 5000 years. At the dawn of written history in Babylonia, when science and religion were one, all nature was seen as alive. Animating nature, giving it its living qualities, was the life force as seen by early man. Astrology/astronomy, alchemy/chemistry, and a belief in many gods ruled human knowledge.

Babylonian knowledge and lore spread through and out from the middle-east, west to Egypt, northwest to Greece, and east to India and China, merging into the already advanced early civilizations in these places. Almost all of them had something like a life force concept, or a related god or gods-in-nature concept, or both. Astrological beliefs were widespread among the advanced early civilizations. The astrological beliefs in the influence of the stars and planets on earthly events and human fate needed a medium to convey the influence from its heavenly source to its target. That medium, stated or unstated, is that aspect of nature I call "the life force."[3]

LIFE FORCE

An early elaboration of the life force concept, with roots extending 2000 years before Christ, occurred in India, with the Vedic and Hindu idea of the *prana*. The prana is defined as the principle or the breath of life. Some branches of Hinduism incorporate an idea of prana that is quite similar in its properties to the life force concept that is developed on the pages of this book.

The old Chinese concept of the life force is called the *chi* or *ki*, a widely used term in Chinese martial arts such as akido and t'ai chi, disciplines popular in western countries today.[4] (Chi is here pronounced "chee" and not "kie" like the Greek letter of the same spelling.) The chi is a widely used explanatory concept, not only in body oriented practices like t'ai chi and acupuncture, but much more universally, as a natural force in the physical environment. Start with acupuncture and the body. The chi is believed to flow in channels in the body referred to as meridians. In medical acupuncture meridians are tapped into at acupuncture points along the body's meridians to provide anesthesia for surgeries, and as treatments for disease in traditional Chinese medicine. Acupuncturists have complex maps of the channels of the body carrying the chi, and theories of their function in health and disease.[5]

The Chinese also see the chi as a free force in space outside the body, an integral and important aspect of the environment, flowing here, blocked by natural or man-built structures there, but manipulable by those having the know-how. Feng Shui, the Chinese "art of placement," popular in architecture and the design of spaces in America today, is a discipline for using techniques to manipulate and work in harmony with the chi in nature in both indoor and outdoor environments.[6]

In the West, other life force concepts grew independently. They were probably rooted, consciously or unconsciously, in pre-Christian pantheistic "god-in-nature" beliefs and practices. In the mid-18th century, Dr. Franz Anton Mesmer, a body-oriented medical psychologist, far ahead of his time, dealt with what he called *animal magnetism* in the human body.[7] He saw animal magnetism as a real, demonstrable and controllable natural force, operating both inside and outside the body. He developed techniques and devices for its use, and demonstrated these across Europe. He was denounced by the scientific orthodoxy of his time.

A century after Mesmer in 19th century Germany, Karl von Reichenbach, an organic chemist of note, discovered and wrote of the *odyl*, or *odic force*, another life force concept.[8] He did not acknowledge a connection between his work with the odic force and Mesmer's work with animal magnetism a century earlier. Applications of his work are the use of magnets and crystals in alternative medicine, practiced to this day.

Vitalism is a 19th and early 20th century school of philosophy incorporating an intangible vital force as a central element.[9] The French vitalistic philosopher Henri Bergson called the life force the *elan vital*. Vitalistic biologist Hans Driesch named it the *entelechy*. Mechanistic western physical science in the seventeenth through nineteenth centuries embraced certain of the essential qualities of the life force in the concept of the ether, while spiritually oriented human beings have embraced other essential qualities of it in the concept of God. Sigmund Freud observed the functioning of the life force in human emotions and termed it *libido*. William MacDougall, the great British-American psychologist of the 1920s, labeled it *hormic energy*. His protégé J.B. Rhine became world famous for his studies of ESP (extra sensory perception) and while at Duke University developed an aspect of MacDougall's model. Among other twentieth century proponents of the concept are Doctors Charles Littlefield and his *vital magnetism* and George Starr White and his *cosmo-electric energy*. Freud's student Wilhelm Reich chose for the life force the name *orgone energy*. His monumental work on the subject occupies our third chapter.

Like Reichenbach, most discoverers were unaware that a predecessor had made what was in essence the same discovery years or centuries ahead of them. This was easy to do because each time the discovery was made it was from a different direction, and from a point of view that was of necessity partial and incomplete. Only in the maturity of their separate discoveries is it clear, for example, that Mesmer, Reichenbach and Reich are talking about the same thing and that the later men might have employed the same or similar terminology.

There have been other reasons for deliberately employing new terminology, however. Knowledge of the life force process is threatening to a certain type of character structure, and there is a strong tendency to try to destroy such knowledge whenever and wherever it appears. This is done by discrediting the discoverer and discovery without really examining what has been found. The most effective weapons are distortion, ridicule and contempt. The "new" concepts are unjustifiably but effectively associated with notions of charlatanism, quackery and pseudo-science. Scientists and scholars, overconscious as they are of intellectual respectability, then shy away from the new knowledge as if it were poison. Thus the concepts are effectively destroyed before they gain a foothold in the intellectual community. The three giants in the history of work with the life force in the West, Mesmer, Reichenbach and Reich, were each discredited in this way, even though they worked in different countries and were separated from one another by a century of time. The life force has been discovered, named and re-named, misunderstood, shunted aside, distorted, ridiculed, and erased from the history of reputable western science again and again, only to crop up anew in someone else's work at another time and place.

Today the life force concept has aroused interest and gained new respect in the West. A change in attitude is taking place. The "far-out" theories and data of "new age" scientists are being met with skepticism, as new and radical ideas should be, but with more openness and less pre-judgmental hostility than was the case even a few decades ago. Science is moving so fast, ideas and news of data requiring new and often strange theory happen in orthodox as well as fringe science. The two are not as far apart as they once were.

My own reasons were primarily scientific for coining yet another term for the life force. I chose the *radix* because it means "root, or primary cause." This not only distinguishes it from prior interpretations of what the life force is, but also represents more accurately what I believe the life force to be – the creative force in nature. The radix process is the process by which the natural world, the only reality, originated and continues to originate both in its subjective and objective aspects. Physical and mental, material and spiritual, come into existence together as a result of the same process.

Since I had immersed myself in Wilhelm Reich's work, I used his terminology until eight years after his death. Reich had originally employed the term *bioelectricity* for the life force, in accord with the physicist's belief in electromagnetic phenomena as the core events in nature. He moved to increasingly general terms, *bioenergy* and finally *orgone energy* when it became clear that the phenomena he worked with were more than electrical in their fundamental nature. But by calling it "energy," Reich showed his inclination to reduce both subjective and objective phenomena to the concepts of physical science. This is the mechanistic error. The term "energy" has a precise well-defined meaning to the physical scientist, and it must fit into the scientific concept of the nature and properties of energy. This, I discovered, the life force does not do.

Just as the mechanist tries to fit the life force into the physicist's domain, so the mystic interprets the life force as something supernatural. One may ask: If the radix process is the creative process in nature, isn't it just another name for God? Indeed, the mystical character psychologizes the process of creation, and so makes it intangible and unreal, out of the reach of direct experience and natural observation, experimentation and control. A popular concept is the personification of the life force as a being who has omniscient, omnipotent and other extra-natural powers.

To study the life force we need to be free of preconceptions imposed by the views of either academic science or of religion. There is something of value to retain from both domains. From religion we need the feeling of wonder, from science the curiosity of the mind; from religion the cosmic sense of awe at this process which produces the deepest in us and in this world we are part of; from science the determination to explore, to experiment and measure, to touch, to fathom the mystery of the radix by making it comprehensible to the reasoning mind.

Chapter Notes

[1] Reich, Wilhelm, 1942, THE FUNCTION OF THE ORGASM (VOL. 1, THE DISCOVERY OF THE ORGONE). New York: Orgone Institute Press. Subsequently reprinted by Farrar, Straus & Cudahy, New York.

_____, 1948, THE CANCER BIOPATHY (VOL. 2, THE DISCOVERY OF THE ORGONE). New York: Orgone Institute Press.

_____, 1949, ETHER GOD AND DEVIL. Orgone Institute Press. Reprinted by Farrar, Straus & Giroux, 1973.

_____, 1951, COSMIC SUPERIMPOSITION. New York: Orgone Institute Press. Reissued by Farrar, Straus & Giroux, 1973.

[2] See Appendix H for more detailed annotated landmarks in the evolution of the life force concept.

[3] Eysenck, H.J. and Nins, D.K.B., 1982. ASTROLOGY: SCIENCE OR SUPERSTITION. New York: Penguin Books.

[4] Allison, Nancy (Ed.) 1999, THE ILLUSTRATED ENCYCLOPEDIA OF BODY-MIND DISCIPLINES. New York: Rosen Publishing Group.

[5] Mann, Felix M.B., 1962, 1973. ACUPUNCTURE: THE ANCIENT CHINESE ART OF HEALING AND HOW IT WORKS SCIENTIFICALLY. New York: Random House. Reprinted by Vintage Books.

Wallnöfer, Heinrich and Von Rottauscher, Anna. (1965) CHINESE FOLK MEDICINE AND ACUPUNCTURE. New York: Bell Publishing Co.

[6] Lin, Henry B., 2000. THE ART AND SCIENCE OF FENG SHUI. St. Paul, Minnesota: Llewellen Publications.

[7] Mesmer, F.A. (1957) MEMOIR. Mount Vernon, N.Y.: The Eden Press. Translated, and with a preface by Jerome Eden. The Memoir was first

published in France in 1799. Eden's translation is out of print. A good short article relating Mesmer's work to Reich's is:

Shapiro, Mark. "Mesmer, Reich and the Living Process." *The Creative Process,* Vol. IV No. 2, June 1965, pp. 64-71. Vancouver, WA: K/R Publications.

[8] Reichenbach, Charles Von (1851) PHYSICO-PHYSIOLOGICAL RESEARCHES. London: Hippolyte Bailliere.

Starz, Kenneth (1963) "The Researches of Karl (Charles) Von Reichenbach," *The Creative Process,* Part 1. Vol. III No. 1, August 1963, pp. 25-33; Part 2, Vol. III No. 2, March 1964, pp. 67-77; Part 3, Vol. IV No. 2, June 1965, pp. 91-103. Vancouver, WA: K/R Publications.

[9] The work of Bergson, Dreisch, MacDougall, Freud, and Rhine are readily available in good libraries. Readers are advised to read works by the originators in this area. Most of the secondary sources are very poor.

LIFE FORCE

Chapter 2

SCIENCE AND RELIGION

Hans Jonas wrote:[1]

"When man first began to interpret the nature of things -- and this he did when he began to be man -- life was to him everywhere, and being the same as being alive. Animism was the widespread expression of this stage....Bare matter, that is, truly inanimate, "dead" matter, was yet to be discovered -- as indeed its concept, so familiar to us, is anything but obvious. That the world is alive is really the most natural view....

In such a world-view, the riddle confronting man is death;....To the extent that life is accepted as the primary state of things, death looms as the disturbing mystery.... Before there was wonder at the miracle of life, there was wonder about death and what it might mean. If life is the natural and comprehensible thing, death -- its apparent negation -- is a thing unnatural and cannot be truly real.... As early man's practice is embodied in his tools, so his thought is embodied in his tombs which acknowledge and negate death at the same time.

Modern thought which began with the Renaissance is placed in exactly the opposite theoretic situation. Death is the natural thing, life the problem. The lifeless has become the knowable par excellence and is for that reason also considered the true and only foundation of reality. It is the "natural" as well as the original state of things.... Nonlife is the rule, life the puzzling exception in physical existence.

Accordingly, it is the existence of life within a mechanical universe which now calls for an explanation, and explanation has to be in terms of the lifeless....That there is life at all, and how such a thing is possible in a world of mere matter, is now the problem posed to thought."

Today, in the world as depicted by science, life has all but disappeared from the universe. Untold billions of galaxies of stars, distributed in space in uneven clumps, comprise a visible universe of bright disks or spirals. There is an exceedingly thin soup of dark matter distributed between, and as rings encircling, stars and galaxies. Each galaxy is itself composed of hundreds of millions of spheres of incandescent matter, the stars. Until very recently, scientific cosmology believed that many billions of years ago all of the content of the universe was clumped together in a tiny tight fantastically heavy hot ball. The ball exploded in the mother of all explosions, "the big bang," to begin the universe. The force of the "big bang" propelled the content of the universe apart until, over billions of years, local forces came to form the local structures making up our expanding universe. Near the edge of one spiral galaxy in this expanding universe, an average star (a class B dwarf), was kept incandescent like other stars by hydrogen fusion. Circling it at various distances for hundreds of millions of years have been nine smaller and cooler round chunks of matter, a planetary system. Eons ago on the third planet out from this star, in a lightening-struck corner of a sun-bathed sea, an astounding coincidence brought something new and strange into the universe: a cell that reproduced itself. In time such one-celled creatures filled the sea. They mutated, evolved, developed more complex forms, for some two and a half billion years; and here we are! Such is the scientistic world-view and mythology of this time. The greatest of mysteries to this world-view is life, or the nature of the non-dead.

Between the animistic dawn of history and modern myths of scientism yet another spirit and mythology grew and held sway, and rules millions today. Its main concern is death and its defeat. One version of this myth tells us creation is the work of a superbeing, who at the dawn of history said, "Let there be light," and there was light; and in six days created the universe and everything in it, including the first human beings, Adam and Eve. These two became sinful by learning to know good and evil, and in punishment were cast out of paradise. They founded the human race, and their original sin taints all their descendants, i.e., all human beings.

To redeem these descendants, a few thousand years later the superbeing sent his son to earth to provide salvation and immortality to human beings. One only had to believe and accept the son as "the savior" and the believer would not die, but would have everlasting life, thereby defeating death. This is the spirit and mythology of Judeo-Christianity, probably the most powerful and influential belief system in human history.

Primitive people at the dawn of history recognized no split between religion and science. To them, life existed everywhere and filled everything. The conscious sun and seeing stars watched over the earth, where winds, clouds, storms, trees, flowers, and animals and their spirits lived. Medicine men and women, priests and priestesses gathered mixtures of facts and myths in an effort to deal with all this life, and passed the knowledge down through the generations. A ring around the moon meant that rain would come. Cessation of menstruation meant pregnancy. A bad storm meant a god was angry, and should be propitiated. The leaves of a certain plant could form a healing poultice for a wound. A dream of flying foretold good fortune and power to the dreamer. A certain dance could bring on rain. On and on, scores of facts and myths were remembered, retold, and incorporated into the beliefs of a tribe or a people. Science and religion were part and parcel of a single whole.

Dualism

For primitive animistic peoples, spiritual guidance, healing, and scientific information all came from the same persons. This didn't change until the unitary animistic view split apart, and dualistic belief developed. The split developed around death, the great exception to living nature. As primitive tribes developed into early civilizations, death, the great mystery, occupied more and more human attention. Tremendous effort and wealth went into death: for tombs, funeral artifacts, burial grounds, and ceremonies for the dead. The beautiful Imperial Tombs of China traveling exhibit of artifacts from ancient Chinese tombs illustrates the point, as do the

LIFE FORCE

greatest buildings surviving from early civilizations, which are pyramids and other tombs.

The belief in life was strong enough to discount the reality and nature of dead bodies. The consciousness of a person who died could be thought to continue somehow in an existence akin to the life we experience in dreams. In dreams it seems we leave our sleeping bodies to live and move about in some other reality, in a different way than when we are awake. This collective experience supported the spiritualistic idea of life after death and the separation of consciousness and spirit, the animating principle, from the physical body.

And thus humanity created the myth of survival of the individual soul after death. It attempts to circumvent death even in the face of the finality of death and the decay of the dead body, and in spite of the contradiction to the myth presented by every real death. With the survival myth, systematic unreality entered religion, and the great spiritualistic distortion of human knowledge began.

I use the term "spiritualistic" to differentiate the distorted point of view from "spiritual" which, as I use the term, does not imply distortion.[2] Spiritualistic distortions include irrational beliefs about the spiritual nature of things, e.g., belief in the supernatural, the miraculous, and revealed truth. But it is not a distortion to believe we have a spiritual as well as a physical nature, and that there are great mysteries as yet beyond our ken. Survival myths of life beyond the grave are unrealistic, spiritualistic rather than spiritual.

Believing one unreality opened the door to believing many others. After the myth of survival of the individual soul after death came other unrealities: stories of heaven and hell, angels and devils, miracles and curses, and of a god or gods in the form of one or more superpersons watching over us from an unseen world. Thus developed the mass irrationality that is spiritualistic religion. If only one or two people believed it we would recognize it as insane, but spiritualistic thought affects entire populations. Most, but by no means all, religion is spiritualistic. Spiritualistic religion is rooted in myth and fable, in "revealed" texts of allegedly divine origin, in miracles and in the belief that we have a supernatural afterlife. Hundreds of millions grow up being taught a religious belief system that contradicts reality. It is a socially accepted form of psychosis.

Science and the Rise of Scientism

A serious challenge to religion, however, began in the renaissance and expanded with the enlightenment. It is associated with the rise of technology and science. Alongside spiritualistic religion and its claim to one's soul grew the secular fields of endeavor dealing with daily life on this earth. These included farming and agriculture, building and architecture, transportation and trade, industry and manufacture, government and law, weaponry and the military, and medicine, to name but a few. In each one, knowledge and techniques grew and expanded in support of the given field. These fed the growth of science and technology. In all these fields the development, systematizing, storing, and transmission of knowledge and techniques became a central endeavor. It gave rise to widening literacy, libraries, printing, and schools dealing with secular as well as religious subject matter.

There are exceptions, but it is generally true that religion retained its sway over the central features of the living. Religion ruled over mind, soul, spirit, beauty, and the individual's relation to god or to the transpersonal in nature. Gradually technology and science began to develop, and to take over more and more knowledge of the external physical world. With the renaissance, and then the enlightenment, secular knowledge apart from religion grew rapidly. It began to pose a challenge to established spiritualistic religion. As we know, the conflict is alive today.

At the dawn of the history of knowledge, then, religion claimed the entire realm of knowledge as its own. Science was still an interloper. In the pre-Christian west, pagan religion, with its animism, nature worship, and polytheistic myths, provided a base for the growth of science when stable government and long periods of peace allowed it. Babylonians followed by the ancient Greeks had given a foretaste of what human beings left free to think could achieve in philosophy, mathematics, physical science, and the arts. Although the knowledge created by the Greeks persisted, the societal process by which that knowledge had been created was lost when the Greeks fell to the Roman Empire, and the Christian revolution (more accurately, the Judeo-Christian revolution) swept over Rome and the rest of the west.

But the pressure of new developments, knowledge, and discoveries grew, even as spiritualistic religion fought it ruthlessly. "Unbelievers," including scientists whose discoveries contradicted biblical "divine truth," were branded heretics and persecuted by or for the church. For examples, Galileo faced torture and was forced to live out his life under house arrest and Bruno was burned at the stake for their scientific beliefs. Nevertheless, scientific and technological advances continued to grow and gain strength.

Gradually, though, an accommodation began that gave birth to "scientism," the opposite-appearing twin of spiritualism. Science grew, but with the exclusion of mind and spirit, reflecting a scientistic distortion of knowledge. Since spiritualistic religion had already preempted mind, soul, and spirit as its realm, scientistic science had to gain its foothold dealing with physical nature. As science grew and developed in its permitted area, it came to provide a kind of symmetry to spiritualistic religion. The focus on physical nature in scientism balanced the focus on mind, soul, and spirit of spiritualism.

Spiritualistic Religion vs. Scientistic Science

Spiritualistic religion grew to concern itself mostly with the subjective, scientistic science with the objective in nature. This division of interest was a good arrangement in many respects. However, subjective and objective nature are different aspects of reality, and not entirely parallel. The differences are important.

Subjective nature, consciousness, takes place in the living, spontaneously moving, feeling and thinking individual, and depends on the physical integrity of a properly functioning body to sustain it. Death brings an end to individual consciousness, but not to the physical material that comprises the body. The dead body is real, while individual consciousness after death of the body is a ghost, a spirit, a fantasy. This is where the symmetry between scientism and spiritualism breaks down. The realm left by religion to the scientist deals with a part of reality, the reality of dead inanimate matter, i.e., of the physical universe. The corresponding realm left to religion, human consciousness without the body, deals with no reality at all, but only religious myths and fantasies.

As a consequence, science is left with a much stronger position than religion from the standpoint of efficacy. The spiritualist is fundamentally impotent to change physical reality. Religious myths, wishful thinking, and faith in the miraculous change nothing in the world except as they influence others to act. The deterministic causality of the scientist corresponds to an important reality, however: that of inanimate physical nature. The laws of the physical sciences -- mechanics, thermodynamics, electricity, chemistry -- work. They apply to real events, and knowledge of them has made possible humanity's ability to control physical nature. The magical causality of spiritualistic religion corresponds to no external reality at all, though, and results in no control over that reality. Blessings, curses, charms, and prayers for divine intercession do not impact the physical world; dams, bridges, and internal combustion engines do. Scientistic science grew apace.

The realm of scientistic physical science tried to take in the rest of the domain once ruled by animism, i.e., life, consciousness, mind and their place in nature. The realm left to life under the impact of the scientistic distortion of knowledge shrank to an almost insignificant corner of the real physical world.

Scientistic science and spiritualistic religion are inherently unequal forces competing over the centuries for our minds. Dealing as it does with an important though partial aspect of reality, science has had the virtue of being able to learn, develop, and advance over the centuries. And advance it has, of course, enormously, though only with respect to physical processes and mechanical aspects of life. There has been no corresponding scientific advance in dealing with spiritual and conscious processes, with mind, spirit, esthetics, ethics. They, too, are real and in need of understanding! But the magical causality of spiritualistic religion deals with no reality and so has made no advance. Fashions in spiritualistic thought change, but it is today in essence just what it was 2,000 years ago. Spiritualists often even make a virtue of the unchanging quality of their beliefs. But the sad truth is that because of spiritualistic belief, humanity has made only slight progress over the centuries in understanding the spiritual and the subjective. Soul, spirit, consciousness, mind, beauty, love and their place in life remain an unfathomed mystery to scientistic thought.

Scientism and Socialism

In the 19th and 20th centuries, thoughtful searching people, aware of the irrationalities and horrors of spiritualistic religion, turned in droves to scientism to produce a better world. Officially anti-religious socialist regimes gained power over country after country, and anti-religious Marxist thought enjoyed (and continues to enjoy) a vogue among Western intellectuals. But by rejecting all religion, socialism itself became a quasi-religious irrational belief system about the fundamental nature of humanity. The role of soul, spirit, ethics, beauty was distorted, minimized, or ruled out of human life. Based on the irrationality of scientism, socialism has degenerated into ugliness and horror in every country in which it has been seriously tried.

Those in search of a reasonable alternative to the twin irrationalities of scientistic science and spiritualistic religion are hard pressed indeed. What went into creating these great errors gives us an idea of the direction to be followed, and of the difficult long-range nature of the task of helping society recover.

Science and Religion

Irrationality of Belief and the Cruelty Required to Sustain It

The belief system underlying spiritualistic, as opposed to spiritual, religion is, of course, only one feature of a spiritualistic church or denomination. All spiritualistic religion is irrational in important elements of belief and dogma. That is the nature of spiritualistic belief, the way it has evolved over the millenia. Irrationality and violence against dissenters have been major features of the system. This irrationality forms a guarding function protecting against deeper knowledge of the life force, the creative process or, if one prefers, God.

Once people give up their rationality to the point that they accept an irrational belief or dogma, their reason is broached. Those who accept the truth of one miracle, one religious myth of the supernatural, no longer see that the world operates according to universal laws of nature. Then there can just as well be two, ten, or a thousand exceptions to nature's laws. Rationality has been abandoned, and the door opened to more extreme and often more cruel irrationalities. The irrationalities are important because they are irrational. Accepting irrationality means giving up reason for faith, and faith is the cornerstone of spiritualistic religion. Many of the rituals and special practices of spiritualistic religion are built around its more far-fetched beliefs. It is necessary to ask why.

Those who subscribe to irrational beliefs in the name of religion tend to become sensitive and aggressively protective of them, especially when they hold power in a society. Reich pointed out that the more irrational a group's belief system, the more cruelty and violence are required to maintain it. The cruelty and violence create "respect," or more accurately pseudo-respect, a silence born of fear.

In countries ruled by spiritualistic religious "fundamentalism," this protection of irrational beliefs often escalates to killing those who express disbelief. The worst crime in such societies is exposing its irrationalities of belief. Such exposure is condemned as heresy or blasphemy. The source of the cruelty directed against the Jews by fundamentalist Christians across the centuries, the pogroms, inquisitions, and cruel discriminations, is that Jewish religious doctrine denies the central irrational belief of spiritualistic Christianity, the divinity of Christ. Witness the same cruelty to "unbelievers" issuing from primitive Islamic fundamentalist societies today when irrational Islamic beliefs and practices are questioned.

The principle applies as well to scientistic socialist irrationality. Consider the cruelty and horror of socialist prison states, with their suppression of dissenting speech and writing, the "brain-washing" indoctrination groups, the hordes of residents trying to escape the borders lined with walls or barbed wire and/or patrolled by armed guards, and the gulags for dissenters who are caught questioning or expressing disbelief in the system. Exposure of the irrationalities of the beliefs that underlie a system, either scientistic socialism or spiritualistic theocracy, mobilizes the anxieties that fuel militant "true believers," and galvanizes them to violence against the source of the exposure.

Cruelty and violence against dissent characterizes all countries governed by irrational beliefs, then. It is the government-fostered irrationality that creates the essential difference between the spiritual and the spiritualistic and between the scientific and the scientistic systems of belief.

Very early in the 20th century scientistic socialism could be regarded as a reasonable, potentially benevolent, untried system of belief. Since then it has been tried in country after country, with results ranging from dismal repeated failures in democratic countries to the extremes of horror in those countries where socialism is complete. It can be regarded as reasonable or benevolent no longer.

Unfortunately, major criticisms of the beliefs of spiritualistic religion and of scientistic socialism come mostly from each other, from the opposed belief system, not from the rational center. Active militant support of their own irrational beliefs and criticism of opposing irrational beliefs is often a substitute for thought when either spiritualism or scientism is involved.

The drive toward unity of knowledge is universal. Existence has the two realms, subjective and objective, but they are aspects of one underlying reality. Nature must at the deepest level be unitary. But how do the two realms or aspects fit together in the reality they are both part of?

Spiritualism tries to achieve unity at the expense of objective physical reality, which is made derivative and secondary in consequence. This gave impetus to the rise of scientism to deal with physical reality, and scientism was, in consequence, split off from the reality of subjective experience, of spirit, mind, and consciousness. This is the point where the wholeness of knowledge was split in two. Spiritualism and scientism became antithetical intellectual forces that have dominated human history to the present time. Table 1 gives a systematic comparison of them.

Table 1
A Comparison of Spiritualistic vs. Scientistic Distortions of Thought:[3]

Spiritualistic Religion	Scientistic Science
Over-focus on consciousness, mind, spirit, subjective nature. "Mind is primary."	Over-focus on physical world, body, energy, objective nature. "Energy is primary."
Belief that objective nature arises from subjective processes; mind creates energy.	Belief that subjective nature arises from objective processes; energy creates mind.
Minimizes and even scorns the body and its physical processes.	Minimizes and even scorns consciousness and spirit and the role they play in behavior.
Belief that life arose by plan from a "supermind" -- the mind of God.	Belief that life arose as a consequence of accidental purposeless physical processes.
Philosophy of idealistic monism (subjective idealism).	Philosophy of materialistic monism (mechanism in physics, reductionism in biology, behaviorism in psychology).
Belief that the deepest truths are revelations by God, conveyed through special messengers, and written into sacred texts.	Belief that the deepest truths are the discoveries of scientists.
Belief in magical causality through suspension of natural law by divine intervention, e.g., miracles, response to prayers. blessings.	Belief in scientific causality made up entirely of deterministic and chance physical processes.
Good comes from living according to God's supernaturally revealed laws; evil comes from disobeying them.	Since man has no free will there is no good and evil in the religious sense, only ignorance and illness.
The essence of a person is a disembodied soul, that which lives after death.	The essence of a person is physical processes that sustain and further his life.

Science and Religion

These are some of the essentials of the two opposed belief systems I call spiritualism and scientism. Spiritualism means belief in revealed truth, life after death, faith above reason, miracles, divine texts, revealed truth, the primacy of consciousness, mind, and spirit. Scientism means belief in the primacy of the physical, of the laws of "dead" matter, of deterministic physical causality. It means materialism, reductionism, behaviorism, mechanism, rejection of belief in revealed truth or miracles, of faith as a path to knowledge, or in the survival of the individual personality after death.

But underlying spiritualism and scientism is the little-understood unity that underlies all nature, the subjective branch, the physical branch, and their deeper joint source, which I call the radix. Error and conflict occur when either branch of this identity is treated as primary and the other as secondary in human knowledge. That which is primary is the source of both.

Let me close this section on the spiritualistic and scientistic errors in the development of human knowledge with a quotation from Wilhelm Reich. Reich used the term "mystical" in very much the same sense that I use the word "spiritualistic," and the term "mechanistic" in the sense that I use "scientistic." Reich's terms of fifty years ago carry too much baggage of other meanings for me to use in my writing today, but his meaning is clear. He said:

> "And so the mechanistic, like the mystical human being, stands within the boundaries of his civilization which is ruled by a contradictory and murderous mixture of machines and gods. This civilization forms the mechanistic-mystical structures of men, and the mechanistic-mystical character structures reproduce the machine-mystical civilization. Mechanists as well as mystics find themselves within the given framework of mechanico-mystically conditioned civilization. They cannot grasp the basic problems of this civilization since their thinking and their world picture correspond exactly to that very condition which they reflect and perpetually reproduce. One need only think of the murderous civil war between the Hindus and

> Mohammedans following the division of India to realize the disastrous influence of mysticism. And one need only think of the "Age of the Atomic Bomb" to understand what mechanistic civilization is."
>
> Wilhelm Reich
ETHER, GOD AND DEVIL[4]

The Quiet Millions

It is fortunate that many religious people, including those in spiritualistic denominations, are not spiritualistic, and that many scientists, including the best, are not scientistic in their belief systems. In "true believers," accepting and protecting the central irrationalities of spiritualistic or scientific beliefs often creates aggressive or militant behavior to defend the irrationality. For most people, the belief system supporting a church or denomination is not its primary feature. Many people are indifferent to doctrine, but want to belong to a religious community where the members support each other and are concerned with doing the right thing. Parents often want religious education groups for their children because they want their children to grow into good human beings. Honesty, compassion, and consideration for others are of central importance to most of us. Anyone who has ever belonged to a strong and effective religious congregation, whatever its doctrine, knows the power of its fellowship and mutual friendship, the support and charity toward members in sorrow or in need, the striving after meaning in life, something other than work, entertainment, and recreation. Churches are often places of beauty and quiet where daily cares and turmoils can be left behind, and one can search for a deeper level of meaning than most people's daily lives offer them.

The quiet millions who are not "true believers" know that one needn't believe a church's stories and dogma to experience gratitude and wonder at the gift of life, the blessing of loving and being loved, the joy of community -- and of periods of meditative solitude.

To support the teachings of Jesus, one need not believe that Jesus was conceived of the "Holy Ghost," born of a virgin, performed miracles, died for other people's sins, was resurrected from death and rose bodily into heaven, and that in a ritual called "communion" a cracker and a thimbleful of wine are actually changed into his flesh and blood. One can quietly reject such spiritualistic myths and yet see that Jesus was a wise and good man, an exemplary human being. The Bible (or Torah or Koran) can be accepted as a mixture of history, myth, advice, and cautions, rich in wisdom, even though human and imperfect rather than a sacred revelation from God. Belief in miracles, magic, revelation, saints, and devils is not the essence of religion but its distortion and degradation.

By the same token, scientism is a distortion and degradation of science. Because science has gone so far in discovering the laws of dead matter and the physical aspects of living things does not earn it any expertise in the realm of mind and spirit, e.g., in psychology, human relations, religion or politics. In this realm its explanations fail to explain and its methods and laws do not work. The material of consciousness is not matter nor other forms of energy. It has no mass, and is not gravitational, electromagnetic, or made up of weak or strong nuclear forces. Science has as yet not an inkling of how it is that mind changes the course of events in our bodies and changes the course of the movements of these bodies as a consequence of feelings, thoughts, and intentions. Scientistic science is blind to new energy coming into the physical world as a "first cause," bending events to the will of a conscious individual. "Freedom of the will" looks anti-scientific to the scientistic mind because it is not in accord with the laws of physics. To the scientific mind, on the other hand, "freedom of the will" is an obvious fact of nature, even though physical science does not yet know how to explain it. To claim that ideas, feelings, and thoughts do not bring changes in the course of physical events is a mark of scientistic irrationality.

Most scientists are not that insane. It is science, not religion, which has given us technology and the control we have over the physical world. It has opened the world to exploration as it lifted people out of poverty, disease, and starvation. It has made it possible for the most productive and technologically advanced nations to have a way of life that is the envy of the rest of the world. It has provided most of the people in advanced nations with decent housing, made knowledge available to the population, brought heat and light, music, books, telephones, computers, and television into our homes, automobiles onto our roads, aircraft to our skies. It has opened space to exploration of the moon, solar system and universe beyond.

And it has exacted a heavy price for these benefits. It has brought us war and implements of mass destruction, the pollution and degeneration of much of the natural environment and, through scientistic Marxism, the degradation of the social and political environment, the imprisonment and deaths of tens of millions unfortunate enough to live under it, and the disappearance of spirituality and meaning from the lives of its followers.

It is when science overreaches the physical and technological and tries to apply its methods and discoveries to the questions of spirit, mind, human conduct, and societal and political organization that it becomes scientistic and irrational. The "social sciences" are not sciences. Even though psychology, sociology, political science, and economics have discovered many important and interesting facts, they are more art than science, lacking as they do knowledge of the fundamental nature of mind, spirit, and the creative process in nature.

The quiet millions who are neither spiritualistic nor scientistic often operate from intuition rather than spiritualistic "faith" or scientistic "logic." Unlike faith, intuition is a legitimate stage of knowledge, an early unformed sense of what might be true, before secure knowledge is developed or available. With so many spiritualistic and scientistic obfuscations of knowledge, the quiet millions need to trust their intuition that neither spiritualism nor scientism knows the deeper nature of things. It is not that the deeper nature of things is unknowable, it is that it isn't yet known. Those who are wise will keep their mind open to new ideas and directions. We need a coming together of science without scientism and religion without spiritualism. The spiritualistic and the scientistic need to be abandoned to the dustbin of history. The reasonable, sane bodies of science and of religion can merge. There is much evidence that this is trying to happen, and from both sides. What is needed are ways to bridge the separate spheres of human knowledge that are science and religion today.

The quiet millions avoid the animosities and irrationalities of spiritualistic and scientistic belief systems by withdrawing interest and involvement in doctrine and theory in science and religion, and instead focusing on their other aspects -- perhaps technology and applications in science, and/or music, organization, or any of the many other functions that are required to make a religious community operate successfully, irrespective of doctrine or creed.

As science and religion shed their irrationalities, individual autonomy grows. Fundamental beliefs take on new importance to people. How is the universe created? What is the nature of right and wrong? Is there a God, and if there is, what is God's nature? If there is not a God, what is the highest, the ultimate in the universe, and how do we relate to it? How did the universe arise? What is the nature of the creative process?

When individual freedom of thought is allowed, we tend to give up miracles, magic, and divine revelations. It becomes possible for us each to approach fundamental questions free of preconceptions and claims of special authority by groups, individuals, bibles, books, religious or scientific "authorities." It is not only permitted, but safe and sensible to be skeptical, to doubt, and to question why people believe as they do.

The door is opening for the quiet millions to form opinions, enter dialogs, and develop their own personal beliefs. Some seek to know the nature of the universe they find themselves part of, and the nature of their own deepest selves -- if you will, of their own souls. And they are turning toward the two spheres of human knowledge that are becoming less separate from each other: religion and science.

Chapter Notes

[1] The quotes are from Jonas, Hans, 1966, THE PHENOMENON OF LIFE. New York: Harper and Row. The views expressed in this chapter were influenced, not only by this book, but in a graduate course taught by Jonas at the New School for Social Research.

[2] In past writing I have used the term *mechanism* to refer to materialistic distortion of thought, and *mysticism* to refer to religious distortions. The meanings of these terms have undergone change in many people's minds. I have switched to the terms *scientistic* and *spiritualistic* to shed some of the old baggage of meaning. My precise meaning is made clear by Table 1.

[3] Revised from the comparison in *Mechanism in Scientific Thought* by C.R. Kelley, an invited "New Fellow" address to the Society of Engineering Psychologists, Division 21 of the American Psychological Association Convention, Honolulu, Hawaii, September 2, 1972.

[4] Reich uses the terms *mechanism* and *mysticism* to describe distortions in scientific and religious thought in a way that is similar but not identical to my use of *scientistic* and *spiritualistic* in this chapter. See Reich, Wilhelm, 1949, ETHER, GOD AND DEVIL. New York: Orgone Institute Press.

Chapter 3

MUSCULAR ARMOR AND ORGONE ENERGY:
The Legacy of Wilhelm Reich

As a boy I wanted more than anything to understand nature. The stars, clouds, weather, trees, flowers and creatures of the world filled me with wonder. *"All things bright and beautiful, All creatures great and small, All things wise and wonderful;"* yes, but I never believed that *"The Lord God made them all."*

I could not believe in the literal biblical Lord God, Superperson, and the biblical creation myth as taught by my fundamentalist minister father. The universe, its laws, and the life in it didn't "just happen," but the physicist's "big bang" theory made no more sense to me than the story of Adam and Eve, and as a myth I found it less attractive.

My school science classes and texts explained some things about life and the world, but lacked the wonder I felt for it all. I played truant to reclaim that feeling, tramping the streets of Los Angeles as well as the Hollywood hills and parks. The plants and animals interested me as much as the books I devoured in the public library and the displays in museums. As I got older, I rounded out my high school truancies with trips to one of the burlesque shows down town, a different side of life. My varied experiences exposed me to many aspects of nature and the world, and deepened my understanding of it in ways schoolteachers and books never could.

Soon after I returned from army duty in World War 2, a friend handed me a book by Wilhelm Reich, a body-oriented psychologist and former student of Freud. Reich's profound discoveries about body, mind, sexuality, character structure, and things he called "muscular armor" and "orgone energy" sent me back to the library for more. Reich had hit on something important. He went where others feared to tread. I read everything I could find by or about him, and I knew I had to become involved with this man. I wrote to him while I was still an undergraduate at the University of Hawaii, and his reply started me organizing my life around plans to study with him in New York. I would do graduate training in psychology, get a job in New York to support myself, and learn from Reich and his colleagues about his work and the radical scientific beliefs growing out of it.

My own discoveries about the life force are built on a foundation laid by Reich. He began with Freud's *libido*, a life force concept limited to the human and animal body. He made the libido more physically tangible and, he thought, scientifically accessible, by at first equating it with "bioelectricity," later "bioenergy," and finally "orgone energy." Reich went on to see the existence of this force in physical nature quite apart from organic life. Why did the life force appear in non-living nature?

A great switch in conception grew in Reich's mind. He concluded that life developed out of the life force, and not the other way round. The life force pre-existed "life" as we know it, instead of being a property of life. By building on this extraordinary insight he realized that the force created matter; and that meant he was dealing not just with a force inherent in organic life, but with the creative force in the universe itself. After that he spoke of cosmic orgone energy, because it operated everywhere and in all kinds of ways in the universe. A special and limited expression of it made living things, but the evolution of living things did not generate it.

I understand "life force" to be the cosmic force that is creating and evolving with the universe. This meaning is consistent with Reich's orgone energy and my radix. To me, as to Reich, the life force is cosmic and primordial, the original and primary force in nature.

In September 1950 I arrived in New York with great excitement. I had my job as a research psychologist and was ready to become involved with Reich's work. The Reichian movement was in upheaval. Reich had decided to move from New York and live year-round at his summer retreat on a large property in the Maine woods. He continued his scientific work full time, but had ceased to practice Orgone Therapy or to train others. This meant I would see him less often, and depend more on his colleagues and associates. I was disappointed at the time, but it proved to give me more than I would ever have imagined.

I entered Orgone Therapy with Dr. William Thorburn, an osteopathic physician in New York who had been trained extensively in Orgone Therapy by Reich. During sessions I lay naked on my back on a couch, while Dr. T worked physically with my body and breathing. He used his hands and a very few, carefully chosen words to release patterns of muscular tension in my body. After months, emotion poured out of me. I cried deeply for the first time in twenty years.

By contrast, the traditional psychotherapies I'd tried in the past had left me strangely unmoved. I talked about my childhood, which I remembered well, and I talked about people and scenes and things that had happened. I talked about experiences, some traumatic. But I didn't laugh or cry or get angry. I became able to release feelings in sessions with Dr. Thorburn because the pattern of muscle tension, the specific muscular armor in throat, chest and diaphragm that had blocked the discharge of my life force, softened. The racking sobs coming from me with my first large release were my long-blocked life force reasserting what the muscular armor had taken from me years before -- the ability to cry when hurt.[1] *"Now the cork is out of your bottle,"* Dr. Thorburn said.

The emotional releases affected my vision, and in a different way than had occurred in the Bates lessons that had so improved my eyesight a few years before.[2] Crying freed my eyes and changed the quality of my visual experience. It "opened my eyes" in a different sense than Bates lessons had. On the way to and from Dr. Thorburn's office I passed the window of a large, well-arranged florist shop. After my therapy appointment the colors and arrangements of these flowers appeared strikingly vivid, and affected me deeply. I would stop and gaze at them in a kind of awe. The whole visual world opened up to me in a new direct intense form of visual perception. I began to understand a little about Reich's work on the *muscular armor* and the force he called the *orgone*.

Muscular Armor

Reich began building his new framework of knowledge while practicing as a psychoanalyst and student of Freud in the twenties. His work departed from Freud's because instead of focusing on the content, meaning, and history of the associations of his patients, he began to pay special attention to their emotional expression. He looked less at *what* the patient said and more at *how*, at the process rather than the content. He was becoming the first truly body-oriented psychologist.

Instead of sitting at the head of the couch, out of the patient's sight, Reich worked beside it. He looked into the patient's eyes, noticed if they looked away from him as important material emerged. He observed the breathing. When did it pause and when did it slow down? When did it race? He noticed the flatness of the voice and the agitation or stillness of bodily expression as the patient recounted emotional events. He noticed when tears broke through and when they didn't, identifying tensions in the body that played the crucial role in blocking the affect -- the experience or the expression of feeling. He realized that words often distracted from and obscured the underlying emotional processes. When he had his patient remain silent, the bodily expression then spoke the truth. The jaw might clamp shut with gritted teeth, the eyes open wide in anxiety, the chest remain inflated, etc.

Reich suspected that physical tension and emotional holding expressed the same thing. He noted a kind of identity between patterns of muscular armor in the body and patterns of rigidity in the character. This provided a key to the mind-body problem. He said,

> *"...muscular and character attitudes serve the same function in the psychic apparatus; they can influence and replace each other. Basically, they cannot be separated...."*

Thus Reich developed his concept of muscular armor to describe the blocking of feelings by patterns of muscle tensions in the body.³ He refined his discovery to correlate specific patterns of character defenses with patterns of bodily tensions and behaviors. He saw the patterns of muscle tension in the body as resistances: resistance to the expression of emotion, the freeing of the feelings, and the progress of the therapy. The character defends itself against change, Reich said, against letting go of these patterns of resistance. It does this by holding back and blocking the release of tension within the body that would otherwise make the patient change. I would say it now a little differently: The patterns of muscle tension block the discharge of the life force that would otherwise be experienced and expressed as feelings.

As Reich developed his concept of a muscular armor that blocked feelings and emotions, he faced the ancient mind-body problem. The armor was made up of patterns of tense muscles. How could physical tensions in the body block things that weren't physical but mental or emotional, like thoughts or feelings? Muscle tensions are objective, tangible. They can be directly observed by others. Thoughts, feelings, ideas aren't objective but subjective. They cannot be directly observed by others. One could observe the muscle tensions, but had to infer the feelings, thoughts, emotions, or ideas behind them. How did the interaction between body and mind take place?

The Function of the Orgasm

Reich's contribution developed from the idea that the Freudian libido is the life force, having real and tangible properties one can observe, describe and work with. Reich did direct sexual research. He observed the body charging and discharging the life force in sex, and he perceived the orgasm as a key to understanding what he observed. He saw the orgasm as the epitome of life force at its most intense, when its properties are most evident, and he used this as his point of reference, exploring the rest of nature from this vantage.

Reich came to view the life force as an unrecognized physical energy building up in the body and discharging in orgasm. The internal regulation of the life force that was built around charge and discharge in orgasm he referred to as the "sex economy" of the body. His "orgone" acted as currency in this economy, building up and charging the body until it was discharged in orgasm. Reich saw the muscular armor's disruption of orgasm as the primary source of human suffering and illness.

The function of the orgasm, including the process of charge and discharge in sexuality, remained the core of his work. This is what he called his "red thread" as he built his new framework for understanding nature, applying the same principle in ever-wider fields and branches of scientific research that included biology, meteorology, cosmology, and "pre-atomic" chemistry (the creation of matter).[4]

Reich's concept of the life force differed from the life force concept of most others, e.g., of Europe's "vitalists" or of eastern religions, because of the way he observed it and tied it to real natural processes. Reich went from Freud's libido and the energy of the instincts to the pulsation of the body in sexuality, and to emotion and the action of the muscular armor in blocked emotion. He saw all of these as natural processes expressing the life force. Reich's life force was real, actual, of the body and of nature, rather than of an intangible, intellectual or spiritual world. The Reichian life force lacked the mystical and religious element with which many life force concepts, including the Hindu *prana* and the Chinese *chi*, have been associated. And this again resulted from Reich's unwavering focus on process rather than content; on expression rather than meaning;

and on events and their causes in the body and mind at the present moment rather than their history.

Reich viewed sex then as cosmic and religious as well as natural and practical. Reich saw the form and potency of the sexual embrace, the coming together of male and female, expressed at the cosmic level in the spiral galaxy and, in the earth's atmosphere, in the hurricane. Both of these were to him discharges of the orgone in superimposition and mating. Reich believed the orgasm could be the individual's most powerful experience of the creative process in nature and the closest approach one can have to the cosmic.[5] I can only agree with my teacher. This position is as central to my work as it is to Reich's. Reich saw sex and orgasm in their proper dimension and glory, and lamented that the armored character made them small and dirty. This happens because the reality is too powerful for the heavily armored to encompass. Early in life he blocks and inhibits his own sexuality, and then diminishes the importance of sex in the world to mirror his own self-limited experience.

The Genital Character Myth

In another closely related respect, I came to part company with Reich. He believed orgastically potent people had established an armor-free genital character structure. The appearance in therapy of the orgasm reflex was said to signal "orgastic potency" to the Reichian therapist, who judged the appearance in therapy of this supposed signal of health and freedom from armor.

Reich's concept of the armor-free genital character had a profound and unfortunate effect. When I arrived in New York in 1950 I found the Reichian movement structured hierarchically around the concept of the superior being, the orgastically potent, armor-free genital character. The concept grew naturally from what seemed to be happening in the progress of orgone therapy, where the reduction of armor produced a softened character, more open, direct, loving and sexual. Orgone therapists only rarely claimed to see anyone become a full-fledged genital character, but they did regularly see changes in that direction. By extrapolation, these changes seemed to support Reich's genital character concept. We students in the Reichian movement experienced these changes in ourselves and saw them in our friends. We therefore tended to accept the genital character myth, and judged human beings by it,[6] even though it was woefully lacking in clear scientific description and validation.

We therefore viewed Reich unrealistically, sitting as he did at the pinnacle of the genital character hierarchy. Worshipful students made him out to be unarmored and ideally healthy. Mystified as nearly a god, his associates and therapists became angels since they'd been freed of their armor by Reich himself. All this fed a paranoid streak in Reich. He was well shy of psychosis, but also shy of the best mental health. He was a truly great man, but not a Superman. He was, after all, human.

The myth of Reich's genital character had no more reality than any other story of divine personalities, the "fully enlightened masters" of Eastern cults, the "saints" of Christian mythology, or the hang-up-free Scientology "clears" who have processed away all their engrams by auditing. Add to these the thousands who have been "reborn" and often given a new name in a religion or personal growth group, or the millions who have had their sins washed away through baptism or other religious ceremony. These practices are sometimes helpful to people, but are not magical. There are no genital characters, and the people Reich helped free from their armor, his doctors, his orgonomists, and the children of the orgonomists, are not bigger characterologically nor better people in a moral sense as a result of what they've done. For many the reverse is true. They do not think more clearly than other people or behave more decently because they've been stripped of their armor. Many of them are decent and honorable people, but de-armoring has not made them more so. They haven't achieved more in the world than non-armored characters, or realized their potential more fully. Many of them would have achieved a great deal more if they had been more armored, but in a more balanced way.

Reich observed the characterological smallness of so many of his followers. He became disillusioned with the struggle to turn patients into genital characters, and quit practicing and training orgonomists. In 1955, he wrote in the Reichian journal **Orgonomic Medicine**:

> ...Nothing can be done with grownups. I am rather experienced in psychiatry and biology, human biology. Nothing can be done. Once a tree didn't grow straight, but crooked, you can't straighten it out.[7]

To this day Reich's disciples avoid dealing with this statement by Reich. It is quite a change from the brave hope offered the readers of CHARACTER ANALYSIS and FUNCTION OF THE ORGASM![8] Reich's excessive and unreal hope for his therapeutic technique brought this disillusion. He became discouraged with a great achievement because he failed to understand the origin and true nature of the muscular armor. He never saw the defect in his theory of the armor, and as his student I didn't see it until several years after his death.

Reich himself never abandoned his dream of the unarmored genital character. He merely decided that this character could be produced only by raising children free of armor, and not by removing armor through therapy with adults. In 1949 he launched a research project on the rearing of armor-free healthy children. When he died, he left his estate, "The Wilhelm Reich Infant Trust Fund," to this and related purposes.

To my knowledge, no one in orgonomy has yet succeeded in raising his child as an armor-free genital character. I have met dozens of children raised according to Reichian principles by Reichian therapists and other parents who have had extensive Reichian therapy. When intelligently applied by healthy and loving parents, I judge the Reichian techniques to have sometimes been of real value, and the children to have benefited. Often, though, children of Reich's disciples received over-permissive upbringing not in their best interests. Every child, including those of Reichian parents, has problems and hangups and, fortunately for them, all normal children past the age of four or five have their defenses, their armor, Reichian upbringing or not. The unarmored child is as much a myth as the unarmored, defense-free adult, and for the same reason. The armor has a function Reich did not suspect. After his death, discovering that function became central to my own work.

Religion and the Reichians

It is easy to look back now and see that our little group of followers of Reich and Orgonomy were engaged in part in a religious pursuit. I would have scoffed at the idea at the time. I was an agnostic and scornful of every religious "authority," as were a majority of my Reichian friends. At that time I did not clearly understand that religious authority is not the basis of religion but is instead its major perversion. By closing my eyes to the religious element in the Reichian movement, I blinded myself for years to one of its central dimensions.

However, we Reichians struggled in our own ways with two religious questions involved in Reich's work, questions at the root of human existence. Question One: What is the nature of the creative process in nature, the source, that from which all the universe, ourselves included, has arisen? Question Two: How did good and evil arise in the world, and what is their nature? -- Perhaps a full answer to the first question would entail an answer to the second.

Of course, we didn't phrase the second question in the words "good and evil," which are religious rather than scientific concepts. Nonetheless, central to the Reichian movement was belief in the good. The goal of Orgone Therapy was to free people from the armor and make them more open, genuine, loving and alive – surely all "good" qualities. We believed that hate, chronic anger or fear, mechanistic rigidity and mystical flight from reality – surely "bad" qualities – resulted from armor and disappeared as the armor did. We had been told that the neurotic armored character structure gave way and a healthy genital character structure grew in its place. Reich said his therapy changed the character structure profoundly, in the direction of the good. He said "...*the whole being of the patient changed so basically that at first I could not understand it.*"[9]

At that time I accepted without question Reich's medical formulation of the problem of good and evil. "Good" equaled "healthy," with virtue the natural concomitant of health. The medical concept of armor replaced the religious concept of evil; the disease process of armor affected masses of people, virtually all of them. Reich attributed the great "evils" of the world -- black and red fascism, mysticism, mechanism, and other mass irrationalities -- to manifestations of the disease of muscular armor. "Free man from his armor and we will live in a much, much better world." -- That was the clear promise of Reich's work. If armor is the disease, then the remedy is to remove it from adults and prevent its formation in children. These were and are the objectives of true Reichians in therapy and in the Reichian rearing of children.

Reich's formulations are still attractive. They seem to solve the religious problem of the existence of evil by tracing it to the armor. We are, basically, entirely good, the theory indicated. The armor makes us evil. It is a medical problem, amenable to treatment by medical orgone therapy. And, armor can be prevented in the first place by proper child rearing. But the mystery of the origin and nature of evil is not solved by this reformulation. It is merely replaced by the equally great mystery of the origin and nature of the armor, a question Reich could never solve. The solution to this problem, and the development of personal growth work based on the solution, resulted in the divergence of my work on the life force from Reich's.[10]

Sex and religion deal, in their different ways, with the most powerful human impulses within and around us. They, more than anything else in our lives, concern the creative process in man and nature, the deeply felt problems of life and death, romantic attachment, children and family life. That is why they involve so much distortion. The loveless sex of the pornographer and the sexless love of the celibate religious disciple are two sides of the same coin, equal and opposite distortions of the loving sexual creative impulse. We understood this in the Reichian movement. And though there were and are no genital characters embodying the ideal fusion of the loving and the sexual, there often was a degree of this fusion taking place as a result of good Reichian therapy. We experienced it in ourselves and our friends. It is the same change that we see take place in friends when they fall deeply in love. The new seriousness and depth of feeling reflect a surrender of superficial defenses in the deep giving of ourselves in the sexual embrace. Yet at the same time and as a result of the same process, long continued de-armoring, there was often something significant lost in the character, a serious change for the worse. It took me years to understand it.

The Great Mystery: The Origin of Muscular Armor

One theoretical problem raised by Reich's work then stood out from all others: the origin of the muscular armor. Reich had discovered that human life is disastrously affected by the chronic patterns of muscular tension he called the muscular armor. It was his first major discovery and, together with discoveries about the life force or orgone, formed the basis of his work. Reich called himself a "good engineer" of the body. He noted not only how the armor blocked feeling and deadened the body, but which patterns of muscle tension blocked which feelings and impulses. He observed how certain patterns of tension in the body result in corresponding patterns of character and, over time, predisposition to certain physical illnesses. Thus one's armor expressed a good deal about a person to those who could read it.

Furthermore, destructive patterns of armor occurred in groups or societies and resulted in the distinctive mass characterological expressions of each society. When Reich wrote books such as THE CANCER BIOPATHY or THE MASS PSYCHOLOGY OF FASCISM, he was writing about patterns of armor, their expression and effects on millions of people. The armor blocked the feelings, and acted the "villain of the piece" in Reich's psychiatric view of the world.

The armor is indeed the mechanism of emotional repression. Many serious individual and societal ills are traceable to bodies chronically tightened and deadened against the feelings by their armor. These ills include insanity, heart disease, cancer and, in society, gratuitous violence, communism, fascism, and religious fanaticism. The armor contributes in a major way to each one of these. It forms distinctive patterns of muscular tension in particular large groups of people, creating widespread physical and social disorders unique to the human species.

But despite being a fine engineer of the human body with an extraordinary sensitivity to its patterns of tension and expression, Reich could never understand why the armor existed. Where did it come from, and what did it mean? To his credit he saw that it had to have some value. "*There's a logic to it somewhere,*" he said, "*...a rational element we don't grasp yet.*"

I believe that if Reich had lived, he would have gone in the direction I doggedly pursued after his death. After he died in 1957, I seized on the problem of the origin of the armor. I asked for my readers' help, and worked on the problem from the first volume of the Reichian journal, **The Creative Process**, that I published from 1961-1965. Five years later I was still without a satisfactory solution.[11]

I had made one advance beyond Reich on this problem. Reich thought that the armor originated prehistorically in the course of the evolution of the species. Once in existence, he reasoned, it perpetuated itself by social processes, e.g., armored societies with armored families produce armored children. This self-perpetuation continued across the thousands of years after the prehistoric originating event had long since been forgotten. Reich said this event introduced an irrational element into human life, able to reproduce itself anew in each generation.

LIFE FORCE

My analysis showed that this could not be true. The biological disadvantages of the armor are enormous. They hurt and handicap a person sexually and socially so much that natural evolutionary processes would eliminate them in the species over the generations, unless whatever caused it originally has persisted and is causing it still. Thus I wrote in 1961:

> "The original cause of the armor is still in existence, and has been in existence throughout human history..."[12]

This insight, and a deepening personal understanding of the nature of the life force, were the major intellectual legacy I received from my Reichian period. They set the stage for the discoveries soon to come that would establish the direction and meaning of my own work.

My personal orgone therapy was central to my understanding of the life force. By the end of my Reichian period I had had more than fifteen years of it, nine with Dr. Thorburn, whom Reich had trained, and six with second-generation Reichian therapists. I changed profoundly as a consequence of therapy, and so got closer to the functioning of my own life processes, apart from therapy. Feeling the life force express itself through me, I opened myself to feelings I had blocked all my life. I became able to cry and to surrender myself more deeply in orgasm. These were first-hand experiences of my own life force no scientific experiment could convey. In therapy, I repeatedly felt my muscular armor give way and the life processes that armor had been impeding complete themselves. This indicated to me that armor works by patterns of muscle tension blocking the pulsation-charge-discharge process through which emotions take place. Reich had only begun to understand this process when he died.

I experienced the life force in myself as the bridge between mind and body, consciousness and my physical being, the subjective and the objective realms of nature. The life force operated in both realms, and held the key to the interaction between them. As I said earlier in this chapter, the mind-body problem, the mystery of freedom of the will, so puzzling to philosophers for more than 2,000 years, had its solution in the understanding of the life force. We had not yet reached the solution, but had moved much closer to it with Reich's discovery of the muscular armor. The muscle tensions making up the armor were objective, physical, and socially observable. Feelings blocked by these tensions were subjective, mental (in the broadest sense), and not socially observable. How something physical like a tense muscle could block something non-physical like a feeling or emotion lay at the very heart of the mind-body problem.

We needed a life force concept in philosophy and in science. The lack of understanding of the role the life force plays in natural processes had allowed philosophy to become split into the unreconciled opposites of philosophic idealism which leads into mystical thinking, and philosophic materialism which leads into mechanistic thinking. The split extended to all of knowledge, resulting in the unreconciled division between a science rooted in mechanism and religious beliefs rooted in mysticism.

The life force was the key to understanding and integrating these opposites, but I didn't at first understand how. My developing theory of causation pushed me toward the solution. It suddenly became clear to me that new physical energy had to be created in the mind-body process. "Freedom of the will" required that changed physical outcomes could come about as a result of the operation of thought and will. The changed physical outcomes required that new physical energy issue in some way from thought and will to bring about the changes. Mind, consciousness, had to carry with it new physical energy that brought the changed outcomes about. The life force had to be the root of thought and will, and the newly created energy the source of change in the physical world. I didn't yet understand that process well, but I would.[13]

Hazards of Working with the Life Force

There were two different aspects of work with the life force holding hazards that I had not anticipated. The first was a straightforward physical one as I worked with Reich's experimental devices and procedures, such as his powerful "cloudbuster" to control the weather.[14] This instrument could manipulate movement of the life force, much as Chinese acupuncture and Feng Shui can, though I had heard nothing of these disciplines in the fifties. What if I triggered a violent storm or other severe reaction that I could neither prevent nor remedy? I needed to learn fast the limits I could go with my experiments.

The second hazard was insidious and more serious. I called it the "guarding function," an emotional reaction of people committed to a particular opinion who cannot tolerate a point of view that threatens their position. Established science is as intolerant of scientific heresy as fundamentalist religion is of religious heresy. They have together evolved great unconscious vested interests in protecting the "veils obscuring the face of god," obscuring knowledge of the creative force in the universe, closing ranks against those lonely religious and scientific pioneers who pursued the unveiling. Anyone getting too close to the central mysteries of nature and of human life comes up against the guarding function in all its power. The reaction to them is often outrage. Punish the unbeliever, burn the witch, persecute the Jews, kill the heretic and distort, ridicule, ban and outlaw and burn his work, his heresy. Do anything to prevent it from being read and discussed objectively and seriously.

Established science labeled Reich a heretic, and he became its victim.[15] He pulled back the veils a little, only to be attacked and vilified. His scientific publications were burned. Reich was sent to prison, where he died in 1957 at the age of 60. This happened in the 20th century, by order of the U.S. Government and to the applause of its medical and scientific establishments.[16] Those who doubt the connection between Reich's discoveries about the creative force in nature and the banning and burning of his publications should remember the condition included in the court order obtained by the Federal Food and Drug Administration against his publications. It stated that his books could be used provided that all reference to the existence of orgone energy were deleted from them.

At the time I could not understand the extraordinarily cruel and hate-filled nature of the persecution of Reich, the burning of his writings, his death in prison, and the collusion with the persecutors by established scientific and medical organizations. It was only years later, when I understood Reich's identification as a heretic, that the dynamics became clear to me.

The danger to my own work increased in proportion to my progress toward my primary objective, delving ever further into the mysteries of the creative process. Protected at the outset because of my ignorance of the subject, I became more of a threat the more I learned. I was often considered presumptuous and brash, particularly to Reich's followers who considered his work "sacred." I became an outcast. (To colleagues in my orthodox scientific career, if they knew of my moonlighting work with the life force, I was simply a little eccentric.) As I came to understand the dynamics of the guarding function, however, I could eventually protect myself from it. The grip of scientific and religious orthodoxy continues to loosen, too, at least in the developed free world, but thinking for oneself about the deepest questions of creation and nature can nonetheless still be a perilous activity.

The End of My Reichian Period

Looking over my Reichian period now, decades after it ended in 1965, is for me a little like looking back on my adolescence. I view it with a mixture of pride and embarrassment. The embarrassment is with respect to a hung-up, cultish quality in much of the Reichian movement, in which I then played a significant part. Sometimes this quality got into my own writing. A gulf separated my naive expectations of Reich's disciples and the reality. My disillusionment stemmed less from them than from myself. The reality had been there all along: believers in Reich and his work, ordinary decent people caught up in the dynamics of work with the life force and its guarding function. In 1965 I put the story into words in the final issue of **The Creative Process**, and began to get some perspective.[17]

LIFE FORCE

" *The problem areas to be faced in conducting research on the creative process are these two:*

a.   What is the creative force in nature? How does it work?.... How can we use it technologically?

b.   <u>What are the incredible forces at work that cloud our vision, twist our judgment, paralyze our productive ability, the forces that deflect, defeat or destroy us when we try to advance scientifically in this one direction?</u>

The second problem is the key to the first.

...My identification with and work on behalf of orgonomy is now at an end. It has been the center, the core of nearly fifteen years of my life as a scientist. I believe that because my career has had this root, it has a potential significance that it could otherwise have never had. Whether that significance is realized only the years ahead will decide. I am eager to face them.

Thus ended my Reichian period.

Chapter Notes

[1] For a further personal description of orgone therapy, see Bean, Orson, 1971, ME AND THE ORGONE. New York: St. Martin's Press.

[2] See Kelley, C.R., 1958. PSYCHOLOGICAL FACTORS IN MYOPIA, Ph.D. dissertation. New York, N.Y.: The New School for Social Research.

[3] Mitchell, Meredith B., 1964, *Reich's Theory of Armor*, **The Creative Process**, Vol. III No. 2, March. Also Kelley, C. R. 1978, *Basic Concepts in Radix Feeling Work*, **The Radix Journal**, Vol. I No. 1, Fall.

[4] Reich, Wilhelm, 1942. THE FUNCTION OF THE ORGASM. New York: Orgone Institue Press. Subsequently reprinted by Farrar, Straus & Giroux, New York.

[5] Reich's cosmic view of sex is best expressed in his book COSMIC SUPERIMPOSITION. New York: Orgone Institute Press, 1951. (Reprinted by Farrar, Straus & Giroux, 1973.)

[6] For a thorough critique and discussion of this issue, see Kelley, 1972, *Post Primal and Genital Character: A Critique of Janov and Reich*, **Journal of Humanistic Psychology**, Vol. 12 No. 2, Fall 1972. First printed by Kelley/Radix Publications as "Primal Scream and Genital Character."

[7] Reich, Wilhelm. 1955. *The Source of the Human 'No'*. From the **Archives of the Orgone Institute in Orgonomic Medicine**, *Vol. I, No. 2*.

[8] Reich, Wilhelm, 1949, CHARACTER ANALYSIS (3rd enlarged edition). New York: Orgone Institute Press, and
Reich, Wilhelm, 1942, THE FUNCTION OF THE ORGASM. New York: Orgone Institute Press. Both subsequently reprinted by Farrar, Straus & Giroux/The Noonday Press.

[9] Reich, Wilhelm, 1942, THE FUNCTION OF THE ORGASM. New York: Orgone Institute Press. Subsequently reprinted by Farrar, Straus & Giroux, New York.

[10] Kelley, C. R. 1970, revised 1974, *Education in Feeling and Purpose*. In THE RADIX, VOL. I: RADIX PERSONAL GROWTH WORK, 1992. Vancouver, WA: K/R Publications.

[11] I had many first-rate minds working on the problem of the origin of muscular armor, including Adam Margoshes, Frank Beddoe, Lawrence Barth, Roger Wescott...A couple of them got closer to the ultimate solution than did I in those years, but in the final issue of **The Creative Process** the problem remained unsolved.

[12] Kelley, C.R. et al, 1961, *The Origin of Armoring*, **The Creative Process**, Vol. I No. 2, p. 104.

[13] I first published my concept that new energy was created in the mind-body process and was the basis of "freedom of the will" in a footnote to an article in **The Creative Process**, 1962, Vol. II No. 4, p. 142.

[14] See Appendix A, "Cloudbusting and Rainmaking," and Kelley, C.R., 1961, A NEW METHOD OF WEATHER CONTROL. Technical Report 60-1. Also published in German, EINE NEUE METHODE DER WETTERKONTROLLE. Vancouver, WA: K/R Publications.

[15] See Reich's book, THE MURDER OF CHRIST, 1953. Rangeley, Maine: Orgone Institute Press.

[16] For more detailed factual information about the persecution of Reich and the burning and banning of his writings, see my monograph "The Ending of Wilhelm Reich's Researches," (1966), available today through K/R Publications, and the far more extensive later book by Greenfield, Jerome, 1974, WILHELM REICH VS. THE U.S.A. New York: W.W. Norton & Co.

[17] Kelley, C.R., 1965, *Orgonomy Since the Death of Reich.* **The Creative Process**, the whole of Volume 5. Copies available through K/R Publications, Vancouver, WA.

Chapter 4

WHY HUMAN BEINGS ARE "ARMORED"

The young child is a creature dominated by feeling, and the feelings tend to flow directly into action. Spontaneous, expressive, innocent, vulnerable, the young child is also a victim of his feelings. They control him, for he cannot block them. If hurt, he must cry, even if it is not in his self-interest, because he has not learned how not to. He has not yet developed the muscular armor to prevent it.

In a few years it will be very different. The child will have lost the spontaneous innocent quality of the very young as, with great effort, he learned to block feelings that once ruled him. With this learning has come a self-awareness, a self-scrutiny. It comes as part of the blocking process that made him turn inward to control his spontaneous feelings. His parents may view the loss of spontaneity and innocence with regret. Their child is no longer the open, guileless creature he was. He has become armored. No longer a victim of his feelings, he has, through the armor, achieved a degree of mastery over them. The price of this mastery is high.

The armor first develops in large undifferentiated contractions that prevent the unwanted feeling from running its course. This is most evident in the young child still learning to hold back anger or tears. The breathing almost stops, muscles become massively rigid in specific patterns familiar to every Radix teacher. As months and years pass, the blocks become less massive and more selective. The breathing slows in a pattern reflecting the emotion blocked. The muscle tension forming the armor differentiates to a few contractions directed against specific feeling expressions. Attention is thus diverted by the armor from the feeling blocked. And, like other skilled patterns of behavior, this armoring process becomes habitual and automatic, no longer requiring conscious control. With this becoming automatic of the armoring process, the child who was once a victim of his feelings is their victim no longer. The price he has paid is to become a victim of his armor.

The process is symbolized in the biblical myth of the eating of the apple by Adam and Eve in the Garden of Eden. They eat from the tree of knowledge and so become like God, knowing good and evil. Knowledge gives them the power to see future consequences of their acts. Thus they become, for the first time, capable of good and of evil. In the process they become self-aware, notice their own nakedness, and seek to cover it. Innocent no longer, they are cast out of the bliss of childhood, out of the garden, and into the world of work, of personal responsibility, success and failure.

And so Adam and Eve, the unarmored children of God, ate of the tree of knowledge and became armored in consequence. Every human being repeats the process as he or she learns to control the feelings that are, for the child, all-powerful. In so doing, each progresses from being a victim of the feelings to being a victim of blocks to feelings, of the armor.

In 1966, the year following my separation from Orgonomy, I discovered the origin, purpose and meaning of the muscular armor, why there is an armor. This was the turning point in my life. It set me on the track of the discovery of the radix process, nature's primary activity of creation. Other significant discoveries followed. The period of discovery was the consequence of changes, personal and intellectual, that I went through at that time.

I closed down **The Creative Process**, the Reichian journal I published from 1960 to 1965. I was leaving the framework of thought that Reich's work provided me during young adulthood. I moved back to California after nearly fifteen years in the east, involved with the Reichian movement. My character was in turmoil, my world view, my values, my sense of self undergoing transformation. The principles and values I used to govern my life no longer worked or helped me, but instead were constricting me unbearably.

I had lost all respect for Washington politicians and bureaucrats and for the medical and scientific establishments as a result of their contributions to Reich's persecution and death. My political views had failed me. I underwent a radical change away from the socialistic welfare state collectivism of my youth. I read Ayn Rand, the novelist and political philosopher.[1] She was a champion of individualism, and called her way of being in the world "objectivism." Her writings, -- ANTHEM, WE THE LIVING, THE FOUNTAINHEAD, ATLAS SHRUGGED and the rest -- had an electrifying effect on me. Though I was never her disciple – I was never anyone's disciple – Ayn Rand's books were, like Reich's, a monumental contribution to knowledge, one of the most important of her century. Ayn Rand expressed something new to me that was crucially important for understanding human character. She knew something I couldn't yet fully grasp. And she wrote that she believed man to be a heroic being, with his own happiness the moral purpose of his life, productive achievement his noblest activity, and reason his only absolute. This was in stark contrast to the self-negating altruism in which I had been raised.

Ayn Rand and the Armored Character

In 1965 I needed toughness to deal with the difficult decisions my life faced, the kind of toughness Ayn Rand's heroic figures demonstrated again and again as they took hard paths through the years of their purposive and difficult lives. How she was hated by Politically Correct academics! There was little in my years of Reichian work that prepared me for the difficult decision, the tough move, for dealing effectively with the harsh and painful realities of my life. I opened my feelings on the Reichian couch, become able to cry. My sexual experience deepened and I became better able to contact other people and myself. I was in many ways a different person than the one taking his first Reichian session fifteen years before. But I was not tough, and I needed toughness to deal with the difficult life decisions I faced. I needed a better capacity for self-discipline, denial, for taking the hard path. Sometimes the hard path hurts other people. Little in my years of Reichian work prepared me for that, and it was the hardest path of all. Sensitive and tender hearted as I was, I suffered for it.

Ayn Rand's characters were tough. They were armored, no question about that, and their armor seemed to be a virtue, playing an as yet unclear role in their achievements, their triumphs of mind and will over feelings. What a problem this posed for me, with my Reichian point of view concerning the armor! How could the armor, the central agency in human suffering, illness, mass insanities, the catastrophes that make up so much of human history, ever be regarded as a "virtue?"

On one point I was clear. My judgment, my capacity to act according to my own thought and will I valued above my feelings. Feelings came second to me, no matter how intense, how deep the longing, how desperate the fear or agonizing the pain. But Reichian work focused on freeing and opening feeling processes, something I needed and welcomed. Had I undergone all those years of Reichian work to learn that it was pushing me in a wrong direction, a direction that limited rather than expanded my human potential? Was the Reichian therapist, the technologist hired to break down the armor and free us from its noxious effects, the enemy of mind and will?

I had reasoned that armor originated and continued to exist because, even though it is a biological handicap of the most severe sort, it had survival value. Armored man was in some way better suited to life on this planet than unarmored man. The mystery was how.[2] I was making progress, and thought that I would soon solve that mystery.

A more immediate problem was how to change my own confused and unsatisfying life. Despite every effort, my marriage did not work. It had become joyless over its years. Nothing I did breathed life into it. I was effective in my job as a research scientist, but the work itself lacked significance. I functioned day to day out of duty and habit, desperately unhappy. I was drinking, overweight, depressed. I had to do something.

I started the fierce, uncompromising process required to get my life on track. What I needed now was not to open my feelings, but to do what I had to do. I admitted that my marriage had failed, and moved out from my home and family to a small apartment, where I lived like a monk in a cell. I stopped drinking, followed a strict diet to shed 20 pounds, and began a regular exercise program. I required myself to work regularly on a book on applied experimental psychology that I had agreed to write.[3] Most difficult of all for me, in the year that followed I met and gradually fell deeply in love with a colleague. For a year I would not face that fact. Finally, I did, and I offered a commitment to Erica, the woman I loved. After the painful collapse of my marriage, I found this as frightening as facing death. I have never done anything harder for me. Finally I had opened my heart to love, and it was terrifying. I knew that I had to deal with these personal problems to be able to devote myself effectively to the scientific problems of the life force and its role in the creative process in nature.

Erica had moved to Europe, and I wrote her a letter proposal. Before I received her answer I formulated another commitment, this one to myself. The life force as I, standing on Reich's shoulders, had come to see it, was real and understandable, the agency of the creative process. In 1965 Reich had been dead for eight years. I had to confront the life force for myself, independent of what Reich had thought about it. What was my own mission concerning the life force? I found I knew, once I began to state it. I hand-printed on parchment these words:

> *I have now one resolve, preeminent above all else, and that is to do my work and do it as it should be done. My work is to study and write of the creative process in nature and its expression in man. To me this is the most important and difficult task in the world, and I believe that I am one of the few people in the world who can do it and do it well.*
>
> *I will not be content to do it well; I intend to do it superbly, which is to say, to do it clearly, simply, and with integrity, utilizing every resource at my command; -- to do it without blunting a phrase, without compromising an inch,*

without trying to please any other soul on earth. I will not be sidetracked.

I can do it and I will.

-- C. R. Kelley
New Years 1966

I framed this commitment to myself, and hung it in my office. It has hung in my office ever since. I read it from time to time, and I strive to live up to it. This book can be read as a chronicle of my struggle to do so.

A few weeks later I had a letter from Europe. Erica was moved by my letter. She was closing off her stay in Europe for a new life with me in America. It would be a couple of months. Suddenly the future changed. -- Entirely.

What is the magic of love? I had never known before. Everything was different now. A certain grimness in my determination to solve the great mysteries which I confronted gave way to happy anticipation. I could let myself see the bubbly pleasure on a baby's face, the colors and scent of the vivid white and blood-red of a bowl of carnations, even the deep misery of a dog when its master leaves for a trip. It was not happiness but life I was sensitized to. Everywhere all around me was life, suddenly become more intense, more moving, more dear. What is the meaning of life? -- Life is itself the meaning. The blessings and the curses of it come with opening oneself to it. Blessings and curses have no meaning to the dead.

I went back to my studies of the life force with a new sense of excitement and enthusiasm. I was surely one of the most fortunate of the human race. I was creative, searching, exposed to cosmic mysteries, privileged to have learned from great teachers. Now I was addressing those mysteries for myself. My power of thought was keen, my sense of wonder intact. And I was in love with a beautiful woman who loved me and in a few weeks was coming to spend her life with me.

I focused in on the mystery that would occupy me for the next months, the origin of the muscular armor, the agency of the emotional disaster afflicting our species. I had new clues. Through Ayn Rand I had gained the insight that the armor had an important but not yet clear positive function in human life. She did not speak of armor,of course, but of the virtues of men (and women) with hard faces, steely self-control and the discipline to pursue long-range goals through years of great difficulty. They had to face down animosity from the enemies of life, who by nature hated these intensely alive, autonomous, creative, figures.

I was getting close, but I needed something more, another piece of the puzzle. I read and re-read, looking for a bridge between those chronic life-destroying muscular tensions that were the armor to tough disciplined characters able to stay focused on long-range goals, such as Ayn Rand's heroes. Of my sources, only Reich showed knowledge that there was a muscular armor shaping the character. But wait, there was another, closely related, who might help me.

Ribot and Voluntary Attention

I remembered a book I had read more than fifteen years before at the suggestion of Margaret D. Corbett, who had helped me so much in improving my eyesight and training me to teach the techniques of vision improvement to others. Mrs. Corbett, like her mentor, William H. Bates, worked consciously to free muscular tensions associated with seeing. Though these two hadn't used the word "armor," I recognized that in Reich's terms they were loosening the muscular armoring of the visual apparatus in order to improve their clients' vision. Bates made his discoveries before I was born,[4] well before Reich discovered the muscular armor. The book that helped them and that Mrs. Corbett recommended to me two decades later was THE PSYCHOLOGY OF ATTENTION, an old classic by the 19th century French psychologist Theodule Ribot.[5] I hadn't known about Reich and the armor when I read Ribot before. Might he have written something in the 1890's that would help me now?

55

Ribot had made a profound discovery. He wrote that living animals showed two forms of attention, *spontaneous* and *voluntary*. The biologically old form, *spontaneous* attention, we share with the other animals. As animals our attention is drawn toward, and we spontaneously bring our attention to, things tagged as significant by our experience, and by those effects of the experience of our ancestors that have been stored in our genes. But the human species alone of all the animals has evolved another form of attention of a different sort, *voluntary* attention. Voluntary attention is forced rather than spontaneous, something we make ourselves do by act of will.

Ribot said that voluntary attention occurred *only in the human species*. Reich had asked, *Why is the human animal the only species that is armored? -- Why not the deer or the chipmunk?*

Ribot explained that voluntary attention was a late and special development in human evolution, much different from the spontaneous attention man shares with the animals. Voluntary attention is forced and artificial, learned by great effort in childhood.

The answer hit me. Close as I had come, the connection had not been complete before. Then came the flash, and my "Eureka -- I have found it." (With me it was *Erica*, I have found it!) Suddenly I knew. The muscular armor is the mechanism of the human will. Its contractions enable us to block, direct, and focus our own life force, and thus our attention. *That* is what makes voluntary attention possible.

Ribot studied attention, an aspect of consciousness, and discovered voluntary attention, the unique human capacity to direct one's attention and form one's thoughts at will. He observed carefully, and noticed that voluntary attention was always associated with effort, muscular tension, breathing changes. Reich observed muscle tensions and breathing changes as they interfered with spontaneous processes, feelings and emotions. I needed only to put Ribot and Reich together, and *voila!* Combining Ribot and Reich gave me more than the sum of their parts.

I knew this was the insight I'd been looking for. My heart was pounding. I was so excited I couldn't keep reading without a pause. I had grasped something of extraordinary importance!

Ribot noted that voluntary attention was a late and special human development, always involving muscular tension and breathing changes. These quotes from Ribot illustrate the point:[6]

"....every act of volition *acts only upon muscles and through muscles.*" (p. 43, emphasis Ribot's)

The armor is a *muscular* activity, Reich had explained.

"....voluntary attention is always accompanied by a feeling of effort...." (Ribot, p. 56)

The armor is formed by patterns of tension requiring effort, Reich said.

". . . with all persons and in all cases there are modifications in the rhythm of respiration." (Ribot, p. 61)

The muscular armor *always* involves inhibition of respiration, Reich taught us.

Thus, with the help of Ribot, I suddenly came to understand the great problem Reich had never been able to work out. The origin and meaning of the muscular armor was a mystery no longer.

Volition, what we do by choice, is an effort because it involves a conflict of impulses. It is the conflict between what we want to do and what we decide to do, between old and new systems of motivation, between the "built in" spontaneous motivation operating through the feelings, and the new motivation underlying voluntary human purpose, the laboriously acquired product of human culture, operating through thought and will. Judgments, decisions to act based on beliefs, values and thought, must overcome the attraction of short-range activities and the interference of emotions that are incompatible with the long-range goal, or volition fails. The armor is how we block and shape the activity of our life force to control and guide our life in the face of short-range impulses

LIFE FORCE

and interfering distractions. Feelings are life force processes. It is these processes before they are expressed as feelings that the "armor" blocks and shapes.

Armor as an Aid to Survival

Quite suddenly a whole host of perplexing and important scientific problems in psychology became clear.

- *Why is it that man alone of all the animals developed a muscular armor?*
  Because man alone developed a will, and **the armor is the mechanism of that will**.

- *What is the function of the muscular armor?*
  To restrict, focus and channel the activity of one's life force as required for voluntary attention and voluntary movement. This is how the will operates. Voluntary attention and voluntary movement give us control over our own lives.

- *Why is the muscular armor, the mechanism of the will, so terribly destructive, so damaging to health and to rationality?*
  Because it is new (in an evolutionary sense) and partial and imperfect in its development. When an important and new evolutionary step is made in an animal species, there often must be a long difficult period of adaptation because the new step is not yet perfected. We are like a species just evolving the capacity for flight that doesn't know how to do it well as yet. We are only beginning to develop and use the power of the muscular armor.

- *Why is it that many of those individuals that are highly armored are also people I consider interesting, attractive, admirable in their character structure, when Reichian theory would predict the opposite?*
  It is because these people have a high degree of will power, and often exhibit an unusual degree of self-discipline and ability to do difficult things, and so control the direction of

their lives. Ayn Rand admired and championed such armored human beings.

Muscular armor has survived biological evolution despite its terrible destructiveness because it has a survival function. That survival function is volition, the human will. The armor is an expression of our life force turning back in on itself, making us self-aware and helping us gain control over life processes and behaviors that up to that point in human development had been spontaneous.

Volition and the armor, which is its mechanism, together with conceptual thought and judgment, which makes volition of value, form the source of our power as humans over ourselves and our environment. Those best able to suppress and control the spontaneous impulses that interfere with their long-range direction in life achieve long-range goals. This gives them great power. This is true even when the goals they work for represent the warped values of individuals -- or whole societies -- that have adopted life-negative values. If thinking and volition are well developed, these societies will prevail over emotionally "healthier" societies (in Reich's sense) in which feelings are more open but thought and volition are less well developed. The relatively unarmored "happy loving primitive" has no chance against the armored "dour and joyless missionary" in the long run, because the latter exhibits much stronger volition and long-range purpose, and can work toward his values and goals with a singleness of direction that is beyond the primitive's capability. Over time the missionary will establish control over the primitive culture, and his values will come to prevail. They will prevail, not because they were imposed by force (though they often are), but because they are the values of the more evolved more powerful culture. Its power is a product of its people's greater capacity for thought and volition. Conceptual thought and volition are the basis of virtually every new achievement of human civilization, good or bad.[7]

The Radix Block: The Positive Function of Muscular Armor

Reich's great mystery was a mystery no longer. The human species developed muscular armor as it evolved the ability for its members to think conceptually, judge right possible courses of action, and *do what was judged to be right despite feelings pushing toward a different choice.* An entirely new process of motivation based on this new ability was coming into existence. The old system was rooted in feelings and natural impulses, in which attention and action flowed spontaneously from the feelings. The new system was rooted in the unique human ability to think, develop values and beliefs, exercise judgment about what to pay attention to and how to act, and then force oneself to honor that judgment by an act of will. It is the metaphorical apple eaten by Eve and Adam, enabling them to "know good and evil."

The new system and the old often come into conflict with each other. What one feels like doing and what one thinks he ought to do are often different. The latter depends on the new system of voluntary attention and voluntary action, implemented by the armor. It expresses a new branch of the life force turning back on itself to produce self-awareness and self-control in an individual. It did this through patterns of muscle tension guiding a person's life force. It is much more than "armor" blocking feelings. It is channeling and directing one's life. I came to call this more evolved and purposeful form of armor the *radix block.*

So the armor had a wider function than Reich ever imagined. True, it could be the means of blocking feelings that should be expressed, and so operate as the "villain of the piece" in Reich's psychiatric view of the world. Yes, the muscular armor is the mechanism of emotional repression. Disastrous individual and societal ills are traceable to bodies chronically tightened and deadened against the feelings. Reich had showed us this again and again, beyond all doubt. But now I had discovered Reich's muscular armor was much more. It was the means by which a human being could resist short range impulses, and so stay on track towards long range goals. It made self-awareness, work, study, self-discipline, forbearance, self control, containment and morality possible. Spontaneous attention and the feelings were given us by god or nature, but the voluntary we each have to learn, gradually and painfully, by becoming armored. It is a wonderful gift for which each one of us pays a terrible price, because as it has developed in our species, it must develop in each child.

We armored human beings struggle and grope our way toward the adulthood of ourselves and our species, trying to understand and do the right thing. Our errors in thinking and judgment are many and terrible in their effect, and human suffering in consequence is immense. The armor forms patterns of muscular tension distorting feeling and thought, patterns that feed the characteristic widespread irrational psychological and social disorders pervading the human species, including most wars. There are rational wars, of course, but not many.

Reich discovered and understood that the distortions in feeling and thought came from the armor, and he taught this to us well. I discovered the other half of the equation: Volition, self-discipline, commitment, ethics and personal achievement, the character traits of purpose, are also made possible and mediated by the patterns of muscular tension Reich called the armor and I came to call the radix block. When the patterns of muscle tension which support these positive traits predominate, societies are productive, open, and respectful of individual rights. The finest expressions of human civilization consist of the accumulated achievements of purposive human beings, and so rest on the cumulative positive effects of Reich's "armor" – the radix block. Knowledge, science and technology, literature, human art and music are created by "armored" human beings.

Thus it is not a question of eliminating the armor, as Reich and his followers have tried to do. It is instead a question of understanding it better, dealing with its more terrible side effects, and helping the human race to move in the evolutionary direction.

LIFE FORCE

This is toward the more flexible tensions of the radix block over which we are gradually developing better control. Our present-day challenge is to retain the advantages of the armor and at the same time learn to ameliorate the damage it does in this early point in its evolution.

Chapter Notes

[1] Ayn Rand, champion of Objectivist philosophy, came to the United States from Russia, her birthplace, in 1926 and published her first novel, WE THE LIVING, ten years later. Other works include THE FOUNTAINHEAD (1943), CAPITALISM: THE UNKNOWN IDEAL (1946), ATLAS SHRUGGED (1957). During the sixties she edited, with Nathaniel Branden, a monthly magazine, **The Objectivist**, first called *The Objectivist Newsletter*. Then, from 1971, she wrote and published *The Ayn Rand Newsletter*. Ms. Rand died in 1982.p

[2] Kelley, 1961, *The Origin of Armoring*, in **The Creative Process**, Vol. I No. 2, p. 105. This material on the origin of armoring explored the mystery created by the armor and showed that it had to have a positive value to have persisted through the ages, but I hadn't found what the value was.

[3] Kelley, C.R., 1968, MANUAL AND AUTOMATIC CONTROL. New York: John Wiley & Sons.

[4] William H. Bates was an ophthalmologist far ahead of his time who developed techniques for improving vision by psychological techniques and simple exercises to promote relaxation. Bates died in 1931. His work was carried forward by his student Margaret D. Corbett, who trained many teachers of vision improvement. I entered her teacher training course in 1947. Through Mrs. Corbett's work, I greatly improved my extremely nearsighted eyes. It was in her training course that I was first introduced to the writing of Wilhelm Reich.

[5] Ribot, T.A., 1890 in French, THE PSYCHOLOGY OF ATTENTION. Republished in English by Marcell Rodd, New York, 1946. Ribot's work is relevant to the vision work of Bates and Corbett. It was Mrs. Corbett who arranged for this English edition of Ribot's work to be published.

[6] *Ibid*

[7] I first published my discovery that the armor was the agency of the human will and the basis of purposive behavior in Kelley, C.R., 1970, EDUCATION IN

FEELING AND PURPOSE. Vancouver, WA: K/R Publications. Revised 1974.

Chapter 5

DE-ARMORING TO OPEN THE FEELINGS

Marian

I hardly notice her until she volunteers to take a demonstration Radix "Intensive." This is a large introductory Kelley/Radix workshop on "Opening the Feelings". Marian is one of six students volunteering to work in this particular session. Two of the six will get an individual "intensive" session from me in front of the whole group of fifty people. The rest of the small group will assist me, and my co-leader Erica will be responsible for the rest of the workshop members as needed.

When each of the group of six share their feelings, I get an impression of her. An attractive black woman, she shows a good level of radix charge in her stance and voice, giving an impression of strength, aliveness and awareness. She speaks well -- almost too well -- easily putting together the words and phrases about her feelings. Her eyes open wide and roll just a little -- some fear held there, and more significantly, the words and voice are too "nice" for a structure that projects this much power. Under her adaptiveness there has to be its antithesis, her anger. I look at her vigorous, well-muscled body and feel a challenge. I want to work with this woman.

She lies on the mat on the floor with the group around her as we go through the preliminary instructions. The things I ask her to do that she can do voluntarily are "exercises"; what is called for from her is full participation. If feelings come up, however, that is something else. She is to surrender to and accept the feelings, neither blocking nor trying to "do" them, but letting them happen in their own way. And she is to accept it if no feelings happen, for whatever she feels is what she is "supposed" to feel. She understands.

I begin with her eyes, which are watchful now and show she is thinking -- in her head. I have her stay a long time with an exaggerated lifting and lowering of her eyebrows, moving them up and down, all of the time in eye contact with me, contracting and releasing her whole scalp and area around her eyes. She stays with it, and soon slips out of her headiness and works through a touch of fear that releases in small shudders as she looks at me. Now I ask for a shoulder movement, and begin exploring the tension patterns in her body, keeping her with me in the eyes. Her breathing is deepening, and I'm tuning in to the anger process growing from her body core, expressed in the swelling of her chest, in the growing tension up her back and the sides of her neck, and in the flash that now and then comes at me through her eyes. But the anger process is being choked off in the throat and jaws, which are counterpulsing, working hard to swallow back and clamp down against the body charge pushing up from her chest. Having her kick into a mat and shake her head helps, and she "goes with" the touch of my fingers to open her mouth and free her jaw, allowing the sound to grow and the throat to open better.

It's time that I change our positions. Her eyes are telling me "I'm at a disadvantage lying on my back on this mat while you, big as you are, kneel over me and do these things to me." I ask her to get up to her knees on the mat quickly and I kneel in front of her eye-to-eye at her level. "Hit," I tell her, indicating a rolled mat the group held between us, as per instruction. Mechanically at first, but eyes locked into mine and seeing, she starts pounding, while I work to get her to drop the jaw and make clear, strong sounds into my eyes with every hit. It takes a while; the mouth and throat want to choke back the sound, but soon the process coming up from the chest and belly overwhelm the last resistance. The power of the pounding doubles, the jaw flies open, the sound comes at me loud, strong and clear, and the eyes pour out rage from her depths into mine. Her anger process is in full discharge. I am excited, exhilarated, impressed. What a fantastic woman!

It goes on spontaneously until it's finished. I'm glad that she doesn't stop her discharge before it runs its course. "Accept your feelings," I remind her, and I see her begin to do that.

The discharge of rage clears a space. It says to those around "keep back," and respect requires that we do, whether or not we are afraid. I *still have her eyes, but she is changing direction now, going in, and a significant thing begins to happen. Starting down her body from the eyes, the tensions of the anger process begin to soften. The eyes look inward, the jaw slackens, the sides of her neck stop pushing out, the shoulders go down, the chest begins to drop. Erica, who is behind her, tells me afterwards that she could see the tension pattern in Marion's back surrender gradually from the top down. When it reaches the level of her diaphragm, she begins to sob.*

Still respecting her space I move closer. Her eyes, now full of tears, still hold mine. With their pain is a question which I read as about my feeling towards her. Her crying is deepening, connecting into that same source of power that has gone into her rage, but now she is soft, deeply hurting, bereft. My heart goes out to her. I go nearer: "May I hold you?" -- For reply she opens her arms and I gather her close to me. Her hot tears scald my cheeks, and her whole body convulses with soft anguished sobs. Half the people present are crying with her. Holding her close, I feel such tenderness for her. A virtual stranger to me thirty minutes before, I love her, and feel my love received and accepted.

I am honored and proud, -- honored that she has seen me for what I am and given herself over to me to do what I do well. – And I am proud of myself and this work I have developed that carries such incredible power to unlock and free the deeper self.

How different this session is from sessions done with the student lying on his back on a couch and the professional sitting alone in a chair alongside.

Marion will never be the same again, this I know. A single experience of that depth and intensity and one is changed. She'll know it, as do I. She will find herself in better contact with her core, and her power will be more available to her. She now knows she's able to release her muscular armor, and that it can be safe to do so. This will open the way to a different feeling about herself and a different relation to others. And should we meet again, I know that once we have the chance to work past superficialities, the conventional layer that protects us from our deeper selves, we will have a connection. Our souls have touched each other's, and the soul never forgets.

It is the nature of the life force, the radix, to develop, to grow, to become more. Movement of radix charge from lower toward higher potential was present long before living forms made their appearance on earth. Then, as now, radix charge emerged into the universe, traveled away from its source, going from less charge to more, lower charge to higher. Throughout all space there are always charge gradients and the movement of charge is always up the gradient toward higher concentration. Flows of charge coming from different sources intermingle, still following the law of movement of the life force toward higher charge. Superimposition of radix charges flowing from two different sources can then occur. If it does, radix discharge, the creative process by which consciousness and energy enter the universe, occurs. The chapter which follows is devoted to radix discharge, but it may help us to preview a little of its material. When radix charge is converted to energy and consciousness, the charge disappears. It was fuel that has now been used, the fuel of the creative process. Through this process whole worlds are born, grow and evolve. In our own world at least, life developed, spread, following the universal law of the life force of movement from lower to higher, simpler to more complex, less conscious to more conscious. Living radix systems exhibit the lower to higher direction in their growth, evolution, development. It is the basis of creation, of life, of evolution, of the progress of human civilizations, and the personal growth of individuals who are part of it.

Look at our species. We grew from ancestors less developed in cleverness, skill, and control over the environment. As they evolved they developed and used tools that extended their control over the world around them. Agricultural discovery and development stabilized human communities. The growth of trade connected them. Writing was discovered, and written history began. Human history, like its prehistory, is a story of growth.

De-armoring

Today we humans are learning to work with the life force in a new expression of an old process, a process that characterized the creative force in nature long before life, reproduction, evolution, and social evolution came into being. It is a part of nature that individual human beings experience and express achievement and growth in their own lives. Each one of us strives to discover and fulfill the potentialities his or her unique life holds, and the group may benefit.

In the development of our species, however, something new has been added to human striving that is changing it deeply and irrevocably. Up to this new addition, all our striving toward development has been directed toward the world. It has been as unselfconscious as the way the fruit tree gives its fruit and the flower opens and casts its scent on the air. But for a few tens of thousands of years, the life force in the human body has produced a branch that has turned inward on itself to gain self-awareness and self-control. We have begun to know ourselves and control the force of life within us deliberately and consciously. I repeat that it is in this fateful moment in biological evolution that, as the Bible says, we have eaten of the tree of knowledge to find ourselves "become like God, knowing good and evil." It is exactly this new explosive process of becoming that we sit astride now, each of us, in our own efforts after understanding and personal fulfillment.

One new way we are learning to exercise control over our own life is the means by which we are learning to block, channel, direct and control our own life force. We do it through what Reich called the "muscular armor" and I have come to call the "radix block." The concept of the radix block evolved from Reich's discovery of the armor, to become much more. It expresses the turning back inward of a branch of the life force to explore and understand the self and gain some conscious control over our life process.

The avenues of personal growth to the citizen of a modern nation are many and varied. Each avenue branches, spreads, spawns potential paths of development. How many ways can a human being expand, learn, develop new knowledge and skill, to become larger in consequence? In this book we treat the major areas of growth that lie close to our subject: growing spiritually, opening the feelings, developing purpose, and becoming more autonomous. Each of these is relevant to us because they each express the "lower toward higher" nature of the life force, the central, conscious theme of this book.

The Radix Block

Those who become highly armored in their childhood to protect themselves from oppressive and harsh circumstances in their lives may enter adulthood with an excessive, life-destroying muscular armor. They develop "too much armor too soon" by normal standards, in order to get through the excessive pain, fear and anger their childhood circumstances produce. When young they needed far more self-control, discipline, blocking, than should be expected of a child. Their armor, their capacity to block, was their childhood friend, because it enabled them to survive their harsh circumstances. But the armor became a great handicap in the more normal circumstances most of them entered on reaching adulthood. It is then that the services of a skilled and experienced professional teacher able to help them free some of their muscular armor can be of such great value. Every such teacher has witnessed the remarkable transformation such rigid character structures undergo as their patterns of rigidity soften. They regain the capacity for feeling they had to surrender in childhood, becoming more open, vulnerable, able to love and to cry, to feel the fear and trust, anger and joy, pain and pleasure that are every person's birthright. It is a birthright surrendered to the muscular armor by tens of millions of children each year in their fight to survive.

However, I find myself reluctant and concerned about teaching others the Kelley/Radix technology of opening the feelings through freeing the "muscular armor," the radix block. I have spent the greatest part of the past thirty years doing and teaching others to do this, consciously and deliberately. I have learned, and I hesitate and offer caution now. The Kelley/Radix technology, if used appropriately, is life-giving. It can reverse disease processes rooted in the radix block, open the closed heart to love and to pleasure, replace contraction and dying with expansion and aliveness. But if the "de-armoring" process is carried too far or too long without counterbalancing work to build back (or just to build) the effective flexible patterns of muscle tension needed to control one's undesired, inappropriate, or dangerous feelings, de-armoring (opening the feelings) will in time lead the student to regress in character, become more child-like and less self-disciplined and so less capable of purpose and, over time, to become smaller in character and stature. Wilhelm Reich was only partially aware of this dynamic when he coined the metaphor for such people as "chickens,"[1] and when he quit practicing and teaching others to practice de-armoring (Reichian therapy) with adults. Professional neo-Reichian therapists and bodyworkers practicing de-armoring to open the feelings rarely understand and deal with this crucial point. Yet it is happening not only in professional work to open the feelings; it is happening all around us in our culture today. Our newspapers are full of examples. Note the freedom-peddling politicians with no grasp of the responsibilities necessary to support the freedom they preach. They spawn immature protesters. Senseless property destruction is the mark of people abandoning needed self-control. That control is rooted in the "muscular armor." It is weakened drastically when too much armor is broken down too soon in order to free feelings.

Despite this serious problem, for the over-armored character, effective freeing of the armor can be a godsend, a lifesaver. Rigid armored character structures who have given up the wonder and pleasure of life because of their deeply imbedded muscular armor can get it back, can change so dramatically through the work of body-oriented professional programs to free the feelings that it makes the difference between a life that is fulfilled and happy and one that is not. That is what "Marian" and other examples of de-armoring sessions in this chapter were doing in their work with me. They were freeing armor needed in childhood but that remained to limit adult potential to feel and to achieve.

The radix block, Reich's muscular armor, has developed unevenly in human history. It has produced an extraordinary, drastic, in many ways wonderful and in many ways terrible change in the situation of the human race worldwide. Conscious purpose and the human will are expressions of the radix block, and often provide the blocked person added power and control over his environment and over his less blocked human companions. That is why the radix block persists and grows in the human race despite its terrible side effects.

The terrible and the wonderful effects of the radix block are with us to stay for as long as the human species survives. As I have said, the radix block is a turning back of the individual's life force on itself for purposes of self-understanding and control. When the knowledge is rudimentary and control is exercised blindly (as it usually is) it can be very destructive. The major endemic and epidemic diseases afflicting the human race are the outcome of life turning back on itself via muscular armoring. By "diseases" I refer here to medical diseases such as cancer and heart disease, but also and more importantly to self-destructive societal activities. These bring about their destructive effects through social institutions, especially government, education, police and the military, and religion. These institutions have done great things, but the misery and death produced by them, the nightmares of horror they have produced, especially when they operate coercively, is seldom fully acknowledged and faced.

De-Armoring

As I came to understand more fully the nature of the armor, I used my new knowledge with students I worked with directly. Many of these came to me at the start to improve their visual functioning,[2] then did work to free the body and its blocked feelings. My knowledge of the life force grew by leaps and bounds as I worked with the muscular armor in my students. Exploring the expressions of the life force in their eyes and in their bodies opened my own eyes. I developed a highly interactive technique of working with the body in "feeling" work, i.e., de-armoring, to open blocked feelings of my students. I made eye contact with the student as I worked and, keeping such contact, freed armor from the eyes down. I handled the body, explored the armor, became involved directly and intimately in life force processes that underlie the chemistry and physiology of the body. I developed techniques and rules to make it safe for my students to express the most powerful feelings, some of them towards me, in their sessions. They had to follow my instructions closely to do the work. There could be no acting out of the feelings. Most emphatically, there could be no violence or threat of violence, and no acting out of sexual feelings. Everyone has feeling impulses which should not be acted on. Learning this is in itself an important part of learning how to use the armor to contain the feelings and to release it when and only when it is safe and appropriate to do so.

Through doing this work I became a skilled technician of the life force, especially in the release of blocks to the life force in the body. I recognized and freed muscular armor, loosening the muscular tensions in my students that held back the life force processes giving rise to pain and pleasure, fear and trust, anger and love. My students dissolved in sobs held back for years or decades by tense throats and diaphragms. Releases of anxiety, fear, and often terror or horror opened not only the natural and important capacity to experience fear, but also the antithetical capacity to be open and vulnerable and learn to trust. And my work freed furious outpourings of rage "in my face." I insisted that feelings be released eyes open, "in the 'now'" with my student aware of where they were and who I was. That awareness in the presence of powerful "old" feelings kept the student's grip on present-time reality as painful, frightening or angry feelings of great intensity were released by their muscular armor. They were learning through the experience of their sessions that even very powerful feelings could be safe to express, and that one could learn to release them with the aid of a teacher who understood how the muscular armor blocked the processes that created the feelings. At the same time they learned how to keep and even increase their ability to block the expression of feelings when release was not safe or not wise.

The work with vision added an important dimension to my work with the feelings. Keeping the student visually aware as strong feelings erupted kept present-time reality the framework within which we worked. I did not allow students to sink into their memories or fantasies while cutting off from the here-and-now, where our lives are lived. Memories of the past and anticipations of the future add dimension and meaning to our lives as long as the visual perception of present-time reality provides the grounding, the context and frame of reference for what is remembered and anticipated. Just as visual perception in the most direct physical sense lets us see the possibilities present for movement and action in the physical world, memory and understanding add meaning to what is seen. Then vision in the larger sense can let us see the possibilities our lives offer, and the framework within which a chosen possibility must be pursued. Purpose and direction in life thus arise from here-and-now visual perception to become vision in this larger sense.[3]

It is "muscular armor," or better, the "radix block," that allows us to direct, shape, and sustain our long range vision. I addressed it most directly while teaching specifically what I have called "education in purpose" as presented in the next chapter, but I learned most about the life force in the body by developing my work with visual perception and by freeing feelings by teaching over-armored character structures how to soften their excessive muscular armor.

Jim

The big-chested red-faced burly man on the mat that I'm kneeling beside is ready to take his first intensive session. This is a week-long workshop in "opening the feelings" that I'm conducting with Erica at the Esalen Institute in Big Sur, California. Jim contacted me before his session to tell me some things about himself. He has heart disease, and had open-heart surgery less than 8 months before. He is convinced that the basic problem is the blocked anger in his body. He had recovered quickly and well from his operation. He exercises regularly and vigorously, and no longer has to limit his physical activity, but his problem with anger remains. He had heard about my work in his home state of Arkansas. He enrolled in the workshop, and watched me work with fellow participants, some of whom had intense and explosive discharges of emotion. That was what he needed to do, he was convinced. It was dangerous, he thought, but a risk he was ready to take. He wanted me to know about his heart condition and hoped I was willing to do my work with him despite it.

I like Jim. He is real, direct, and courageous and I am glad to work with him. I tell him I am not a physician, and know nothing about cardiology, but if he'll work with me I'll work just as I have with the others he's seen. I will not soft-pedal his session or avoid intense feelings in the least. Trying to inhibit feelings would be dangerous and counterproductive. Jim needs to participate in the exercises I give him without reservation, and accept whatever feelings come up, angry or otherwise, without either pushing them or avoiding them. I remind him that the risk he is taking is his, not mine. I would not die from his heart attack.

Now he is lying on his mat on the floor as I kneel beside him. Others in his six-person group form a circle around his mat. They will help me. The other workshop participants form a larger seated circle around this inner group. I begin by moving a pen-light flashlight in front of his eyes in random patterns, as he follows with his eyes wherever it goes.[4] Once the exercise is taught and underway I ask the group member sitting behind his head to take the flashlight and move it as I have been doing. I use my freed-up hands to encourage fuller breathing, especially full, regular exhalation, and help him let go of tensions in the side of his neck which are restricting head movement. I ask first that he begin shrugging his shoulders, then hitting the mat he is lying on, still following the flashlight. His group brings up and holds a mat and large cushion at his feet for him to kick into. I stand beside the mat, and ask Jim to transfer his gaze from the flashlight to my eyes. I direct the former

LIFE FORCE

flashlight holder now to sit on the floor behind Jim's head so that he can place his stockinged feet on Jim's shoulders. Now as Jim kicks into the mat and cushion being held at his feet he doesn't push himself up and off the top of the mat.

Now Jim is hitting, kicking, breathing fully, and looking at me. I ask him to do one more thing -- to make clear sustained sounds with each breath. "See me and make the sounds into my eyes. Let go of your jaw, and let go of inner words. Stay in this room, aware of where you are and what you're doing. Don't try to have feelings. Let the exercise grow as it will. Keep breathing, let the movement be smoother and more fluid. Do it harder, louder, and faster, until you're ready to stop. Don't force yourself."

The release of feeling isn't long coming. Jim's exercise "takes off," overcomes inhibitions, intensifies in power and sound. It becomes a big spontaneous discharge of feeling, especially for a man with a gimpy heart. He "goes with" his explosion in anger well. When I see that the discharge has climaxed and is running down, I slow him to a gradual stop. "Accept what you did and how you feel." The group and I settle on the floor around the mat. I kneel, resting my hand on his big chest, and meet his gaze as he catches his breath.

After a moment of silence, I ask "How do you feel, and what did you feel during that exercise?"

He thinks about it a bit. "Angry and desperate as I got into the kicking and all. Now I feel relieved and spent. There's a weight lifted from my chest. I needed that."

Jim completed the remaining sessions of the workshop effectively. Several months later he wrote me:

"Maybe the work with you was dangerous to my life. I don't think it was. I think it saved my life. I'm different since then, you know. I'm lots easier with myself, and with other people."

The Wizard of Oz

In five prior group meetings arranged with me by her psychotherapist I have not succeeded in helping Pauline reach her feelings. It's been my failure, not hers. The feelings were there; the trust to release those feelings was not. She thinks the feelings that pour out of some of the other group members in their sessions with me are not genuine. It would be frightening to her to see that they are real. We go around the circle of six, each expressing present-time feelings. Pauline says:

"Here we are with the Wizard of Oz again. He points a finger or touches someone here and there on their body and they rage or scream or dissolve in sobs. It's very impressive, but I just can't forget that the Wizard turned out to be a fraud in the end."

When it comes her time to work, I stand Pauline on her feet, knees a little bent and apart, her back propped against a foam rubber mattress standing on its end against the wall behind her. When I am satisfied with her position, I sit on a stool that puts my eyes on a level with hers. The group forms a semicircle close around. Pauline and I look at each other silently for a time. Then I speak.

"You're right, Pauline. If I'm supposed to create feelings in those who work with me, I'm a complete fraud.

"The Wizard of Oz couldn't give the scarecrow intelligence, a brain, he could only give him a diploma. The cowardly lion asked for courage, but all the Wizard could give him was a medal..."

I pause. My confession of impotence to create feelings in her is being heard and acknowledged. She is beginning to connect with me. I skip the Tin Woodman's watch.

"Fraud that I am, I do workshops in "opening the feelings," and I can't give anybody feelings. They take work with me, and all I can give them are exercises, things they can do voluntarily, on request, like breathe more fully, look at me eye to eye, pound a mat with their fists or make certain sounds or say sentences under rules I give them. Exercises aren't feelings. I've never "given" a student a feeling. If feelings come up, <u>any</u>

genuine feeling, it comes from inside them, not from me. I wouldn't presume to try to give you feelings, Pauline.

"But breathe a little more deeply, and stay with me in the eyes. Do I seem to be here for you right now? Accept your own feelings. You have such strong ones underneath!"

Our eyes meet and hold. She lets herself breathe a little more deeply. A profound silence, anchored in Pauline, grows to cover the group.

There are silences and silences. Simple silences are just the cessation of noise. Pauline's silence has substance, is thick, tangible, charged with significance. I tell her to listen to it. I listen with her, as does the group. Her eyes stay riveted to mine, her pretty face becomes rapt, her jaw slackens and her mouth opens a little. Tears are beginning to form. She is trusting me more now and surrendering a little to the process that wants to happen. I believe that she is dealing with a large auditory fear. I risk a small push.

"Are you afraid that if you make any sound someone will come, and you don't want that?"

The eyes open wider, the impending tears start. A sob locks in her throat.

"Let this happen. It's safe to make noise now. Nothing bad can happen here from making noise."

Pauline gradually surrenders to crying. First the tears pour out, and the beginning sobs fight to come out of her throat. I have her stay looking at me and deliberately make sounds into my face -- louder and louder -- until she is crying and screaming out her pain at me, gulping in huge breaths to support the sounds. I have an impulse to offer to hold her, but know that isn't what she needs. She needs to stand there separate, and let the powerful feelings pour out, knowing that I am present to support her, but that I will not intrude.

And the agonizing fear and pain do pour out as she opens herself to them, eye to eye with me, standing on her own feet, owning the power of her own voice, not comforted but empowered.

When the discharge subsides I offer her tissues and a moment to recover. Then I have her look in turn at each of her group in the semicircle around us, with no touching or words exchanged. When she gets back to me we take big breaths together. I offer my hands, not in support, which isn't needed, but in acknowledgment. What she did took courage, and I am proud of her. She looks different now, strong and self-connected. Soon I will invite her to speak.

And, yes, she is a different person. A silent fear she has carried all her life has been faced and vanquished, and she can now become easier with herself and with others.

Sara

Sara, a nineteen-year old girl, is taking her eighth once-a-week intensive session in a vision and feeling group. She lies down on her back on the mat on the floor and, with encouragement, her breathing relaxes and she surrenders to feelings that she brought in with her. She cries a little. The crying soon stops of its own accord, and she connects warmly one by one with the group members kneeling around her, who have come to feel very close to her in the course of the group's work. I free her jaw and help her relax her breathing as our eyes met. She moves to a deeper level. Her face softens, her mouth opens, her breathing deepens further and begins to become automatic. With each exhalation a wave of motion flows in each direction from her solar plexus, and her head and pelvis begin to rock gently forward and back in synchrony with her breathing. Her mouth opens in an expression of wonder; she is experiencing a growing, highly pleasurable flow of current through her body. The movement and feeling, which are expressions of a slow pulsatory contraction and expansion of her life force, build spontaneously to a climax of soft involuntary pelvic motions in synchrony with her breathing. These then gently subside. She looks glowing and beautiful and in complete possession of herself, utterly without the self-consciousness that is *part of her usual expression. Normally nearsighted, she tells us that she can see with perfect clarity.*

~~~~~~

It was by doing hundreds of these sessions, each one different, that I learned most about the life force and how its expressions are blocked, shaped and channeled by the muscular armor in the body. Then I realized that the term "muscular armor" was an anachronism. It froze a damaging misconception about the true nature of the chronic muscle tensions that shape and channel the activity and flow of the body's life force into the language. I resolved to try harder to use my new term, "radix block," instead.

Chapter Notes

[1] Reich's "eagles and chickens" metaphor first appeared in his small book, LISTEN LITTLE MAN, 1948, New York: Orgone Institute Press, and Farrar, Strauss & Cudahy. I developed and expanded the metaphor in Kelley, C.R., 1989, revised 2004, THE MAKING OF CHICKENS AND OF EAGLES. Vancouver, WA, K/R Publications.

[2] From 1948, the year I graduated from the Teacher Training Program of Mrs. Margaret Corbett's "School of Eye Education," I had students coming to me to improve their sight. I received the Bachelor's degree in psychology, the Master's and Doctor's degrees in applied experimental psychology specializing in vision and the philosophy of science. I served as an Assistant Professor and Director of the Division of Applied Vision Research in the Psychology Department of North Carolina State University in Raleigh, N.C. As I studied Reich and the muscular armor, I worked consciously to free muscular blocks to perception and feeling (armoring) associated with my students' vision. In Reichian work myself at the time, I gradually extended what I learned to the bodies and minds of my students.

[3] For basic professional material on "opening the feelings," see the collection Kelley, C.R., 1992, THE RADIX: VOL. I, RADIX PERSONAL GROWTH WORK, Part Two, *Radix Feeling Work*, pp. 89-164. Vancouver, WA: K/R Publications.

[4] Use of the penlight has always been an important part of Radix work. I learned it from its originator, Dr. Barbara Goldenberg (now Dr. Goldenberg Koopman), a friend and medical orgonomist. I have used it for thirty years in

workshops all over the world, and taught it to 150-plus trainees who trained in my work. The published description of the technique by Dr. Goldenberg appeared in: Baker, Elsworth, 1967, MAN IN THE TRAP. New York: MacMillan Company, p. 50.

Chapter 6

PURPOSE

The learning of purpose requires the building of the radix block in all its subtlety. The radix block, which grows from Reich's muscular armor, is the physical basis of the new motivational system being evolved by the human species. This system is providing and perfecting the capacity of individuals to take action based on judgment rather than feelings. This newly evolving human capacity depends for its effectiveness on the complex set of muscular habit patterns that form the radix block. These block and channel the flow of the life force in the body into the actions that judgment calls for, in the face of feelings pushing in a different direction. Thus the individual can learn to take an action even though afraid, or despite angry impulses, or in the presence of a strongly attractive but unwise or wrong course of action. The set of habit patterns of the radix block are the "mechanism" of the human will. These habit patterns rechannel the life force from its "instinctive" spontaneous course into a new course when thought and will require it. The purposive life rests on the appropriateness of the judgments produced by thought, plus the effectiveness of the radix block in rechanneling the life force in this way, i.e., on the will.[1]

Building the Radix Block

The technical problem of building a student's radix block, the positive form of muscular armor, is much harder than that of "opening the feelings." This is because of the nature of the task. Tearing down a building is easier than constructing it. Dismantling chronic patterns of muscle tension to free the feelings is much easier than building such patterns to begin with. Muscular armor develops in the day-after-day life of the child over the years of infancy and childhood. It is difficult and often painful for the child to bring spontaneous life processes, especially feeling processes, under control. Discovering how to produce the muscle tensions that block, channel and shape the flow of the life force in the body that produces feelings and thoughts is an exceedingly complex unconscious skill.

First formed are the patterns of tensions required to control feeling processes that are particularly threatening, the ones that lead to disapproval and sometimes punishment by significant adults. These tensions become articulated, practiced, skilled and effective in their job of containment, even as they become habitual and automatic. Some of these patterns become obsolete as the child grows up, but they hang on unconsciously and stubbornly. They need to be cleared away to make room for new development, new construction, new growth. Opening the feelings is the clearing away process, the learning of purpose is the new construction. Some part of the function of the pattern of tensions that is to be cleared away is usually still needed. Demolition (opening the feelings) therefore requires some care, and should involve a preservation or building back of a more flexible pattern of tension in place of the pattern dismantled to free the feelings.

Thus when a body-oriented personal growth teacher helps a student who has for years or decades been unable to get angry, say, or to cry, the ingrained pattern of muscular tensions, the radix block against rage or crying, gives way. The dammed up life force is freed, which means that the body is opened to a safe outpouring of the resulting feeling discharges: rage or sobs. The short-range consequence of the session is the opening of the deeper self that had been difficult or impossible to access because of the radix block. The longer-range process is the student learning the capacity to choose between expressing and containing these powerful feelings.

The primary goal of purpose work, then, is not to open and free the feelings, but to build spontaneity and feeling in balance with a strengthened capacity to contain feelings and to function thoughtfully in the face of strong feelings. As muscularly rigid armored structures need feeling work to let themselves soften and get in touch with their feelings, softer structures need purpose work to build armor, to hold and contain higher radix charge, and so hold back and channel feelings. Containment allows them to delay discharge, and to delay short-range pursuits for the sake of long-range ones. This raises serious resistances and problems, however, which I learned the hard way in developing my own skills and trying to teach what I called "education in feeling and purpose" in the 1970's and 1980's.

When students' armor is effectively dismantled in a conscious and deliberate way, time after time over a long period, and in the absence of equally effective work on purpose, I learned that character structure changes in one direction. Students become less armored and, like children, more strongly feeling, open, perceptive, often able and energetic. But they also become less capable of self-discipline, toughness, and thoughtfulness, and less able to exercise their will to realize the potential their lives hold. Acting on or from the feelings becomes an ever more powerful motive, and ever more likely. Delaying gratification becomes more difficult, and hard work in the service of long-range objectives occurs less and less. The difficult task does not get done, the assignment does not get written, the onerous but needed work is neglected. Without a parent figure present to impose requirements and set limits, long-range interests are more and more sacrificed for short.

One especially damaging result was that students often resisted doing the work that would help build their radix block and keep balance in their character. Tough, structured, confrontive work on their self-direction and purpose in life is anathema to people reveling over being in touch with their long-suppressed feelings.

Not only did these students resist learning "purpose," but often their regression in character was manifested in childish, impulsive, inconsiderate and, under pressure or stress, even malicious behavior. In my personal experience, this showed up in procrastination, a glaring lack of contributions to the technical and scientific development of their field, irresponsibility, and a penchant for falling under the spell of fads and cults. I was disillusioned and chagrined as these things happened within the Radix community I had founded, particularly because it had taken me so long to understand and face up to the dynamics of it. The effects of long-term feeling work without counterbalancing purpose work, that is, armor dismantling without effective rebuilding, were predictable from my first discoveries about the nature of the armor and the relationship between feeling and purpose in human life. But as students flocked in for the "feeling" programs, I was unable to entice more than a few into counter-balancing "purpose" programs. Study and teach "purpose" I did, however, after schooling myself intensively in disciplines closely related to purpose work.

Three Purposive Programs

Three programs particularly impressed me for the building of purpose: Nathaniel Branden's Biocentric Psychology, Synanon, and Reuven Bar Levav 's Crisis Mobilization Therapy. I studied them each in depth. I always began studying a promising program by entering it as a participant for at least a year or two, and I did this with these three.

Nathaniel Branden and Objectivism

My own concept of purposive individuals owes much to the work of Ayn Rand. The purposiveness, determination, toughness and long-range vision of her characters impressed me. I was purposive in character, but lacked the quality of "toughness." I needed to develop it in myself.

In the early '60's I was a supporter of the Nathaniel Branden Institute in New York. The Institute was based on Ayn Rand's thought,[2] and sponsored lectures by her, as well as classes and lectures by Branden and his former wife, Barbara. The Institute published the **Objectivist Newsletter**, later replaced by the journal, **The Objectivist**. Branden, an applied psychologist, has written many books,[3] lectured widely, and worked for several decades in the field of personal growth. Aspects of Branden's work that contributed to

Purpose

and helped shape Radix purpose work were the attitudes and values his work conveys, the concepts he developed and expresses, and the techniques and procedures he employs.

Attitudes and values are a largely unconscious projection of who we are and how we live rather than what we believe or profess to believe. Branden projects self-confidence, self-responsibility, and competence. He is a man who sees life as an exciting challenge, and enjoys it. His practice is run in a businesslike way, smoothly, on schedule, and well. This is something not true of many professionals in the "new age" field. Branden does not "take care" of his clients, but he respects them, and projects the expectation that they can and will take care of themselves. He does help them work on their problem areas, but doesn't presume to make their life decisions for them.

I liked going to Branden's groups, and I personally got lots out of a series of monthly weekend workshops with the same 20-25 participants. Branden values intelligence and purpose, and brings it out in the bright and talented people who are attracted into his practice. They are mostly purposive, in charge of their lives, but with problems, and seeking to become better integrated and more effective. The atmosphere infuses those coming from less positive places, and inspires most of them to a higher level of functioning. It is gratifying to see someone as charismatic as Branden who does not use his charisma to cultivate dependency and a cult of followers.

Few leaders in the personal growth field have described the concepts underlying their work as fully and well as has Branden. His many books, including several self-help manuals, further our understanding of the development of the self concept, and the role it plays in the successful life (see Note 3). His central conceptual message remains one of self-reliance and taking responsibility.

Branden originated and adapted verbal techniques that speeded self-discovery and insight. He developed an old technique out of experimental psychology, the completion of unfinished sentences, into a clinical procedure of great efficiency and power. It

LIFE FORCE

came to be a hallmark of his work, and his books are a goldmine of illustrations and exercises employing sentence completion. It enables him to move into and around a student's defenses while staying focused on a given problem or process.

As his books became popular and his success grew, Branden began working in large workshop groups, often of one or two hundred people or more, in cities across the country and the world. I admit to mixed feelings about the large workshops. On the one hand, they have enabled him to reach a much larger number of people at some level, and encouraged many in the direction of personal growth and expansion in their lives. Branden is a purveyor of health, and his workshops have a health-enhancing effect. But for me, the most interesting process of personal growth is with long-term clients, seen in small groups and/or individually, over long enough periods of time to produce profound changes in their being. Thus my personal interest is in the narrower, deeper focus as opposed to the broader more popular one. Yet the world needs both directions of work from its wiser members.

Synanon: Confrontation Encounter

Synanon was a drug rehabilitation center run by ex-addicts, as opposed to mental health professionals. An impressively large number of drug abusers of the most serious, extreme types went to Synanon and reformed, quitting drugs entirely. They acquired the toughness and discipline for a decision that in the short run "felt" terrible, and they stayed with it. I participated in Synanon confrontation encounters two or three times a week for more than a year. They called their encounters the "Synanon Game."

What happened in the Games varied a lot. Sometimes they were funny, sometimes (often) angry, sometimes moving, sometimes just boring. The central rule was that there could be no violence or threat of violence. This rule was ironclad, and never relaxed. Break the rule and you were out of the organization on the spot, for good.

It's strange to me how confrontation encounters run by mental health professionals often lack a clear, enforced stricture against violence or the threat of violence. I went to many of that sort. Such groups are often led by good "liberals" who form the majority of the mental health establishment, and their groups are frequently dominated emotionally by one or two aggressive short-fused bullies and the fear that their threats engender. Deep rage is never safe to express in such groups. By contrast, at Synanon the violence rules were kept. Their groups contained men with violent histories, many of them convicted felons. Yet in hundreds of hours of work I never saw the rule broken. Synanon's groups were safe.

Reich originated character analysis, but never practiced it in groups.[4] The Synanon Game is a primitive form of group character analysis. The effectiveness of the process depends on discovering and exposing defensiveness, hidden moral shortcomings, pretenses, falseness, posturing. A good group finds and confronts the character defenses and flaws. My Reichian background helped me read the character defenses expressed in the over-friendly smile, the too-soft voice, the averted gaze. I had my own share of such defenses, and it was painful and yet useful when they were effectively pointed out.

On a personal level I found Synanon stimulating and challenging, and I gained confidence and assertiveness from it. Technically, I saw that it built awareness, exposed defenses, and developed a greater capacity for purpose in its participants. Group members became more self aware and learned better self control, had improved self images, and acted out less.

I asked a Synanon chief who was also a professional what he saw as the difference between Synanon groups and psychotherapy and encounter groups run by professionals. He described the character change that often took place through the Game:

Our groups deal with a different strata of society. Most of the "dope fiends" crawl in here off the streets, never having learned how to live with people at all. Lots of them don't know the simplest, most basic things. They don't know how to take a bath, change their underwear, empty their ashtrays, turn down their radio when someone is trying to sleep. They don't know not to steal from their neighbors, much less strangers. They haven't learned to do an honest day's work for a day's pay, nor that they need to be able to apply themselves day after day, learn a trade, build some kind of future for themselves. We have to pound it in to them in the "Game." We make them look at themselves and become aware and ashamed when they're jerks, and when they aren't thinking. At least we make them uncomfortable enough that they change their behavior, so that we can live with them. -- And we have a big advantage over academic professional types. There's no one who can teach them like the person who's been there, who grew up like they did, and then made their life into something better.

There was another aspect of the life of Synanon residents. One evening I had coffee with "Judy", a young woman I'd often seen in previous weeks sitting in the living room holding hands with "Robert", another young Synanon resident. She told me their story -- a Synanon romance.

Judy had been a whore [her term] for eight years. From the age of 16 she "turned tricks" to pay for her drug habit. Typically, Synanon women had supported their drug habits with prostitution, the men with burglary. Judy was high on drugs during virtually every trick she turned. One day she just got mad about the life she had fallen into, and made a decision to try for something more. She entered Synanon. Three months later she had met Robert in the "stew," an ongoing (for a time "perpetual") Synanon Game. Robert was an ex-burglar and ex-junkie, also relatively new to life off the street.

They had some special attraction in their chemistries from the moment they met but, being relative Synanon newcomers, their behavior was strictly supervised seven days a week. In the first weeks they saw each other only in group and, the few odd times their paths crossed, living and working at Synanon. Then their Synanon "parents" conferred, and Robert and Judy were allowed to sit together in the living room for an hour most evenings, where the permitted level of intimacy for them for the next two months was to talk and hold hands. Judy told me she needed those *restrictions; they made it safe to be with Robert, and to let herself learn to care more deeply without having to deal with the new and frightening issue of sex with a man she cared about.*

A month before I met her, Judy and Robert's enforced courtship period had served its purpose. They were given permission to consummate their relationship, and with gifts of flowers and heart-felt good wishes from members of their newfound family, and after a suitable ceremony, Robert took his blushing beloved to the room that was their bower. Judy said she should have been dressed in white because she felt like a virgin bride. In an emotional sense she was. It was the first real emotional relationship with a man she had ever had.

The story of Judy and Robert is touching, but it raised questions for me. How much of the change that took place in Synanon was due to the confrontation group process that the Game residents were exposed to 8-12 hours each week, and how much was due to the residential addict-operated life-style, the structure and rules, the surrogate family outside of and apart from the group process? Surely both were important. The Game forged the family, confronted the members with what was required of them to grow, monitored their progress, dealt with backsliding, and kept their eyes open to reality.

The process of growth, as I see it, is a progressive breaking down of old armor, old structure, early and no longer appropriate blocks to life force processes that create feelings. These blocks need to be replaced by more articulated, differentiated patterns of tension, giving more effective control over the life force. With the rebuilding the armor was not less effective but more so, yet the person had more freedom, new flexibility and gradations of response. As the power of the will expands, the individual gains choice. Where the early massive primitive armor can only say "yes" or "no" to feelings, the more developed, flexible armor can provide a wide variety of responses between these extremes, a range of choice adaptable to a range of situations. The contradiction between feeling and purpose softens a little in practice as the tensions damming the feeling processes in the service of purpose begin to be less an on-or-off block or barrier, and become more a flexible structure that channels and directs the life force, enabling an appropriate, differentiated feeling response that is both feeling and thoughtful, i.e., the radix block.

And so Synanon residents were verbally battered and beaten into consciousness in the Game, exposed, disciplined, and taught. They were nurtured, too, like Judy and Robert, and they responded, grew and changed, often achieving development as human beings in ways they'd never known before, in the best family they had ever had. However, the glaring weakness of Synanon was that the residents, the children of the Synanon "family," were never helped to prepare to leave "home."

Synanon had no program to transition people back to the community. There was no support for finding housing, jobs, or compatible organizations to join. The motivations and skills necessary to develop friendships, other groups, interests and support systems for a life outside of Synanon were never taught. Synanon provided a ready-made support system for its residents, and did not encourage "graduating." Residents were groomed to stay with the organization, work at its industries, bring in money, and make Synanon their permanent way of life. Thus Synanon became a non-religious cult, and the Synanon Game became a tool to advance it.

The groups abounded in a kind of threat to residents whenever they brought up anything suggesting that they might be leaving. "*You'll never make it. You'll be shooting dope in a week.*" "*I'll buy an insurance policy on you; in six months you'll be dead.*" "*You haven't a chance; you know that, don't you?*" At first I took such remarks as cautionary advice, in customary Synanon Game overstatement. I presumed that they were really saying, "*Don't go too soon.*" "*You aren't ready yet.*" "*It takes longer than you've given it.*" But some of the threats couldn't be interpreted that way. "*A dope fiend is a cripple, and don't forget it.*" "*This, right here, is your only chance to stay alive.*" "*Maury was your friend, wasn't he? He was here five years, and he O.D.'d [he died from a drug overdose] three months after he skipped. Did you go to his funeral?" "Walk out that door and you can never come back. You know that." "You can't make a cripple into a whole person. Don't kid yourself, you need us." "We're the only decent family you've ever had. We've diapered you and taken care of you for six years. Now you're going to walk out. Fuck you, I hope you do croak."

I didn't mind people being being "beaten up" verbally in group for not thinking, for being inconsiderate, bad friends or neighbors, not carrying their weight – those are issues that need to be brought up. What I can't condone is attacking a person's adequacy, potency, sense of self. To damage the self-concept is to damage the person. Attack bad behavior, confront unconsciousness, but the sense of self is, for me, sacred.

The authoritarianism of Synanon went much too far. The group assumed the parental role permanently, not, as I first assumed, just for a temporary period while the residents "grew up." It preempted the members' efforts to grow up in order to establish and perpetuate a fixed authority relation. This created obedient children who, even though they were purposive, were denied independence. Bad parents sometimes do this to their children, making them afraid to cut the parental bond. Well-to-do families supporting adult children for years of professional school often fall into this pattern. In this situation parents provide a "life" for a dependent adult child that does not further autonomy. Synanon provided an ideal situation for furthering the cult, but not for furthering an autonomous life for individual members striving for growth beyond what Synanon provided.

Synanon gradually sank. It gave up its fine facility on the beach in Santa Monica, and took its faithful to a site in Northern California at Tomales Bay. Synanon men had vasectomies (guess who decided). Married couples were required to separate and find new partners. The organization moved increasingly into paranoid paramilitary behavior. Newspapers reported the arrest of two Synanon "marines" for placing a rattlesnake in the mailbox of a Synanon "enemy" -- an attorney who had successfully pressed litigation against them. This was allegedly done with the encouragement of Synanon's brass. An objective history of the whole Synanon story, the good and the bad of it, has been written by Janzen.[5] It was a fascinating social experiment that eventually went wrong.

Despite their ultimate failure, Synanon illustrates how the confrontation group can be used as a tool of extraordinary power. It has been misused to further the purposes of myriad authorities and groups, from political and religious sects and cults to mystical and charismatic movements of all kinds. It can be used in the service of autonomy if the power can be placed in the hands of the one undergoing the process, to be used by that person for good or bad, in the pursuit of his or her individual life.

Crisis Mobilization Therapy (Bar-Levav Work)

The late Dr. Reuven Bar-Levav was a psychiatrist and group psychotherapist practicing in Detroit.[6] He referred to his form of work as "Crisis Mobilization Therapy" because crisis-level feelings are often generated in participants during sessions. Bar-Levav created the most powerful purpose-type program I have ever seen, although I thought it defective in dealing with autonomy and dependency. He trained many professionals in his extraordinary techniques.

Crisis Mobilization Therapy (CMT) combines virtues of confrontation encounter and Reich's individual character analysis, and goes beyond both. Bar-Levav succeeded in developing group character analytic techniques of great effectiveness, focusing on process above history or content, on how something is expressed above what is said. During CMT the staff members use their character-analytic skills to expose the character and defenses. This often generates high levels of feeling in the group. Group members sometimes contribute to this, as many of them have themselves developed professional-level skills after years in Bar-Levav work. I've seen no program where character defenses are opened more skillfully.

New insights and strong feelings result from the CMT opening process, and all participants are required to exercise control at all times. The confrontation group stricture against violence or threat of violence is carried a step further, prohibiting any spontaneous behavior at all. There is no holding, no touching even, without permission. Character insights are gained, accompanied by a high level of feeling and strict self control, thus building a flexible, aware, purposive radix block, such that feelings are encouraged but not acted on.

People in CMT are usually seen at least two times per week in small ongoing groups, with a weekly individual session and a large group marathon every few months. This level of exposure is continued for years. Most of the people that I met in CMT had been coming at least four or five years, many twice that long and some even more.

Bar-Levav was committed to the medical model, which suited his humane but highly autocratic character. The patients were treated as sick; he, the doctor, took over responsibility for their treatment and a great deal of responsibility for their lives. Since he was a psychiatrist, his practice went beyond counseling. Many of his patients were deeply troubled, though most held jobs and a high proportion were professionals.

CMT is here-and-now process oriented. How a message is expressed is much more important than its content. Manner, voice, body, all the tools of expression, then, are the focus of CMT. The emphasis on body and feeling is similar to Reich's but they differed in this important respect. Reich emphasized exposing the armor, freeing and discharging the blocked feelings, while Bar-Levav emphasized exposing the armor while intensifying and yet containing the feelings.

There is discharge in both cases, but the direction of the work is, in a crucial respect, diametrically opposite. In Radix conceptual terms, the primary task of Reichian-type sessions, including Radix feeling work, is loosening armor, freeing the flow of the life force and opening the feelings of the client. The primary task of purpose work, however, is to help the client consciously build their radix block to channel and contain their life force in order to control and direct their feelings and ultimately the direction of their life.

The objective of feeling work is to free and open the feelings, but the objective of purpose work is to do difficult things in the face of and in spite of the feelings. The first loosens the radix block, the second builds it. Some people have found it hard to distinguish between feeling and purpose personal growth work because both are done best in the presence of high levels of feeling, yet they are opposite directions of work.

"Face him Nora. See him. Breathe. Let yourself feel what you feel as you do the exercise. I'll remind you of the procedure: You'll give Michael three reasons, three things about him that lead you to want him to be your partner for this workshop. Then tell him three things about yourself that make you a good choice for him. Finally, ask him to be your partner. If you are one of Michael's two pre-selections, he can accept you as a partner. Otherwise, he will reject you. Now see if you can get through it all, seeing, breathing and staying conscious, without prompting from me."

"I hate these Bar-Levav exercises. They are torture."

"I know -- you feel like you'd rather stay unconscious and ease into some kind of partnership or other without effort, risk or pain. But that's not why you're here, and that's not the way for you to grow. You know that. You've been here long enough. Now, do the exercise."

"I know. I know. I just need to bitch about it."

Feeling challenged, Nora went through the exercise better than had any one of those who had gone before her. She told Michael clearly what it was about him that attracted her to him as a partner and, harder for her, what were the things about her that would make her a good choice as a partner for him. She asked him, then, if he would be her partner for the rest of the workshop. Then she stayed in contact with Michael's eyes as he pronounced the almost inevitable words. "I reject you as my partner for the workshop." *She released a held breath, let the reply sink in and said,*

"Thank you, Michael."

Nora stood up and returned to her seat.

CMT does not use many exercises, but this one typifies its style. Nora is required to seek a partner under tightly specified conditions that virtually guarantee a high level of feeling. She must expose her feelings about Michael in front of the group, telling Michael what she likes about him, and worse, what she has to offer him. It is likely that she is not one of Michael's pre-selected choices, so she will probably be rejected for her efforts. It may be equally hard for Michael, who probably likes her. He must take in her solicitation, see her struggle, then stay in eye contact with her as he pronounces the hurtful words, "I reject you."

If this exercise were done with a feeling emphasis, it would be changed to promote discharge of the feelings generated. Nora might overflow with tears and be encouraged to cry over the pain of rejection. Michael might do almost the same over inflicting the pain of rejection on a person he cared about. A feeling work teacher or therapist might do bodywork to loosen and free the muscular blocks to feelings in one or both participants. But these are not the objectives of this purpose exercise.

Nora indeed might have cried doing the purpose exercise, but she would have gone ahead anyway. Someone would have pushed her the kleenex, and the exercise would have continued as soon as she was able.

In CMT work, the feelings mobilized are often so strong that the patient feels as if the issue is emotional survival. Nevertheless, the patient is required to keep the "observing ego" active at all costs. It provides the guide to behavior in the crisis, and assures that control will not be lost, despite emotions that seem close to being overwhelming. And it develops consciousness of feeling and thought processes in the participant.

Sometimes the "crisis level" feelings are generated by an exercise, but most frequently they come out of the work itself, which involves scrupulous attention to expression. Obviously, too, all of the work cannot be at crisis level, and will often require months and years of painstaking unraveling of the defenses.

Of central interest are the changes undergone by CMT clients. Having seen and worked professionally with some of them for a five to ten year period, long enough to judge over-time changes first hand, I can say with certainty that CMT clients change a lot. Sometimes change is sudden and dramatic, followed by long periods of integration, and sometimes it is slow and gradual. In both cases, though, I see clients develop impulse control they once lacked. They individuate, become more aware, and establish better boundaries, all of which indicate the development of more effective armor. Most CMT clients also do much to straighten out their lives. They become better organized and more responsible. I have seen several become more intelligent in speech and behavior. They take better care of their health and appearance. They become more effective and often upgrade their work through promotion or job change. Many of these changes are comparable with those at Synanon, but Bar-Levav's work is more potent than was Synanon's, considering that his people are seen fewer hours per week and without the residential control that Synanon had over its regular members.

There is a serious shortcoming of CMT work, however, and that is its failure to develop self-reliance, independence, and autonomy in its patients. (Note that Synanon had the same problem.) While he was alive and running the practice, Reuven Bar-Levav's own authoritarian personality played a pivotal role in preventing this important area of growth from being developed in his patients. Autonomy was stunted by his procedures. One cannot gain autonomy and self-reliance by years of submission to a benevolent despot. The very benevolence of that despotism disarms the impulse to rebel in those seeking independence. I speak from my personal experience of CMT, and of Synanon, which had the same dynamic. Religious cults promote the same dependency among members.

The atmosphere in the CMT practice is much like that of Synanon and very different from that of Branden, who breeds self-confidence and self-responsibility in his clients. At CMT and Synanon, patients are required to assume a dependent role. The staff assume authoritarian parental control over them. Staff members pronounce edicts and make unilateral decisions of all kinds affecting the patient's therapy and life. The patient *must* maintain a dependent posture on pain of being thrown out of therapy. From my point of view, patients are infantilized outrageously in order to press home their dependent status. This feeds and sustains the child-parent relationship to their therapist/leader. Being infantilized psychologically creates in them dependent behavior and a dependent psychology that is, in my opinion, profoundly anti-therapeutic, damaging to the self-concept, sense of potency and (hence) to autonomy. With psychotics, near-psychotics and serious character disorders, one can argue a case for such dependence. But when mature adults leading responsible lives come in to therapy and are forced to assume a child-like dependent role as a fixed matter of procedure, it reflects, in my view, something amiss in the practice.

I agree that there are times when dependency may be a necessary stage in a therapeutic or personal growth practice, but for a different reason than that given by Bar-Levav. He claimed that dependency was an essential ingredient of deep-reaching therapy, necessary for the patient to re-experience the terror of infantile experience in which the baby was helpless and dependent. He claimed that the deepest feeling experiences require that such dependency be present, and justified the cultivation of dependency in his practice on these grounds.

I consider this argument specious, and claim that dependency is a temporary result of, not the necessary permanent condition for, deep work on purpose and dependency. There are some defenses, patterns of armor, so integral to a client's functioning that as one of them dissolves he feels as if he is facing annihilation. It is often experienced as impending insanity or death. The schizoid head defense is an example where this is apt to occur. The client's relationship with teacher or therapist is the anchor for working this fear through, and for integrating the character changes in progress. While going through a terrifying period of character disorganization, a client is likely to become temporarily highly dependent. He feels himself coming unglued in the foundations of his being. A solid dependable committed relationship with teacher or therapist sustains him through this difficult period, which lasts from a few weeks to a few months in the course of ongoing work of much longer duration.

Purpose and Autonomy

Autonomy as I use the word is an advanced stage of the development of purpose. Leading a conscious purposive life leads one toward autonomy. Autonomy cannot be imposed on someone else, since it is a state achieved as an act of self-possession, but in teaching purpose I strive to create an awareness of the possibility of autonomy in students. Self-understanding, self-direction, self-chosen values, principles and goals governing one's life, toughness and self-discipline in the pursuit of one's goals, living one's life consciously and exercising the options required to move effectively toward one's long-range goals – this is the purposive life. We achieve it by developing a flexible conscious armor that supports us in difficult situations, but that can then soften by choice to allow full spontaneous emotional experiences when these are safe and appropriate.

Personal growth along the dimension of purpose is in many ways the opposite of growth along the dimension of feeling, thus:[7]

EDUCATION IN FEELING	EDUCATION IN PURPOSE
Free blocks to feeling	Establish and sustain one's own direction in life
Gain increased spontaneity	Gain better self control
Learn better to:	Learn better to:
• give and accept love	• clarify one's values and principles
• work through anger and fear	• choose one's own objectives
• laugh and cry	• pursue one's objectives effectively
• surrender in orgasm	• take charge in crises
Feel more deeply	Achieve more meaning
Achieve better contact with others	Become better able to function independently
Develop more capacity for tenderness	Develop more capacity for toughness
Open up emotionally	Focus energy rationally
Attain greater emotional freedom	Attain greater intellectual clarity
Become better able to love	Become better able to work
Learn to enjoy life more deeply	Become better able to realize one's potential.

Both sets of objectives are valid, and the path to autonomy requires that both be respected.

Since one of the goals of purpose work is the ability to think and feel simultaneously, giving due weight to feelings and to judgment, I developed a group process that I commend to mental health professionals. It requires the student to think and feel at the same time

In co-confidant work, a group of students work in pairs, under leader supervision. The students forming each pair alternate in the roles of worker and partner, taking about half an hour in each role.

I developed the co-confidant technique for group work, but often use it also in individual sessions. Students are led through a controlled fantasy by the teacher, often one that triggers strong emotional responses. During the fantasy, the partners assist with simple bodywork and occasional verbal interventions, following instructions from the teacher. Significant stages of the exercise include preparation, transitioning into, doing, and coming out of the exercise.

Co-confidant exercises are distinguished on the basis of the theme of the fantasy, e.g., <u>mother, father, first sexual partner, unfinished (emotional) business, goodbye</u> (about a separation), <u>a frightening experience, a painful experience, an enraging experience, a joyful experience, talk with an old friend, talk with a lover, your deathbed, "self" co-confidant</u> (talking to yourself as a child). There are many others, of course, and they can be improvised. I have presented <u>war trauma, sexual messages from parents, a childhood abuse, a fight, a humiliation,</u> and <u>physical injury</u>, to name a few others.

The technique is best explained by example. In on-going groups, a first co-confidant is often "goodbye," as it is easy to understand and applicable to everyone.

A *co-confidant goodbye exercise is being presented to a 12-person group, with one leader and a co-leader. The workroom is carpeted and soundproof, and it has firm foam mats and two cushions on the floor for each pair of participants.*

The first workers lie on their mats and loosen up by kicking and hitting onto the mats. They then lie supine, knees bent, as partners kneel alongside the mat for a moment of eye contact before the fantasy begins. Then the worker closes his/her eyes, the partner sits on one of the cushions alongside the mat, and the leader begins speaking.

"This exercise is called goodbye. All of us have had separations in our life that left us unfinished emotionally. Perhaps a marriage or love relationship broke up with bad feelings, a friend died unexpectedly, or we or someone close to us changed jobs and moved to a distant location. Maybe leaving home and a parent was especially difficult for you, and you repressed a lot of feeling about it. You can say goodbye to a teacher who you found was important in your life, and you left without thanks, without saying anything. You can even say goodbye to a baby that was aborted or stillborn or a loved animal that died, though I will assume in helping you

build the fantasy that you are speaking to a person who will reply. You'll need to put words in the mouth of the baby or animal when you switch roles and voice the felt reply at one point in the exercise. Oh yes, and if you used a language other than English in speaking in person to the one in your fantasy, use that other language now. It isn't important that your partner understand your words. Partners will focus on your body processes.

"First, some general instructions. Breathe as you work. Partners, touch their chest or their belly when their breathing halts or slows, and touch their mouths when they stop talking. <u>This is your primary responsibility</u>. They must breathe continuously, exhaling deeply but not panting or forcing for the feelings to develop and move. They must talk their way into and through the material that comes up, allowing the feelings as they do. Watch the breathing, keep the words flowing. Communicate unobtrusively with your hands, and avoid talking to them unnecessarily. Stay observant. Are they breathing right now? When they speak, don't get caught up in their material. The leaders will sometimes intervene or ask you partners to intervene by having your workers hit or kick or make sounds.

"Workers, follow the instructions, even though you don't feel like it. Interventions may feel intrusive, interrupting your process. Do what you're asked to do anyway. It will usually help the feeling process even though it may disturb the fantasy. Let your breathing deepen right now, as I speak. Some of you have stopped breathing as you listen and think about what I say. Help them partners! Workers, this exercise asks you to breathe and think at the same time -- breathing helps the feelings to move. Breathe. Exhale fully, but don't force it.

"Now, workers, choose the person you will say goodbye to in fantasy. Don't vacillate on your decision. If it's hard to choose between person A and person B, either will work. You have to choose now. Soon I will have you spend about 10 minutes of saying your feelings and thoughts aloud to the person you create in fantasy. Then you will switch, imagine that you are speaking for the other person, replying with what you think that person might be feeling toward you. Then you'll switch back to *your own identity, reply, and say the last things you have to say. Finally, you will say <u>goodbye</u> and, in your imagination, one or both of you will turn and walk away. Whether you feel ready or not, you must say goodbye. After 'goodbye' you will open your eyes and speak to your partner. You'll be told when to switch and switch back, and when to say 'goodbye'.*

"*Okay, you've chosen the person you will speak to. Where will you speak in your fantasy? You want privacy. Is there a familiar appropriate room? If there is, remember it; if not, create a place to speak in fantasy. Get the feel of being there. What is the place like? Is it day or night? Are there smells? Are there sounds? Perhaps there is a radio in the background. Is there an atmosphere that you remember?*

"*The other person you want to speak to isn't really noticing you yet. How does it feel to be in that person's presence? How is the person dressed? What colors do you notice? What does the body express? The mood? The feeling?*

"*You're going to tell this person out loud your feelings in the relationship and your thoughts. Say what you feel, bad and good, all your feelings, talking in the first person. If there are angry feelings, get them out, say them early on, clearly and directly. If there were hurts at the end of the relationship you had, express it in words. Is there disappointment, appreciation, caring? Is there joy, or love? Put it all into words. Express it aloud, just as if you were there. Strong feelings will require a strong voice. You'll need to speak aloud for the exercise to work for you.*

"*Breathe, and sink into the place and the presence of the person you'll say goodbye to. You're soon going to speak. Move closer in your mind's eye. The person notices you are about to speak and looks at you. Imagine the eye contact, feel it. Look into those eyes, take a breath and start. Talk your way into this now.*

"*Partners, if they don't talk soon, touch their lips.*"

It takes a little time for most participants to get into the exercise, but in a few moments most workers are talking out loud to their "goodbye" person, and some are getting into strong emotion, yelling angrily, crying, or otherwise moved. The leaders move from mat to mat, loosening bodies, encouraging workers to make sounds, hit, kick, and to go on speaking. <u>Non-repetitive talking moves them through their material when their thinking blocks; breathing, appropriate body movements and sounds move them through their blocks to feeling</u>. The leaders go from mat to mat, sometimes giving instructions to partners and sometimes intervening with workers directly. Discharge of feeling often comes with leader interventions.

In about ten minutes the leaders are encouraging individual workers to "switch and become the other person" and to "say what the other person feels." Sometimes a lull will come that lets the leader announce to the group that workers should switch now if they have not done so.

After a moment or two of switched identity, workers switch back to themselves again and reply to their imaginary partners. "Say the last things you have to say now," say the leaders, "it is nearly time to say goodbye." The leaders move from mat to mat as needed to get the instruction across. Very soon after they have all switched back to their own identity, they are told:

"It's time to say <u>goodbye</u>; say the final things you have to say, -- only a few sentences at most. See in your mind's eye and hear their reply as you look at them, then say <u>goodbye</u> out loud, and either they will turn around and walk away, or you will."

The leader gives them a moment, then continues:

"When you have said goodbye in fantasy, stay for a moment with the feeling of goodbye, and what this goodbye means to you. Breathe, let yourself feel it; let it in. There is nothing more now to say. Goodbye means it is over. Understand and feel that it is over."

The leaders go to two or three mats to help get the last instruction across. Some workers are still crying.

"Now it is time to let go of the fantasy, but stay with the thought, 'it is over.' Partners, get in position for eye contact with them. Workers, bring yourselves into the room. Look at your partner, and share with your *partner what you are willing to share about that relationship and that goodbye. Stay with your feelings as you share, knowing that the reality is, 'it is over,' whatever it has left you with in feelings or in memories. Accept the feelings and let them be integrated into your knowledge of here-and-now reality. Tell your partner what you feel and what you think. And see if it can be over for you, or if you'll need to do this again sometime to finish with it. Do you have acceptance and perspective about it? Be honest with yourself, -- and with your partner. Partners, keep them breathing gently and in eye contact. You should be up on your knees where eye contact can be most direct. See each other eye to eye. Go ahead now, workers, and talk to your partners."*

The leaders circulate among the mats, adjusting positions, encouraging workers to talk, partners to listen.

The pairs talk only about five minutes. Partners are allowed to reply, to ask clarifications, but to stay focused on the goodbye, and not lapse into conversations with their workers. There follows a brief interlude of silent, peaceful awareness and touch – perhaps the partner's hand. The workers are then helped to their feet to make standing eye contact with their partner, and the co-confidant goodbye *exercise is complete. Sometimes special body exercises are used to bring the workers' awareness firmly outward from their fantasy to the here-and-now reality of the group.*

The primary objective of co-confidant work is the integration of feeling and thinking into awareness of reality. The area of work chosen for co-confidant exercises usually involves strong feelings and so, frequently, there are strong blocks to feeling and/or thinking. When successful, the blocks are loosened, feeling and thinking processes freed, and an integration can take place.

In individual work, the co-confidant material can be chosen with great precision, since it can be tailored to a student's specific issues. The objectives are the same, -- to loosen the radix block in order to open areas of significant unresolved material and integrate thoughts and feelings that then emerge with the ongoing awareness of reality. The objective of co-confidant work is not emotional discharge. Discharges produced by fantasy are in themselves not useful to students except in certain unusual situations. If practiced repeatedly without proper follow-through and integration with here-and-now reality, such discharges do a disservice to the personal growth of the student. When the strongest feelings occur, not in the context of real face-to-face relationships, but to memories or imagination, it tends to divorce students from what should be most important and real in their lives. It may encourage them to live in memory and fantasy when they do that too much already. The often-emotional co-confidant fantasy is a prop to help the student learn to face emotional situations both thoughtfully and with feelings. The final, essential step in the exercise is to "bring the feelings and thoughts into the room," into the relationship with the partner for the exercise and into the group as it convenes in circle after the exercise. These are the true here-and-now reality. This point is misunderstood by leader after leader trying to use the "Co-confidant technique." The group process must focus on integration, and not allow it to be sucked back into re-stimulating and reliving the old feelings. Those who are addicted to replaying old painful memories and fantasies need to learn that the route out of their addiction is to learn how to finish the painful memories by planting their feet on the floor, gripping with their hands, and moving forward through their eyes into the real world and the life that lies ahead of them. This is a redirection of their life force, and helps them move into a more purposive life. In other words, the learning of purpose requires that the individual learn from the past, live in the present and look to the future.

Discussion of "purpose" and its place in the context of "autonomy" is continued in the chapter of this book entitled **Autonomy**.

Chapter Notes

---

[1] Kelley, C.R., 1992, THE RADIX, VOL. I: RADIX PERSONAL GROWTH WORK. Vancouver, WA: K/R Publications. Includes:
EDUCATION IN FEELING AND PURPOSE, 1970 (revised 1974), pp. 3-86;
Series of articles on *Radix Purpose Work*, in **The Radix Journal**, 1980-83, pp. 179-226; and THE MAKING OF CHICKENS AND OF EAGLES, 1989 (revised 2004) excerpts pp. 227-240.

[2] The primary intellectual supporter of the purposive life in our time is Ayn Rand, who has expressed her political philosophy and values mostly through her novels. I recommend that students of purpose read and reread her works. These are her books that most influenced me (all have been reprinted as Signet books by the New American Library):
1943, THE FOUNTAINHEAD. New York: Bobbs-Merrill.
1946, ANTHEM. Idaho: Caxton Printers.
1957, ATLAS SHRUGGED. New York: Random House.
1959, WE THE LIVING. New York: Random House, 1959.
1961, FOR THE NEW INTELLECTUAL. New York: Random House
1964, THE VIRTUE OF SELFISHNESS. New York: The American Library of World Literature, Inc.

[3] Nathaniel Branden came to my attention in the 1960's as the principal lieutenant of Ayn Rand. He went on to become a primary figure in purposive psychology in his own right, with a long list of fine books to his credit. Among them are the following:
1997, THE ART OF LIVING CONSCIOUSLY. New York: Simon & Schuster.
1996, TAKING RESPONSIBILITY: SELF-RELIANCE AND THE ACCOUNTABLE LIFE. New York: Simon & Schuster.
1994, THE SIX PILLARS OF SELF ESTEEM. New York: Simon & Schuster.
1973, THE DISOWNED SELF. New York: Bantam.
1971, THE PSYCHOLOGY OF SELF ESTEEM. New York: Bantam.

[4] Reich, W.R., 1949, CHARACTER ANALYSIS (3rd enlarged edition). New York: Orgone Institute Press.

[5] Janzen, R., 2001, THE RISE AND FALL OF SYNANON: A CALIFORNIA UTOPIA. Baltimore, MD: Johns Hopkins University Press.

[6] Dr. Reuven Bar-Levav and a patient in his practice were murdered by a drop-out from his practice in his office in Southfield, Michigan on June 11, 1999. The

murderer then killed himself. It is easy to conclude after the fact that the perpetrator was too disturbed to deal with the pressures of Crisis Mobilization therapy as an outpatient. In fact, it is rarely possible for even the finest mental health professional to anticipate that a particular troubled individual will "crack" and commit a once-in-a-lifetime outburst of deadly violence. Dr. Bar-Levav was the finest group psychotherapist and one of the finest individuals I have ever known. His many writings include these:

> EVERY FAMILY NEEDS A C.E.O. Detroit, MI: Fathering, Inc. Press, 1995.
>
> THINKING IN THE SHADOW OF FEELING. New York: Simon and Schuster, 1988.
>
> "The treatment of preverbal hunger and rage in a group." *International Journal of Group Psychotherapy,*
>   Vol. 27, No. 4. New York: International Universities Press, 1977.

[7] List adapted from EDUCATION IN FEELING AND PURPOSE. See Note 1.

Chapter 7

THE RADIX DISCHARGE PROCESS

The end products of the radix discharge process, consciousness and physical energy, rest on earlier, more subtle and less evident foundations. We can study radix discharge directly because its two products enter and change the world in observable ways. Before radix discharge, however, the activity and the nature of the radix must be inferred and studied indirectly.

Imagine a fruit tree in Winter in a cold climate, a flowering tree. In Winter the tree is dark and bare. I infer that its radix charge, which is its life force, has pulled from twigs and branches in and down into the trunk and roots, and so the radix charge is centered.

Imagine the same tree in early Spring. The radix charge is now pushing up and out, making the sap rise. From its action new growth will be created. The tree is soon blossoming. Expansion outward and discharge are signalled by the tree bursting into bloom. Soon blossoms drop away, but fruit and leaves form and there is expansion in the roots, trunk and branches. The tree is growing as the radix is discharging.

Now it is Summer. The tree is in full leaf and heavy with fruit. The outward expansion of the radix charge has reached its peak. The radix charge is in full discharge.

In Fall the radix charge begins to draw back inward. With this centering movement of the radix charge the sap retreats in and down. Growth ends for this season. The fruit drops, the leaves dry out, lose their green color and fall. I infer that the tree's radix charge is again centering in trunk and roots.

Imagine the tree as Winter returns. The tree has grown larger from last year. It has completed a cycle of growth, returning, not to the same place, but to a corresponding place in the next cycle of its spiral of growth. Its radix charge has again centered.

LIFE FORCE

Picture how this would look if recorded on film for years and played back by time lapse camera, flowing repeatedly from Winter (centered)--Spring--(expanding)--Summer (expanded)--Fall (centering)-- Winter (centered)--etc., showing each year in a few seconds of film. This yearly cycle of expansion and centering of its radix as the tree grows across the years is a radix pulsation.

The Orgasm Formula

Reich characterized the central life force process of the body in his "orgasm formula." In orgasm, he said, the animal body develops mechanical tension, which leads to the build up of electrical charge in the membranes, which builds to discharge of the accumulated electrical charge, which results in relaxation of the mechanical tension. Thus Reich's formula:

(mechanical)   (electrical)   (electrical)   (mechanical)
tension → charge → discharge → relaxation

Later the parenthetical terms were dropped, and Reich spoke simply of:

tension → charge → discharge → relaxation.

This change reflected Reich's growing understanding that the life force was other than or more than mechanical and electrical in form.[1]

Reich saw his orgasm formula as <u>the</u> life formula. Living things pulsate in continuing cycles of this formula. This ongoing pulsation of the life force from birth to death was the primary process of life.

I found a problem here. Reich failed to realize that he had the first two terms of his formula interchanged. Tension did not lead to charge, charge led to tension. The life force processes were primary and prior, the mechanical processes secondary and consequential. The formula as I have corrected it is:

charge → tension → discharge → relaxation.

The developing charge of the tissues by the life force, the radix, created tension in the body. In charging, cells absorbed fluid, swelled, and the boundary membrane grew taut. Discharge of the radix resulted in expulsion of fluid, contraction of the cells, relaxation of the boundary with the spending of the radix charge. The radix processes of charge and discharge were primary, governing the mechanical processes of tension and relaxation resulting from them. The rhythmic repetition of the cycle expressed in the orgasm formula is the radix pulsation of living things, and it is, as Reich indicated, the heart of the creative process of life. The corrected orgasm formula is the basis of radix pulsation.

"Orgone Energy" and "Negative Entropy"

Why did Reich make this simple yet monumental error in the sequence of terms in the orgasm formula? Such errors have their cause in the character. Reich had a mechanistic streak. His work was affected by his background in mechanistic medical science and by his rejection of mystical religious belief. That's why he saw the orgone as a "strictly physical" energy. That's why he spent so many years trying to measure it with physical instruments, and to quantify it into physical/mathematical units. That's why he first called it "bioelectricity." Electromagnetism was once thought to be the basic concept of physics. Later, he changed his name for the life force to bio-_energy_, energy having become the most general concept in physical science. His final change, from bio-energy to orgone energy, expressed his realization that the life force not only was the creative force in living things, it was the creative force in the external physical universe. It brought about the origin of matter itself. But even matter, the physicists had taught us, was a _form_ of energy. So Reich held to the idea that orgone energy was physical energy in its most fundamental form. It did not occur to him that it might be something real and natural but not energy, something even more fundamental than energy and from which energy was born.

To Reich, then, the orgone was energy. It differed from other forms of physical energy in being "negatively entropic." Entropy is the principle of nature that dictates that electromagnetic energy, e.g., heat, light, and electrical charge, flow from higher toward lower concentrations. Thus the heat of a hot stove, -- or a star or an animal body -- flows from its source out toward cooler surroundings, a room, an empty space, or cooler air outside the body, the heat flowing ever from higher to lower temperature. Buildups of free electrical charge (static electricity) leak away unless renewed. The loss of energy has to be replenished by a store of fuel, like wood or heating oil consumed by the stove, the hydrogen consumed by the fusion process in heating the star, or in the body by food consumed, digested and metabolized by the animal, or by a friction or other process producing static electricity to offset electrical leakage. When all the fuel is exhausted, the room, the star, and the animal body alike cease to produce heat and grow cold, the electrical charge dissipates. The principle of entropy, the second law of thermodynamics, prevails. Entropy increases, while order and organization decrease. Concentrations of heat and light and electricity are dispersed and equalized with that of their surroundings. To the scientist, the sun is dying, its heat flowing out into space, never to be recovered. Such things express the law of entropy.

But no, said Reich, orgone energy processes go the other way, are "negatively entropic," and flow "uphill" from lower to higher concentration. Organization increases. The orgone, Reich said, gathers energy back from the universe. From this inflowing of orgone, matter and life are born. There is a building up, as well as a running down process operating in the universe, said Reich. The orgone runs "uphill," toward greater organization and lower entropy.

I review all this to show something of the breadth of Reich's life force conception, as well as where he made a major mistake, and why. His error in his "orgasm formula" occurred, as I have said, because of the mechanistic tendency in his character. It had brought the error into his otherwise extraordinary grasp of the life process, interfering with further progress until it was corrected. This error occurred even though it was Reich himself who noted and described the mechanistic and the mystical character structure.[2] It was somewhat like Reich's failure to understand the origin and function of the muscular armor, which I have described already. Big men make big mistakes because they are in the forefront, the vanguard of human knowledge. When such men make a wrong turn, their loyal followers go determindly tramping off in the wrong direction after them, magnifying the great man's mistake. It goes on until and unless somebody shows that the direction is wrong. Often the wrong-way momentum of the great man's followers is so great that they never do get back on track. Yet while he was alive, Reich discovered many of his own prior mistakes and his work grew in scope and power as a result.[3]

Correcting Reich's error in his "orgasm formula" led me to examine more closely what I knew -- or thought I knew -- about the life force and its properties. The orgasm formula had been more than a metaphor to Reich; it represented the fundamental life process. Once Reich's error was corrected, I could agree. Rhythmically repeated, its sequence described the pulsation that sustained living things and carried their lives forward. I called it *radix pulsation*. Charge and discharge were life force properties, tension and relaxation their consequences or effects on the physical matter of the body. The body's rhythmic outward and inward physical movement we could actually observe. Radix pulsation, the in and out movement of the life force itself, was not directly observed, but inferred through the body fluids' alternating pulsatory movements in (toward the center) and out (toward the periphery).

Reich's conclusion that the life force was "negatively entropic energy" embodied an error more profound than the inverted terms of the orgasm formula. Yet under the error was a profound truth. The error was thinking that the life force was energy at all. The profound truth was that the life force moved from lower toward higher concentrations. Much of Reich's scientific work on the life force, like my own work in the years following his death, foundered on this error. The vitalists had foundered on much the same problem, i.e., the inability to demonstrate physically their "entelechy" or "elan vital," their life force. In my own work I was in the process of discovering that we could not demonstrate the life force physically because it is not physical. It is real, it is natural, it gives rise to energy, but it is not energy. It is instead that from which both energy and mind are created.

Pulsation, Charge and Discharge

The pulsations of the body, its rhythmic movements in and out at different frequencies, seemed to characterize all living things. The observable physical pulsations of the body in the charge-discharge cycles of sex, of breathing, of the heartbeat, of sleeping and waking, are a few expressions of the underlying pulsatory life process. The pulsations -- I will call them now *radix* pulsations -- always have an objective and a subjective expression. Major radix discharges are strongly felt. Consider orgasm and weeping. When experienced as ecstasy and agony, these are our most intense feeling experiences. Each has powerful subjective as well as objective aspects, expressing a unitary underlying process, the build-up and convulsive discharge of the radix.

Working with pulsation, charge and discharge of the radix in the bodies of my students was central to my personal growth practice. As I freed and encouraged the pulsation in bodies of my students, mostly through release of inhibitions in breathing, radix charge developed. Charge, as I have noted, is associated with the inward stroke of the radix pulsation, with rest and recovery. Increasing radix charge expresses itself in increased excitement as well as increased tension in the body. Chronic tension is not an automatic result of charge. Rather it is learned, a way of containing the growing charge and inhibiting discharge. The "natural" tendency as charge develops is for excitement to grow and reach a threshold at which the radix pulsation quickens and deepens into convulsive discharge. The ultimate convulsive discharges are orgasm and sobbing, experienced with pleasure and pain, respectively. Inhibiting this process slows down and in some cases blocks convulsive discharge altogether. Many people thus find it difficult or impossible to orgasm or to sob or cry, even when it is entirely appropriate to do so. When discharge is inhibited, charge and tension can build up to very high levels. The body uses muscular tension to damp down the pulsation and charge process to prevent discharge.

There are different forms and rhythms of pulsation that take place over time. The most common is associated with developing more radix charge gradually from cycle to cycle, as in sleep or rest. Call these charging pulsations. Other forms appear in discharge of the radix buildup. The regular, normal, quiet pulsation charges the body. Each instroke of the radix brings a greater increment in the body's radix charge level than the discharge stroke of the cycle consumes. As the average charge level grows, the body grows more tense. Excitement gradually increases. The excitement expresses the "spilling over" into small discharges of the charge that has developed. Vigorous, intense activity discharges more rapidly. Thus after sleeping deeply in the charge phase of the diurnal sleeping/waking pulsation of our body, the charge level rises, until the growing charge begins to spill over into discharge, stirring the sleeper's consciousness with dreaming, moving him toward wakefulness and activity. Full consciousness returns with the onset of the discharge phase of the diurnal pulsation, the outstroke.

The "charging" pulsation happens most of the time, as each individual instroke in cycle after cycle of this pulsation brings an increment in the body's charge. But then at times the different form of pulsation associated with increased discharge occurs. There is a deepening and quickening of the rhythm and depth of radix pulsation as discharge takes over. Excitement grows, consciousness intensifies. In major discharges of feeling the body is mobilized in spasmodic convulsive movements, in which pulsation is quick and deep. Consider orgasm and sobbing again as the most intense examples, their convulsions the most strongly felt. With each convulsive contraction the charge level drops appreciably. But sneezing, coughing, laughing, and crying are also convulsive discharges. The life force in the body is regulated by the pulsatory charge-discharge process. We can list types of body pulsation.

Types or Forms of Respiratory Pulsation

1. Sleeping. Deep regular and usually diurnal radix pulsation, with emphasis on the instroke, expressed in the inhalation. Very little consciousness and movement. Radix charge builds regularly and spreads through the body.

2. Resting. Instroke and inhalation still predominate. Movement limited. Thought present but not intense. Charge increases.

3. Mild Activity. Normal easy relaxed thought and activity. Charge and discharge strokes of radix pulsation in approximate balance. Amplitude of pulsation (intensity of charge and discharge) cycle not great.

4. Intense Activity. Vigorous physical and/or intense emotional and mental involvement. Breathing deepens, and amplitude of radix pulsation expands. Charge grows, to give a greater discharge potential. Rate of pulsation may grow.

5. Convulsive Discharge. Pulsation pushes charge sharply higher, to finally initiate deeply felt involuntary convulsive in and out radix discharge cycles driving the respiration. Think again of sobbing and orgasm. Radix charge drops quickly during convulsive discharge.

6. Post-Convulsive Pulsation. When convulsive discharge is allowed to run its course the body then relaxes, the breathing becomes normal, easy and full. Tensions soften and disappear. Typically there is a strong feeling of relief.

Pulsation occurs broadly in nature, taking many different forms. The life of a tree is made up of a series of pulsatory cycles of its radix or life force, pulsations of different rhythms or frequencies. Remember the description at the start of this chapter. And the tree's whole life is itself one cycle in the sequence of lives made up of prior and succeeding generations of trees, for life is continuous and cyclic from generation to generation. Successive generations of animals as well can be regarded as pulsations of the germ plasm, living through the generations and progressing through evolution. As the individual life cycle of a tree is formed by a series of annual cycles, the annual cycle itself is made up of a series of shorter cycles, such as the diurnal (daily) cycle of the tree's existence. The diurnal pulsation is made up of still shorter cycles, etc. The radix process of living things takes place through pulsation, then. Slow cycles of pulsation merge with faster ones, as one rhythm is superimposed on another.

The radix exists before life, and living things evolve out of it. The living individual is above all a pulsating radix system. As a radix system, the living individual has the power to create. First and foremost, it creates itself. The individual's radix system uses the physical materials available to build a body and use it to store in physical form the information needed for it to live, to grow, to evolve across generations. At another level, over time the individual human creates his or her own character structure, influenced but not determined by the environment. The body houses the living radix system and gives it continuity, memory, and the means to acquire and use knowledge. This includes both the biological knowledge of the species and the particular knowledge acquired during the individual's lifetime. The body mediates the radix system's relation to the physical world, but the body is not the individual. We *have* bodies, but *are not* our bodies. Consciousness is not a product of the body but of the radix system that the body houses. The radix system provides the energy and awareness that make the body work. It is supplied by the *radix metabolism* of the individual radix system.

Radix Metabolism

This brings us back once more to radix pulsation, charge and discharge, and close to the mystery of the origin of the subjective and objective, of consciousness and energy in the universe. Radix metabolism is the accumulation and expenditure of radix charge in a radix system. The radix charge provides the living being its potential for feeling and movement, for consciousness and body activity. Radix charge is the "fuel" of the life process. This "fuel" is consumed with radix discharge. When I realized this, the secret of the radix process opened to me.

Radix discharge is the creative process proper, in which the radix charge is converted into energy and awareness. Discharge occurs on the outstroke of the radix pulsation. It is the "burning" of the "fuel" which is the radix charge. There is some discharge that takes place with the outstroke of each cycle of pulsation, and some charge on each instroke. The net charge may accumulate or drop over time, depending on the balance between the rate at which charge is taken in versus that at which it is discharged. The degree or intensity of awareness reflects the extent or amount of discharge taking place. When there is little discharge there is little awareness. An image may help clarify this point.

Imagine a young child sleeping. It is quiet and peaceful. There is little movement and little awareness. The child's radix charge is centered. This is the instroke of the sleep-wakefulness cycle of radix pulsation, and the child is building radix charge.

Imagine the child waking up, stretching and opening its eyes. Awareness and movement are returning, signaling the development of discharge. Consciousness and movement go with discharge. The child's radix charge is expanding, beginning to move out. The rate of charge and of discharge are approximately the same. The child's radix system has been charged by its rest.

Picture the child during the day, running, playing, investigating, doing. It is intensely aware and active as its radix charge is expended. The accumulated radix is discharging, being used.

Now it is bedtime. The child is asleep, and has slowed down as awareness has dimmed, signaling the slowing down of radix discharge. The child's radix charge is centering, and the rate of charge is rising with the reduced rate of discharge. The child's radix system has discharged, and is beginning to build charge again.

Asleep again, and once more charging, the child has completed a cycle in the diurnal radix pulsation that expresses itself in sleeping and wakefulness.

This illustration shows clearly the association of consciousness and activity with radix discharge, and of the abeyance of consciousness and activity during the charging phase of the pulsation, i.e., sleep. **Charge occurs on the instroke.** The principle is general, and applies to other radix pulsations. For example, in the breathing pulsation, inhalation is the instroke, the charge stroke, and exhalation the outward, discharge stroke. **Discharge occurs on the outstroke.** Awareness and activity intensify with the exhalation. Mrs. Margaret Corbett, the finest teacher of vision improvement I have ever known, taught that improvements in vision come on the exhalation. Moshe Feldenkrais, the Israeli expert on body structure and function, taught that in repetitive activity the more active motions take place with exhalation. The tennis player exhales in striking the ball; many players grunt or cry audibly. Awareness and action express radix discharge, then, and discharge intensifies with the exhalation. To prepare for awareness or action, for thought or exertion, one involuntarily inhales and, by inhaling, builds, centers and focuses charge. The discharge phase *is* the thought and/or activity, and occurs on exhalation. It is what the charge was preparation for, and it completes the charge-discharge cycle of the respiratory pulsation.

Charge is the less evident "invisible" side of radix metabolism because it occurs <u>before</u> the birth of energy and awareness. It is a mid-point in the creative process, yet a point prior to the tangible, observable stage. Because it is before energy is created, radix charge cannot be experienced directly but must be inferred. It sometimes appears that we can experience the charge of our own body directly, but I have concluded that this is not really the case. What happens is that the radix charge of our body feeds millions of fast small-scale pulsation-charge-discharges, including nerve and muscle cell processes. An increase in large-scale charge level results in more small-scale discharges. The increased tension reflecting increased charge can be observed objectively and felt subjectively; charge leads to tension in the body. It is from the effect of multitudes of small-scale discharges, fueled by the body's higher charge level, that the higher radix charge of the body can be inferred and experienced. The higher radix charge in and of itself is not observable.

The central features of the creative process in a radix system can now be summarized. The radix system pulsates, and pulsation sustains the radix metabolism, regulating charge and discharge. The radix charge accumulates on the instroke of the pulsation. This accumulation of charge is the first, "invisible" phase of the radix metabolism. The radix charge provides the system's potential for creation. The potential provided by the radix charge is realized, then, on the outward, discharge stroke of the pulsation, in which the charge is consumed.

But I had questions about the process.

The Radix Process as Pulsation, Charge and Discharge

The radix charge of the body builds gradually through pulsation, and the buildup is expressed through tension. At times the pulsation quickens and deepens into discharge. The discharge is, in its fullest form, convulsive, intense, and powerfully felt. After such a discharge the body is dramatically softer. Notice the examples of discharge in the radix sessions of the previous chapter. The tension has disappeared, signifying that the charge is gone. What happened to the radix charge? It vanished quickly and completely with the discharge. Where did it go? I didn't know, but it disappeared, regularly, lawfully, always as a consequence of discharge. I needed to understand why and how.

"Charge → tension → discharge → relaxation" said the orgasm formula as I had revised it. The radix charge developed gradually with pulsation. There was a build-up of tension that I observed on the instroke of the pulsation. I understood it to be a collecting of radix charge that flowed "uphill" from lower to higher charge, from the environment in to the organism, in accord with the principle enunciated by Reich. I would later have more questions about the charge process. At first I simply accepted that the body collected the inflowing radix charge through pulsation. But with discharge did the body just "throw off" the collected charge? If so, where did it go? If not, why did the charge and tension vanish with the discharge?

I looked harder at the charge-discharge process. Charge took place more or less unconsciously with sleep, inhalation, preparation, the instroke of the pulsation. Discharge, however, was conscious. The greater the discharge, the more strongly was it felt. Orgasm and weeping remained the ultimate examples. And so I came to understand that discharge of the radix produced consciousness. The more intense the discharge, the more intense the conscious activity that was experienced with it. Conversely, the absence of consciousness signaled absence of discharge. Charging took place especially in the unconscious sleep phase of the diurnal pulsation. As discharge went with consciousness, charge went with unconsciousness.

Discharge brought not only consciousness, it brought activity. Charge went with stillness. Discharge expressed feeling, thought, and action. The sleeping child woke, became aware, moved, did things. This all reflected discharge of the radix charge that had built during sleep.

I thought of the annual pulsation cycle of the tree in those terms. The tree gathered charge in its roots and trunk during its long winter "sleep." Then spring came, and it "woke up." Its sap moved up under the bark to its branches and twigs. The tree grew, branched further, produced leaves, perhaps flowers, then fruit. That was its discharge phase. Was it also conscious in its way? I could not say it was not. Truthfully, when I "tuned into" the tree in spring or summer in its full aliveness, I thought of it as conscious. I had my

125

kind of consciousness, the tree had a different kind, its own, that I could appreciate and enjoy. There was a subjective side to the tree's life, as there was to mine. I was even willing to think of a beautiful blooming tree or flowering plant as "happy," granted that its happiness was different from mine.

As these insights developed, a new understanding of the life force was taking place in me. It grew most as I worked with my personal growth students in their Radix sessions. I applied what I was learning to my life, to my scientific theories, and to my religious or spiritual outlook. Scientific and spiritual outlook are very much the same thing with me. As I struggled to understand the life force, I was trying to understand the whole universe, the nature of life in general and my own life in particular.

There was something else needed for me to understand radix discharge. It threw me back to an article I had written in 1951, the year after I arrived in New York. Reich had published my article in his **Orgone Energy Bulletin** the following year.[4] I called it *Causality and Freedom*. In it, I speculated that "freedom of the will" was rooted in life force processes, Reich's "orgone." How? Twenty years later in my burgeoning personal growth practice the mystery was unraveling.

When the key insight for understanding "freedom of the will" finally came to me, it was as if I had always known it. I could now describe the radix process in four sentences. These express my second major discovery, the origin and function of the muscular armor being the first. Here is the second:

The Second Discovery

- Consciousness and energy are born into the world simultaneously through one natural process, the radix process, in which mind and matter, spirit and energy, are created from radix charge, through radix discharge.

- <u>Radix charge is or arises from a substratum of nature, the *radix*, that exists before mind or energy come into being.</u>

- <u>Radix discharge is felt as sensation, emotion, feelings, thought, images, etc., processes of consciousness or mind that occur when new energy, primary energy, having no prior history in the physical universe, enters the world.</u>

- <u>Radix charge is fuel that is consumed in the radix discharge process, resulting in the creation of new energy in the form of new movement (growth or action) and of new matter; new movement and new matter are both forms of energy.</u>

There in a few sentences is the second discovery, the radix process, the creative process in nature, acting through the life force. These four sentences are the essence of what I discovered about the creative process in two decades of study.

Important questions that had long troubled me were answered by this formulation. Here are some of them:

Why does radix discharge leave a tense body relaxed and soft? -- Because the tension is produced by the radix charge. With radix discharge, the charge disappears, having been converted to energy in the discharge process. The conversion leaves the body soft and relaxed. The powerful convulsive discharges of weeping and orgasm show the process most clearly. They are strongly felt and energetically expressed, and they drop the charge (and tension) level of the body quickly and dramatically.

How does radix discharge explain the ages-old philosophic problem of "freedom of the will?" -- The problem of freedom of the will occurs because deterministic scientists see the universe as a closed system, fixed in the amount of energy it contains, and as running down, its entropy increasing. To them, natural processes involving energy convert the energy in a closed system from one form to another in ways that are in accord with the laws of conservation of energy and of entropy. But radix systems destroy the determinist's bookkeeping

127

by introducing new unaccounted for energy via radix charge and discharge. Radix systems, with living things as the preeminent example, introduce newly created energy, energy appearing in the physical universe for the first time, whenever and wherever radix charge is discharged. "Freedom of the will" exists because the process of will has new energy at its disposal, the new energy that can be created through radix discharge. Consciousness, a necessary correlate of will, signifies that radix charge is being discharged, and new energy therefore being created.

What is this problem of freedom of the will? At the common sense level, everyone knows that they have "freedom of the will," that they can stop or go, turn this way or that way, get up or sit down, decide to go in any of a number of directions, and do it. Only the bodies of the dead (or unconscious) move in accord with Newton's laws of motion. But deterministic scientists, in order to keep their books balanced, convince themselves that conscious processes of intention and will cannot change the course of physical events, and that the perception that one does so is illusory. Theirs is a silly, ultimately hopeless position, contrary to every person's experience. But traditional science has been totally unable to find a role for subjective events in the workings of physical nature. The world of consciousness, of feelings, images, thought, and will are not a form of energy or an energy process, and have no status as permissible forms of energy or causes of behavior in the physical scientists' dictionary of permissable energy transformations.

Creation and the First Two Laws of Thermodynamics[5]

The first law of thermodynamics is the law of conservation of energy, the second is the law of entropy. These are not so much laws as major principles believed by most scientists to govern the working of nature. There is a long history with mountains of writings and data to support them if mechanistic assumptions are accepted. In the 19th century there were two conservation laws, the conservation of energy and the conservation of matter. The Curies' discovery of the radioactive decay of matter and Einstein's famous elucidation of the equivalence of mass and energy ($E=mc^2$) showed us that the two conservation laws should be consolidated into one, because matter had been proved to be a form of energy. The eternal but running down universe of conservation plus entropy is accepted as an article of faith by the scientific establishment.

Still, many scientific mavericks have been convinced that there is a building up as well as a running down process in the universe, of creation as well as entropic decay. The view is implicit in the work of Mesmer, Reichenbach, the vitalists, and the steady-state cosmologists of the past century. Wilhelm Reich was one of these. His conviction, as has been noted, was that orgone energy was energy's most basic form, and that orgone energy ran "uphill," from lower to higher concentration, thus from higher to lower entropy, in violation of the second law of thermodynamics.

Reich was incorrect in believing his work overturned the law of entropy. Reich's "orgone energy" proved not to be an objective physical energy at all, and so could not be expected to obey the law of entropy. Nevertheless, Reich's orgone existed as something real and natural, a substratum of nature that exists before energy. From it energy is created and life arises. And I called the substratum the "radix."

It is the radix, this substratum of nature before energy, that flows from lower to higher concentration. It forms radix systems, systems that pulsate, driving their charge to higher and higher levels, until they discharge. It is not until there is radix discharge that energy, new energy, appears for the first time in the physical universe. With it comes consciousness, mind, awareness. Objective and subjective nature are born together in radix systems through radix discharge. They come from a level of existence that is neither objective or subjective but underlies both.

Energy is the material of the physical world, of objective nature. Once energy has been born into and becomes a part of the physical world, it obeys that world's laws of energy transformation, including the law of entropy. At the instant of its birth it intrudes into the world from a different dimension or level of existence. Its form and expression at its birth change the events of the world, and at the same time allow us to reconstruct and begin to understand processes in that other level or dimension, including radix pulsation, charge and the creative process proper -- radix discharge.

Radix processes guide the growth, development, and reproduction of all living things, and of much in nature that is not living, at least not in normal scientific frames of reference. Think of the generation of the stars and planets and, here on our own planet, the storms and weather. And, I believe, the creation of new matter takes place here on earth, under our eyes, as in Reich's experiments and mine. Radix processes that we can learn to understand are at work within and around us. I even developed a special formal system of representation, "Radix Algebra," to aid this understanding. It is described in the next chapter.

Chapter Notes

[1] Reich, W., 1942, THE FUNCTION OF THE ORGASM. New York: Orgone Institute Press, pp. 212-223. Subsequently reprinted by Farrar, Straus & Cudahy, New York.

[2] Reich, W., 1949, ETHER, GOD AND DEVIL. Orgone Institute Press. Reprinted by Farrar, Straus & Giroux, 1973. Contains Reich's classic descriptions of mechanism and mysticism.

[3] *Ibid* for Reich's discussion of his own past errors.

[4] Kelley, C.R., 1952, *Causality and Freedom: A Functional Analysis.* **Orgone Energy Bulletin,** Vol. IV No. 1.

[5] Schroedinger's hypothesis involving Heisenberg indeterminacy, and Sheldrake's morphic resonance as causation concern creation and the 1st law of thermodynamics. Hans Jonas is particularly good on the larger implications of this problem. See:
Schroedinger, E., 1945, WHAT IS LIFE. New York: The Macmillan Co.; Sheldrake, R., 1981, A NEW SCIENCE OF LIFE: THE HYPOTHESIS OF FORMATIVE CAUSATION. London: Blond & Briggs; and 1988, THE PRESENCE OF THE PAST: MORPHIC RESONANCE AND THE HABITS OF NATURE. New York: Times Books. (Reprinted by Vintage

Books, 1989); and
Jonas, H., 1966, THE PHENOMENON OF LIFE. New York: Harper & Row.

Chapter 8

THE ALGEBRA OF RADIX DISCHARGE

New discoveries spawn new techniques and ways of applying them. Most central to the development of Radix has been the discovery of the radix discharge process, through which consciousness and new energy are born and come into the familiar world. They enter the world together, the subjective and objective expressions of the same process, the creative process in nature. The intensity of conscious experience corresponds to the rate at which new energy is created, while the quality of the conscious experience, the character or kind of experience it is, reflects the physical structure into which the new energy is born.

It has been interesting and enjoyable to develop and employ a new formal system to represent the radix discharge process with its dual aspects, subjective and objective, and their common root, the radix. These aspects emerge through radix discharge into the familiar world. The symbols of radix algebra represent the radix discharge process in various contexts and configurations, most of them drawn from observations of human life.

Two features of the radix symbolized in the algebra of radix discharge are identity and antithesis. Radix identity refers to the fact that the radix process simultaneously expresses itself in the two realms of nature, the subjective conscious realm and the objective physical realm. The subjective and objective expressions of a radix process refer to the identical event, viewed from the standpoint of an individual consciousness and from that of physical nature. Therefore a radix discharge process in a human body can be understood and expressed as a psychosomatic identity. Most but not all of the radix identities in this chapter are psychosomatic identities.

The second feature of the radix discharge process expressed in the formal system of radix algebra is that of antithesis. Radix identities occur in opposite-appearing pairs. To illustrate, consider the psychosomatic identity of the feeling of mirth and its physical expression, laughing. This psychosomatic identity has as its antithesis the feeling of grief and its physical expression, weeping.

The primary focus of my studies of the radix process has been living creatures, and in particular fellow human beings, with their expressive movements. Expressive movements arise from radix discharge within the body. The discharge is experienced consciously as feelings and awareness, and the energy discharge is expressed through body movement. What the body does reflects the new energy emerging from the radix discharge process. Mind/body and feeling/movement are the subjective/objective expressions, respectively, of the radix process underlying them both.

The paired subjective and objective expressions of an underlying radix process define a set of relations that can be described in the formal language I call radix algebra. As the equal sign "=" is a primary symbol used in algebra, the radix identity sign "⊀" is a primary symbol used in radix algebra. The radix identity is the first formal relationship expressed in radix algebra. When dealing with the living individual, it can express the relation of mind, body, and the radix process in which they are both rooted. In these cases we can refer to radix *psychosomatic* identities. Most applications I have so far made of radix algebra deal with living things and hence have used psychosomatic identities. However, one advantage of the technique is that it helps one to generalize from radix processes of life to some of the same processes in non-living nature.

The radix identity relates a radix process to its subjective and objective expression as follows:

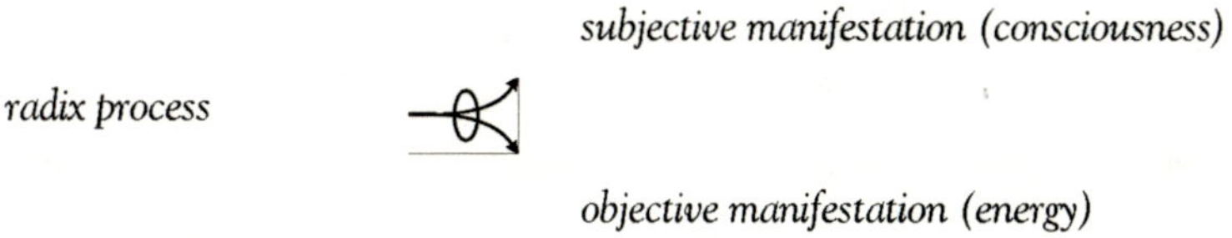

Algebra of Radix Discharge

radix process
subjective manifestation (consciousness)

objective manifestation (energy)

Figure 1.

    The three terms here tied together by the radix identity symbol formalize the radix process. Through the radix process, awareness and energy, "mind and body," are born, to emerge into the world as we know it. The upper term of the identity refers to subjective experience of the radix process, the lower term the physical expression, while the radix process itself is that from which the other two arise. The intensity of consciousness corresponds to the rate at which new energy is created.

    The long-time reader of my writings will recognize the radix identity symbol as the radix logo, trademark of my work. It appeared on the inside cover of the **Radix Journal** for many years in this form:

radix process
(radix discharge)

energy
(objective nature,
growth, spontaneous
movement, action)

spirit
(subjective nature,
awareness, feeling,
consciousness)

Figure 2.

    I learned with time that it was more convenient to rotate and shrink the identity symbol, e.g.,

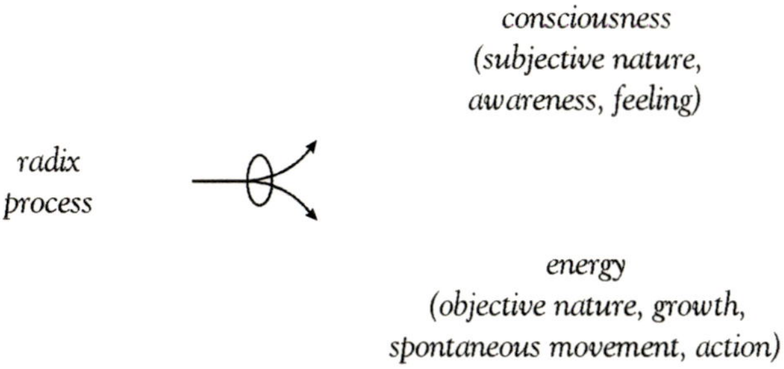

consciousness
(subjective nature,
awareness, feeling)

radix process

energy
(objective nature, growth,
spontaneous movement, action)

Figure 3.

The second formal relationship expressed in radix algebra is of radix antithesis. It is shown by two radix identities that have an oppositional or polarized relationship to each other. As an example, one important radix antithesis is:

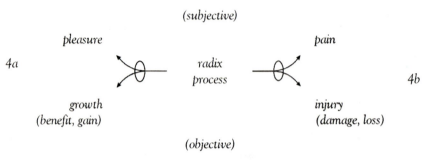

Figure 4.

This radix antithesis represents the living organism's way of reacting to that which furthers, versus that which hurts, its life. The subjective experience of pleasure versus pain attaches a value to an experience that guides learning. Note that a living thing born with the antithetical subjective functions reversed, one that consistently experienced pleasure with damage or harm to the self and pain with growth or benefit to the self, would soon perish.

The radix antithesis involves opposite directions in a radix process that can go either way. My working hypothesis is that for every correct radix identity there is an antithesis, so that when antithesis is not evident, the formulation is not yet fully worked out. Here is another example, used above in the prologue to this chapter:

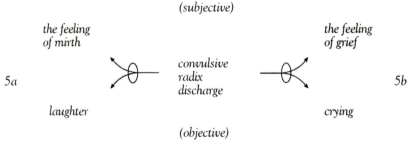

Figure 5.

In convulsive discharge, more radix charge is used on the outstroke of each convulsive cycle than is gained on the instroke, so the process proceeds in pulsatory strokes toward discharge. There is some charging on each instroke of the cycle, however, with this as with every true radix pulsation. It is the extent to which the radix discharge (outstroke) exceeds the charge (instroke) that governs the overall rate of discharge.

In 1872 Darwin expressed the principle of antithesis in emotional expression.[1] The feelings and their expressions in Figures 4 and 5 clearly bear an antithetical relation to each other, and are thus a formal expression of the Darwinian principle. Human emotional responses are a most important class of polarized radix processes. Knowing their antitheses helps to clarify particular feelings and their expression, even as their description has helped to develop the formal technique of radix algebra. In addition, they provide a new avenue toward understanding the radix process they express.

Although Darwin first enunciated the principle of antithesis in emotional expression, radix algebra was influenced more in its development by Reich's work than by Darwin's. Reich was much interested in formulating a system of thought and a formal technique for describing orgone (life force) functions. He described what he called "orgonometric equations" in articles in 1950 and 1951 in the *Orgone Energy Bulletin*.[2] My discovery of the radix process after Reich's death made it possible for me to develop radix algebra, as I present it here. While quite different from Reich's orgonometric equations, radix algebra is consistent with Reich's objective of a formal technique for describing the functioning of the life force. I believe radix algebra is a more developed and powerful tool than Reich's formulations, based as it is on radix discoveries made after Reich's death.

Radix algebra is a precise and systematic way of describing certain radix processes. It clarifies the nature and characteristics of these processes by specifying their subjective and objective identity and polarity (antithesis) relationships. The identities and antitheses of radix algebra describe natural creative processes with more clarity and precision than is possible by word language alone. There are radix algebraic expressions in which it is difficult or impossible to find words to denote the radix process of concern. Once the words are chosen, they are given a highly specific meaning by the context of the radix identity or antithesis in which they are embedded.

Radix algebra does not explain natural creative processes. It is only an improved way of describing them. Newton's law of gravitation and its formal algebraic expression describe the effects of gravity without being in any way an explanation of what gravity is. In the same way, the radix antithesis and identity relations expressed in the formal language of radix algebra describe and may clarify radix processes without in any way explaining them. They are a different framework of description of these processes than word language alone, and as a new descriptive technique they can provide additional insight into creative processes.

One of the powers of radix algebra is that as knowledge is gained about any of the terms in a radix formal expression, it is simultaneously gained about all of the other terms that make up the expression. Thus knowledge of the subjective process included in a radix identity can result in better knowledge of the objective body process it is paired with. The converse is also true. In addition, better knowledge of either the subjective or objective terms of a radix identity can result in better knowledge of the radix process in which both originate. Extending this, better knowledge of any one of the four corner terms in a radix antithesis can clarify understanding of the other three corner terms in the expression, and may also shed light on the polarized radix process that is their root. Thus the nature and characteristics of a radix process become better understood.

The radix in itself is not easily grasped. It is what the radix does, its properties and the natural processes through which it is expressed that throw light on it. Radix algebra is another tool that can be used in trying to understand these processes. The tool is new, and there is no history of its use to guide us. We can use it as we speculate about profound and difficult questions, provided we remember how prone our work may be to error at this early stage. Consider a few fundamental radix processes, and how radix algebra might be used to help understand them.

Individuation

Before life there is the radix substratum from which, and the radix process by which, the living individual develops. I have suggested that living individuals are **radix charge systems**, each one formed around a **radix source**, a center of low charge surrounded by higher charge in all directions. Radix theory is that radix charge flows out from lower to higher charge in every direction at each source. The living individual is a physiological structure built around a radix source. The source is its center of growth, consciousness, being, and contact with the universal. How can we apply radix algebra to help understand this metaphysical position?

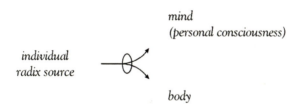

Figure 6.

In Figure 6, the identity is an application to a living individual of the identity with which we began (see Figure 3). Think of the individual radix source as the self or soul, the root of the individual in the universal life force and its connection to a unique person. The body houses the mind and spirit, and gives them their connection to the physical world.

Each living individual incorporates its own source within itself. Figure 6 represents one single unitary individual, having its own separate self-contained radix source. Radix source, mind and

LIFE FORCE

body, characterize the individual, the living physical and mental entity, together with the entity's root in the radix substratum.

It is easy to take for granted that each discrete body has one and only one discrete and individual mind or consciousness, but it is by no means self-evident. One can in principle imagine one body with two or several minds or consciousnesses, or two or several bodies governed by a single mind. In reality, however, I observe that mind and body are unitary and single. This would seem to be because they develop around a single radix source. This source forms the center of their existence as a unique living individual.[3]

Can we complete the identity in Figure 6 by formulating an antithesis, as I said might be possible for all correct radix identities? This means finding the term opposite to individuation. Consider the following as a speculation:

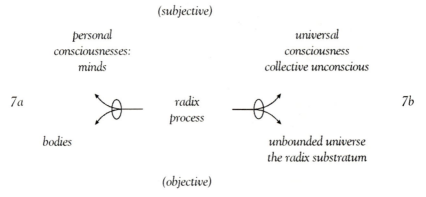

Figure 7.

Can we posit a universal consciousness as opposed to personal consciousness? Perhaps Jung's collective unconscious and Buddhist nirvana belong in Figure 7b. I do believe that there is a transpersonal dimension in life, but it is too early for me to say very much about it in radix terms. I do find radix algebra a useful tool in thinking about it.

The Radix Algebra of the Feelings

Feelings are the primordial form of animal consciousness. In the simplest creatures, feelings in response to the environment (sensations) and those from which responses originate (emotions) are barely differentiated. For them the "emotions" flow almost directly from the sensations. Individual learning hardly exists, and responses are largely instinctive. In simple creatures, responses are modified little by individual learning, but spontaneous variations give rise to some individuals with responses better adapted to the species' survival. These tend to be preserved, to give rise, over the generations, to evolutionary learning by the species.

Early on in the evolutionary process the differentiation grew between the two distinct classes of feelings: those concerned with incoming stimulation (sensation and perception) and those concerned with developing a response (emotion). Increasingly complex neural structures evolved dealing with each class. These grew to include a brain with separate sensory and motor regions. Sensations became refined and developed to form perceptions, which evolved into the capacity to form, from the material of consciousness, a model of the world around the individual. Thus sensation led to perception and, with an increasing contribution by thinking and memory, to some degree of understanding. At the same time the evolving animal developed an ever more elaborate capacity to evaluate through the emotions what was happening, and act accordingly. Growing from the primitive reaction to approach pleasure and avoid pain, the family of emotion so central to higher animal life evolved. Was something enticing to an animal? Arousing? Did another creature stimulate its hunting instinct? A feeling of sexual attraction, fear or anger? At these levels, human beings can readily identify with other higher animals.

Radix algebra describes these developments beginning with the two branches of feeling consciousness that developed between sensations and emotions:

LIFE FORCE

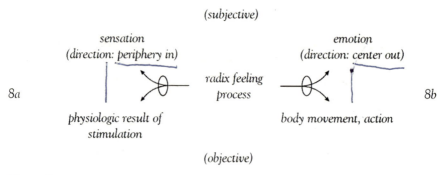

Figure 8.

In *sensation,* the usual sequence is a physical stimulus that excites a physiological response in sensory organs and nerves. This sensory physiological response enables the radix process in Figure 8a to create the sensory experience in consciousness. In *emotion,* the radix process of Figure 8b generates energy through radix discharge that brings about muscular response and action. The mind--body connection goes in from environment to body to radix process and consciousness in Figure 8a, the left identity. It comes out from radix process and consciousness to body and environment (Fig. 8b).

Psychologically, the experiences depicted in Figure 8a consist of sensory and perceptual qualities. Qualities are the materials of consciousness. When experiences derived from memory are added to those of sensation, sensation is enlarged into perception. Examples of sensory qualities are green, or salty, or shrill. Perceptual qualities, however, refer to what we can call a model, however crude, of the perceived world, built with the aid of information from memory as well as from the senses. Something can be perceived not only as green/salty/shrill -- sensory qualities -- but also as dangerous, edible, or inconsequential. These are perceptual qualities.

The perceiving individual is in a position to move about, manipulate, or take action on his environment, but sensations and perceptions are not a guide to action. They give us information about the environment, but not, except in certain reflexes, what to do about it.[4] Movements, actions, are guided by another kind of feelings, the emotions (Fig. 8b). If something rouses our emotions --

frightens, attracts, excites, intrigues, angers us -- action is the usual consequence. Emotions are a non-intellectual evaluation of the material of perception. They tend to lead into action, and guide behavior. Clearly, we behave very differently when angry than when loving, when fearful than when trusting.

Go back to a formulation of the radix antithesis in Figure 4, representing the fundamental psychosomatic process in all animal life:

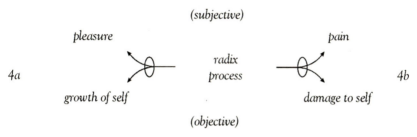

Figure 4.

This general antithesis pervades emotional life. It can be formulated in a variety of ways. Happiness versus sadness is one of importance:

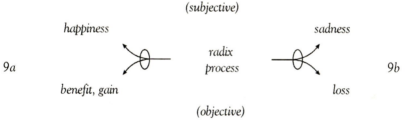

Figure 9.

When the pleasure/pain process is convulsive, another element is added, as in this antithesis already presented in Figure 5:

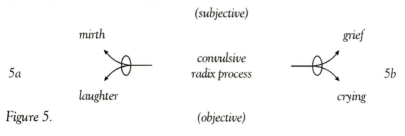

Figure 5.

LIFE FORCE

The convulsive nature of grief and mirth, described earlier, shows something significant about strong radix discharges: a lot of radix charge is discharged quickly in convulsive discharge. This is consistent with such discharge being so strongly felt. Now consider further the quality of the feelings. They are experienced as pleasurable or painful, but differ in their quality from simple happiness and sadness. It is interesting that the convulsive process operates in "both directions," pleasure and unpleasure. The antithesis of Figure 5 represents a convulsive psychosomatic process. It is characteristic of convulsion that the feeling is strongly felt and spontaneous; it overwhelms any voluntary control as it runs its course. A different emotional process illustrating both the pain-pleasure dichotomy and radix convulsion is:

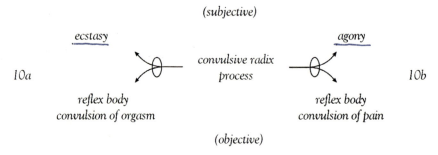

Figure 10.

Ayn Rand, as I noted before, has described the orgasm as "man's only ecstasy." Pain reaches a comparable intensity of feeling only with great agony. When it does, the body is often thrown into powerful convulsions, and the antithesis in Figure 10 is expressed.

"Venture" versus "Protect" Mode Emotions

Consider some non-convulsive emotions that are still part of the pain/pleasure family. The venture versus protect emotions have evolved in the higher animals to guide them in their behavior.

Venture and *protect* modes of emotional response go beyond simple pain and pleasure responses from which they evolved.

Think of the evolution of anticipatory emotion. Simple pain/pleasure are not in themselves anticipatory, but are here-and-now, present-time feelings. They guide the behavior of the simplest primitive animals, which withdraw from pain and advance toward pleasure. With evolution, nervous systems develop through which the anticipation of possible pleasure or pain is made possible. Life begins to be lived across time. So important are the anticipatory emotions that they pervade the life of higher animals.

In the anticipation of possible pain, damage, or loss "protect mode" feelings are triggered. The body tenses; the sympathetic nervous system, a division of the autonomic system, is activated. Adrenalin is pumped into the blood, the heart speeds up, and blood leaves the viscera and moves into the muscles. The body thus moves in the direction of "fight or flight" *protect* mode response. Basic emotions governing the response are fear and/or anger. The *protect* function wards off possible damage and pain by action in advance through the anticipatory emotions.

Consider the antithetical "venture mode" feelings, triggered by the anticipation of possible pleasure or gain. The body relaxes defenses; the parasympathetic nervous system, the other division of the autonomic system, is activated. The body moves into *venture* mode functioning. Blood may move to the stomach if food is on the way, into the genitals if there is possible sexual activity in the offing, or the individual may simply relax into the normal pleasurable activities of daily life.

Figures 11 and 12 express the organizing of the anticipatory emotions into venture and protect modes of function. Figure 11 expresses the center-outward emotions for both venture and protect modes of function:

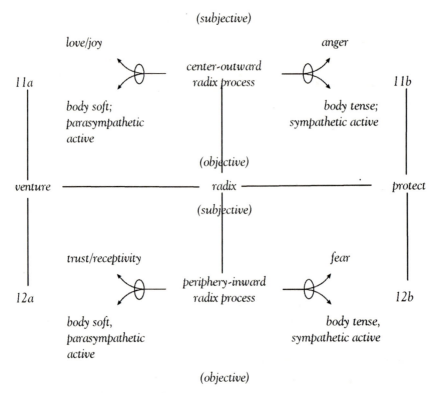

Figures 11 and 12.

Love/joy are venture mode emotions that are directed outward. "Love" is the word we use when the feeling is directed toward another living thing, while "joy" is felt when the expansive venture mode emotion flows out toward the world. With love or joy, the body is relaxed and the parasympathetic is active. In contrast, the protect mode emotion with the direction from center out toward the world is anger. It is antithetical to love/joy, and takes place with the body tense, the sympathetic branch of the autonomic nervous system active, and the body readied to fight.

A similar antithesis can be expressed for venture and protect modes of function for emotions involving the direction, periphery-inward (see Figure 12). In the venture mode the inward direction goes with trust/receptivity. Like love/joy, trust is the name for the feeling when it involves relation to another individual, receptivity

Algebra of Radix Discharge

when it is felt in relation to the environment. (The word "receptivity" is not entirely satisfactory, but seems better here than "openness" or "vulnerability." The radix antithesis describes the meaning better than the words.) The body is relaxed, the parasympathetic active. In the protect mode when the direction is inward, the emotion is fear. The body contracts, the sympathetic nervous system is active.

The antitheses in Figures 11 and 12 together express two radix organizing principles in interaction. The venture-protect principle is expressed in these two antitheses. However, it is just as valid to use the center-out/periphery-in direction of flow as the radix organizing principle for the four emotions, in which case they take the form shown in Figures 13 and 14:

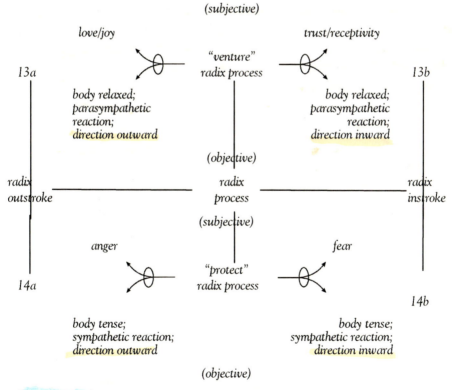

Figures 13 and 14.

LIFE FORCE

These two antitheses, employing the centrifugal (center-out) and the centripetal (periphery-in) radix direction as their antithetical radix principle of organization, are just as valid as those in Figures 11 and 12. This interchangeability can happen when two radix processes interact in our area of study.

Venture versus protect mode expresses a valid radix principle operating in animal life, whatever we name it. It expresses itself in a psychosomatic antithesis of wide validity. Animals evolve under this principle, and complex structures like the autonomic nervous system, with its sympathetic and parasympathetic branches, are the result of the radix principle acting over evolutionary reaches of time. It is not the other way around, with the structures evolving first, and the radix principle then coming into existence.

Venture versus protect emotions are complicated because a second radix principle of organization of equal validity to that of venture--protect is operating simultaneously. This is the radix principle of centrifugal (instroke) versus centripetal (outstroke) direction of radix flow. This antithesis also expresses a principle of wide validity in animal life. It has governed the evolution of what I have called the anticipatory emotions, with their antitheses of (Fig. 13) love versus anger (outstroke) and (Fig. 14) trust versus fear (instroke).

We need to be able to express formally the information in the whole set of antitheses (Figs. 11-14) through one representation. It is needed not just here, but for other duplex radix antitheses that will be encountered. Because the principle of radix psychosomatic identity should remain part of our representation as well, there are really three dimensions to be diagrammed. In algebraic analysis in mathematics, this can be done by assigning each radix principle a dimension in a three-dimensional space. Let X, which is the left-to-right direction in a diagram, represent the centrifugal-centripetal principle. Let Y, which is top to bottom in the diagram, represent the venture--protect principle; and let Z then equal the psychosomatic identity and antithesis principle central to all radix work. The representation in Figure 15 conveys at least an idea of what I have in mind.

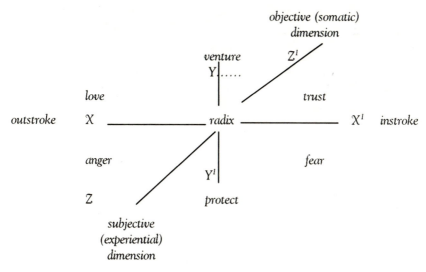

Figure 15. *Three-dimensional representation of radix antitheses illustrated in Figures 11–14.*
The X dimension is left to right; the Y dimension is up--down, and the Z dimension is the third dimension, going near to far.

The four major anticipatory emotions are shown in their correct antithesis relationship. Their objective, somatic counterparts are implicit on the plane behind. Of course, the somatic information not shown is also of major importance in understanding these emotions, doing much to help us discern their nature.

I have presented a radix formal method, examples, and a framework for further development. It is only a beginning. There is a need to extend the method further, for example, to develop further objective antitheses of structure and movement with the corresponding subjective antitheses of enduring versus instantaneous aspects of experience.

Applications of Radix Algebra

I began developing radix algebra in the early 1970s. In 1974 the radix identity symbol became the logo of the Radix organization

I had founded. It went on our letterhead and publications, and was registered as a service mark with the U.S. Patent office. The first published article on radix algebra appeared in **The Radix Journal** in 1979.[5] Articles on the radix algebra of the feelings and the radix algebra of purpose soon followed.[6] Readers were intrigued by the technique, but their comments often carried a question. One of them said, "It's very pretty, you know, very clever, but really, what is it good for? What can you do with it?" Such questions always took me aback a little.

It seems to me what I've presented on radix algebra is just a beginning. In truth, I haven't tried to "accomplish" anything with it. For me, it is like a pretty picture, or a new instrument or other invention that did something very neatly that no one had done before. I've resisted having to justify what I've done by showing its useful applications. Still, I think it is useful, and I believe will prove more useful as it develops because it embodies a new way of describing the facts of reality expressed in radix processes.

When my radix algebra identities and antitheses are correct, they describe creative processes with a kind of precision and elegance that word language alone does not convey. In this respect they are like algebra, geometry, and calculus. The meaning of the terms in a radix antithesis is more than that expressed in the words used for the antithesis. The formal symbols of radix algebra, correctly applied, say something about the radix process that doesn't lend itself as well to strictly verbal expressions. My intuition says that radix algebra will grow, be developed further, and have application to fields and problems I cannot hope to imagine. It has already helped me in my effort to understand the life force and how it functions. The application to the nature and structure of feelings and emotions as described here is still the clearest and best example.

Will radix algebra also aid the understanding of radix physics or metaphysics? I suspect so. As of this writing, that is a dream of the future.

Chapter Notes

[1] Darwin, C., 1872. THE EXPRESSION OF THE EMOTIONS IN MAN AND IN ANIMALS. London: John Murray. Reprinted in 1965 by the University of Chicago Press,.

[2] Reich, W., 1950, "Orgonometric Equations: 1. General Form," *Orgone Energy Bulletin,*, Vol. II No. 4, pp. 161-183. And 1951, "Complete Orgonometric Equations," *Orgone Energy Bulletin*, Vol. III, No. 2, pp. 65-71.

[3] Cases of "split personalities," in which individuals claim their bodies house two or more, up to many dozens of separate personalities, would confirm the existence of separate persons occupying the same body, if the phenomenon were genuine. In my opinion the phenomenon is not genuine, and the various "personalities" that are claimed to inhabit one body are a delusion.

[4] In some simple human reflexes, sensation leads directly to action. Example, touching a live wire or hot stove.

[5] First described in Kelley, C.R., 1979, *The Radix Journal,* Vol. I No. 4, pp. 13-25. Vancouver, WA: K/R Publications.

[6] Kelley, C.R., 1980, "The Radix Algebra of the Feelings," in *The Radix Journal*, Vol. II No. 1&2, and "The Radix Algebra of Purpose," in *The Radix Journal* Vol. II Nos. 3&4. Both reprinted with the original article "Radix Algebra" in Kelley, C.R., 1992, THE RADIX VOL. II: THE SCIENCE OF RADIX PROCESSES, pp. 59-82. Vancouver, WA: K/R Publications.

Chapter 9

CENTERING, SOURCE, SELF AND SOUL

Every human being is a separate and particular manifestation of the life force, an individual example of creation, rooted in, yet differentiated from, the whole. I have my own source, with its pattern of pulsation, different from yours, and I charge and discharge individually and separately from you. My mind, my consciousness, is generated by my radix discharge. Radix charge is the fuel of life, and in discharge the fuel is consumed. As my charge is consumed, feeling and thought are generated -- my feelings, my thoughts. Along with feeling and thought, new energy is born into my body, and through me the new energy, my energy, my physical behavior, changes the physical world I live in. It changes it in small and sometimes large ways, in keeping with my feelings and thoughts. Underlying all this is the pulsation of my life force, into and out from my center, my radix source. This in and out rhythm sustains my life, as the pulsations of other living individuals sustain theirs. It expresses the deepest self, what some call the soul.

Much of my own awareness comes from my will, my peripheral self, while the vital core, the void at center, lies dormant, a half-asleep giant. To realize the power of my vital core I need "only" center; but centering is more than difficult. Sometimes anxiety is in the way, sometimes pain or anger. Tuning in more deeply, I feel an explosion impending. If I am able to center there is a disintegration of the peripheral self. A sudden expansion then pushes beyond the control of my will. When I surrender and accept the expansion, I come into power, intensity, wholeness. Then I lose the objectives of my peripheral self. The cares, considerations, controls that I carry and nurse in my daily life go. The objectives of my center self are not the objectives of my peripheral self, and my day-to-day concerns cease to matter when I center. A deep-lying power at my core is not available to my ego, my periphery, my conscious will. My center self refuses to be involved in the petty matters that consume so much time, attention, and effort. The center self lies deep inside, half asleep when these matters of disinterest to it go on, which is most of the time.

Then I center and suddenly the deeper self is galvanized. Control is turned over to the inmate of the cell at the center of my being. The sleeping giant comes, not to life, for he is always deeply alive, but into awareness. My life force, my personal radix system, is reorganized from the center self, which moves me off along a new path, its own. The peripheral self is left impotent and deserted, pointing ineffectually in another direction: *"But this is where you must go.* ***Stay at work on your monument.*** *What if you die and it isn't finished?"*

The center self doesn't listen. It doesn't care in the least about the program the peripheral self has planned. It has no interest in monument building, no need to please the ego or the world. Its only concern is to fulfill its own nature. Its first task is to discover that nature. Discovering and fulfilling the nature of the center is not an intellectual process of formulating and moving toward goals. It is, rather, a process of tuning in, of opening inwardly, tapping more fully the wellspring of life, the flow of the life force, the radix, from the core. For me, at least, centering involves a surrender of the will and the goals of the periphery. It is a submission to the deeper self.

We are each one unique radix systems, organizations of the life force, with a mind and body different from all others. We each have our own pattern of pulsation, and we each charge and discharge individually and separately from anyone else. Living things are housed in a case or covering. A tree has its bark, an animal its skin. The covering is the boundary separating a person from the world, and we each lead our lives within it. It houses the skeletal structure, and the organs which sustain our individual vital activities. It holds the muscles which enable us to move and act, and the fluid matrix – our personal internal "ocean" –-in which organs, muscles and bones live and are sustained. The organs include the sense organs, the brain and nervous system, which allow us each to perceive, think, remember, and move. They are the physical basis of consciousness and mind.

I grew to understand radix discharge prior to understanding radix charge because freeing blocks to the discharge of feelings, the outstroke, played such a key part in day after day work with students in my personal growth practice. The energy and feeling created through discharge showed readily in their body expression and movements. But in my work I also had to learn to free the instroke, the charging stroke of each student's pulsation. This was more subtle. First I learned that getting a student to repeatedly inhale more deeply raised the radix charge level of the body. Sometimes this "pumping up" of the charge was necessary, especially in freeing blocked fear in the student, yet it was often a superficial and temporary measure. "Centering" exercises, such as helping a student to notice and follow the breath in and out, to become aware of inhibitions to natural respiration and gradually surrender these inhibitions, better encouraged a fuller instroke of the radix pulsation and brought a deeper level of charge. A meditative attitude helped the centering process. The beginning paragraphs of this chapter illustrate, but do not explain, the centering process.

Centering and Radix Source

What happened on this fuller centering instroke of the radix pulsation, I asked myself. What was centering, really? Why was it difficult but, when successful, so potent? It could affect someone profoundly. It usually happened with a quieting of peripheral discharges in the body. But there was more that I needed to understand about radix centering, charging, and the instroke of radix pulsation. The mystery of the spiritual dimension of life was deeply tied up with the instroke and the creation of radix charge.

Why did the body's radix system pulsate? As the charge built, it built most strongly in the periphery, where skin and special senses are located and individual awareness is often vivid. Awareness was tied to the outstroke of the pulsation. The radix in the body was attracted out from the body center toward the more strongly charged periphery. There it discharged each cycle of this pulsation, producing some degree of awareness and energy.[1] On every outstroke the highly charged periphery must, I thought, draw more charge from the less charged interior, following the law of radix flow from lower to higher. Radix discharge normally took place at the periphery. I assumed this dropped the peripheral charge to the level where the gradient of charge from center to periphery reversed. This made the charge flow back inward from the now less charged periphery toward the center. In this way the instroke of the pulsation also followed the well-established "lower to higher" law of radix flow. The essential dynamic seemed to be the peripheral discharge, which reversed the direction of the pulsation with the end of the outstroke of each cycle, whether of respiration, sleeping-waking, or other radix pulsatory rhythm.

Radix charge must, I reasoned, be absorbed into the body at and through its boundary from the lower charged environment. During the instroke the now less charged, less tense, softer and more permeable muscular sheath and skin allowed the charge from the environment to penetrate more freely. This drawing in of charge appeared necessary to maintain the over-all radix metabolism of the body. The body must lose some of its charge with the discharge phase of each cycle. Unless the charge were replenished, the body's general charge level would keep declining.

In sleep the general body charge level is renewed. Discharge during sleep is slight, while the regular full breathing of sleep expresses the underlying radix pulsation, charging the body with each inhalation. The elasticity of the skin, membranes and muscles of the body provide support for the body's pulsatory radix rhythms. Arteries distend and peripheral blood vessels fill on the outstroke of respiration, i.e., exhalation. Elastic tissues that are stretched on the outstroke contract back on the movement in, reversing the outward flow of blood. It seemed technically correct to me, but something was missing. It had to do with the body's radix center, toward which the radix flowed on the instroke of the pulsation.

The movement of the life force back toward the center on the instroke had to be more than a springing inward due to tissue elasticity and the reversal of flow with peripheral discharge. It had to do with the essence of one's being. The center is the vital core of the individual's aliveness. The flowing of charge in from the environment and the periphery was an incomplete story. I saw in my mind a cross section of the body, schematically represented here as:

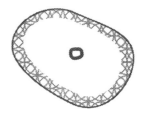

Figure 16. Center and Periphery

The egg-shaped boundary represents the skin, the shaded area just inside the skin the muscular sheath. The unshaded interior holds the support structure and is filled with bone, cartilage, organs and fluids. The circle in the center represents a central area of lowest radix charge, and moves around with the charges that occur in radix metabolism. The pulsatory charge-discharge cycle shows most clearly in skin and muscular sheath, where charge, consciousness, and tension sustain higher levels most of the time. External charge must flow in from the environment to be absorbed, used and discharged every cycle, I had reasoned. But questions about the process nagged at me. How did the charge coming in from the environment become incorporated to become part of <u>me</u>? And how could radix charge flowing out from the center ever get replenished if it came from the place of lowest charge and flowed only from lower toward higher charge?

<u>Radix Sources</u>

The principle of the flow of the life force from lower toward higher charge seemed secure and unassailable. If radix charge is a continuous variable and if it always flows from lower to higher, it means that charge flows in during each instroke cycle from the less charged environment to the body perimeter, the body's highly charged boundary. Inside the boundary the charge is lower again, and there must also be a center of lowest charge. From that center new radix charge must issue. It must enter from the substratum directly into the center of one's being; otherwise the charge at the center would go down, down, down, and never recover. The radix charge flowing out and away from the center of lowest charge would soon make the charge at that center irreversibly low. The center has by definition a lower charge than anything around it in any direction. That's what being the point of lowest charge meant. How could more charge flow out from the point of lowest charge without that point becoming progressively and irreversibly low in its charge? The center of lowest charge had to tap into an as yet unknown source of radix charge. What could it be but something beyond physical space? It must be the radix substratum itself!

Thus was reasoned into existence the idea of a radix source at the center of lowest charge of radix systems. Such systems were built around centers of low charge. These included but were not limited to living beings. It has led to the view that each living thing, animal or plant, develops around a center of low radix charge, its individual radix source within its body or structure. To understand "centering," one must understand why the body's individual radix system pulsates in and out toward its center. To understand that, one must understand something new about radix sources at centers of low charge within pulsating radix systems.

To restate the key point, the central law remains that radix charge always flows from lower toward higher charge levels. That is its nature. Places having lower charge levels than all adjacent surroundings then must be *sources* of radix charge, places where radix charge can only flow out. Where does the charge that flows only out come from? It comes from a different realm of nature. Sources are the places of entry of radix charge from the substratum into the observable universe. All living things and many things we don't think of as living contain a radix source as their vital center. From this center, charge flows out in all directions. This is possible only because the source is rooted in the radix substratum. That root is what connects each of us through our individual source to the universal, and through that vital connection the self or soul is born. In our selves, body and mind, that is the physical self and our individual consciousness, are created together as part of the same process. Radix charge arises from the void at the core within, the place of lowest charge. It flows out into the higher charged areas of the body which surrounds it, creating the mind and body, consciousness and energy, experience and behavior of the individual.

The creative process that we first see originates then with radix charge from the substratum entering the known universe. It enters from another dimension or realm at sources, centers of low charge. From the standpoint of the world in which we live and move, radix charge appears to come from nowhere and everywhere. It emerges from the void in the center of each of us, which connects us to the source of our being and the wellspring of life, which is the origin of the radix flow from the core. Every living thing has its own unique source, from which comes its unique radix charge, the charge that carries its potential to grow, experience and move in the world.

I repeat, at the source the radix flows alternately outward from the radix substratum into the world then back toward the core and into the substratum. This is the outstroke and instroke of that source's pulsation. It is at its vital core that an individual radix system taps into the universal. Like a plant with its roots reaching into the living earth, each individual source taps into the universal radix substratum. It is from the substratum that each pulsating radix system receives the radix charge that gives it being. From it, that individual lives, grows, expands, experiences, moves and evolves. Organic systems such as living animals and plants are one special class of radix system. We understand other classes only a little. We begin with living animals like ourselves.

Thus each living individual is a radix system developed around a source, with a physical structure, a housing evolved over the ages to contain and support the pulsating radix source. Our physical existence is supported by that pulsation. We go through the source into the substratum on the instroke, gathering radix charge; and then go back out of it, through and from the center, toward our body periphery and the world, on the outstroke, using and so discharging our radix charge. Since radix charge is the fuel consumed to sustain our existence, it is through discharge that we are made conscious and able to move and act in the world. In this way both life force and life are renewed with each cycle of radix pulsation.

Center and Self

Centering is a step beyond the instroke of radix pulsation. We go inward not only to replenish the vital "material" of our lives, the radix charge, but also to connect with the universal, our source, our being. In centering we do not think, feel, or do; we simply are. But in the western world we are concerned mostly with striving, thinking, doing -- outward-oriented activities. In centering, attention flows the other way: toward the center! A teacher of Zen, a woman of unusual spiritual development and by any measure a "centered" person, described it to me as emptying the mind of thoughts and letting go of desires, judgments, and effort.

To stop striving, thinking, futurizing, to release restless ambitions and considerations stacked on considerations is a letting go of radix discharge and the pressure toward discharge. The emptiness the Zen teacher spoke of is actually full of meaning and significance. Our lives are busy, but all of us need periods of rest and contemplation. We need to *center* ourselves. I am less than serene by nature, but I take the time to put myself amid serenity – I walk through the woods and over the hill, or beside the river. I get up early in the morning for a cup of tea and a quiet period of communion with nature before I pick up my pen. These moments are instrokes in the pulsatory rhythms of my life force, hence of my life.

In these small simple ways I center, and by centering gain renewal, inspiration, the rebuilding of my radix charge, the refilling of my cup. The peace in my surroundings helps me to connect with my source, and thus with the whole. In centering, I receive directly from the universal, the radix. It took me decades to learn that I must go in rather than out to reach the universal.

When I succeed in centering, I make contact with the greater whole, and I am transformed in ways small and large. I give up tension and effort, open myself to what I have called the radix substratum. Some vital connection I don't yet understand is made. "Veils covering the face of God" drop away, and I see with clear eyes, sometimes with what I have come to call "radix vision." I see the wonder and the horror of life, the radiantly beautiful and the hideous. It is a transcendent experience, and it grows out of centering with the eyes open and seeing.

Radix Vision[2]

Radix vision is a centered form of perception in which the superego relaxes and the id, the biologically old core of the self, takes over. It occurs spontaneously among certain children, psychotics, geniuses, and users of psychedelic drugs. It is learned and can be reached at will by those who pursue its study. Radix vision opens anew an ancient, mysterious, and potent world, much different from the familiar world of everyday life. It bypasses the ego to open a world unencumbered by the impedimenta of words, civilization, conscience; a world of fantastic plastic forms, images, archetypes, visions, nightmares, and sometimes of raw primitive power.

My Mother's Face

During the cold nights of the earliest winters of my life I suffered from the recurrent respiratory ailment we called "the croup." We lived year round in a flimsy summer cabin in a village in the high Rockies. The winters were bitter cold. I had suffered from respiratory problems from birth. In the winter my lungs congested again and again and many nights I could not breathe lying down. My mother would sit me up, stoke the fire under the kettle of our wood-burning stove, then form a cone of newspapers to collect steam from the kettle spout to bring to my face. Inhaling the vapor, my breathing eased a little. My goal was to keep breathing until morning.

Rolled in a blanket on our rocking chair, I silently watched my mother's face. It was 2 or 3 a.m. The censor of my thoughts and images went to sleep, connection to my vital center was made, and radix vision came. Then my mother changed, became strange to me, sometimes monstrous, grotesque. In that altered state of consciousness I saw too much, and I gave deep fears visual forms.

Leaning back in the rocking chair, half my brain dormant, I watched. My mother relaxed part of her own mind as well. The tired dutiful expression gave way and the emotions underneath moved up and over her features. An old bitterness came back to her. The corners of her mouth pulled back. The cords of her neck tightened and protruded. She suppressed a cry. A wad of spit collected over her tongue. She pursed her lips, held them a moment, then swallowed. She drew a breath, held it, then forced a belch. I was fascinated and repelled.

Back to "normalcy" and its different point of view, I came to respect the fortitude with which my mother forced herself through her difficult overworked days and nights. But while seeing her from the standpoint of a child with radix vision, I viewed her without kindness or consideration. She was necessary to my life; I accepted her ministrations on my behalf, and I found her gross.

Masks of Armor

In New York in the fifties I would ride the subway from my Reichian therapist's mid-town office back to my walk-up apartment in Greenwich Village. Centered and opened by my session, the vibration of the train lulled the wordy half of my brain to sleep. Then radix vision would come, and I'd find myself seeing too much. People changed as I tuned into their armor. Fear, pain, blocked sexuality and anger appeared on almost every face, covered by grotesque masks, much uglier than the feelings they were designed to hide. People's faces became caricatures of their deeper selves. I felt alienated, alone.

The power and strangeness of radix vision made it fascinating to me, and accentuated the distortions of expression. The fears of the unconscious combined with heightened perception to create grotesque images. Yet this is only one side of the process. Radix vision is not only negative in its images.

Child on the Subway

Once after a Reichian session during the Christmas season in 1950, a boy of two or three and his mother sat on the seat ahead of me on the subway ride home. My eyes softened, my thoughts suspended. The child had a remarkable beautiful radiant quality. I surrendered into radix vision and the radiance expanded and deepened. The child was unusually free of defenses, with special aliveness and sweetness. I watched from behind, transfixed, and felt myself open to that lovely young being. He took in everything on the subway car with intelligent curiosity except -- I thought -- me. I was sitting behind him. In a few stops he and his mother got up to leave. He was standing beside my seat with the other exiting passengers who were waiting in the aisle of the subway getting ready to get off. As the doors began to open, he suddenly picked up my hand and kissed it gently, then looked up and smiled into my eyes. He turned and walked out of the car with his mother, and I never saw him again. I was thunderstruck and, when I had a moment to recover, deeply honored.

Flowers

There was a florist near my Reichian therapist's office, and I passed it going to and from sessions. I hardly noticed the florist's windows on my way to sessions, but coming back from them was something else. I stood in front of the window, thought suspended, slack jawed, mouth open like a little boy as the flowers showed their beauty to me.[3] The colors flowed vividly into my consciousness. I don't know how long I stayed. Altered states of consciousness play tricks with the sense of time.

Flowers can help to open radix vision because they do not threaten. I remember an experience I had living in Hawaii, years before I became involved with Reich. Hawaii has, I believe, the most beautiful flowers in the world. I was there in 1947-49 as an undergraduate student and a Bates Vision Teacher. Another student, an attractive Korean girl in my neighborhood, picked me up mornings to drive me to the university with her. I met her at the circle on top of our hill by a large wild double-hibiscus bush. Each morning she stopped there and chose one of the lovely red flowers for her magnificent black hair.

One lazy, lovely sunny spring morning I got to the hibiscus bush a few minutes early. While I waited, I looked into the throat of an especially striking vermilion blossom. All thought left me, and I stood stunned, transfixed, transported by the sheer intense loveliness of what I saw. I had no words that did it justice, but the effects of that flower stayed with me, and I was changed by it. I thought of it at the time as some form of mystical experience.

Such is Radix Vision. Many people experience it, usually as a mysterious, wordless, semi-conscious activity that is easily lost to memory, even though it can come with power and inspire wonder. It frightens many who have it, and they rarely speak of it. Renan Suhl, the first teacher to incorporate it systematically into **Radix** personal growth work, used it consciously in sessions I took from her in 1977 and 1978. Renan is one of the most powerful of the **Radix** teachers I have trained. Since the work with Renan I enter **Radix** Vision more easily. It brings me into the world of image, symbol, dream, and myth. I see them in a new way, and through them face new questions about myself and the universe.

I am fortunate that my unconscious has always been close to the surface. It scared me in childhood, but drew me nevertheless with the power of its images, and as my rational ego grew stronger I was less frightened by it. In adolescence I gained confidence, and could sometimes accept it without panic. Now I sink in deliberately, beckon to radix vision, open myself to the power of the id. It's a fascinating world, close to the core, the center, the source of my creativity and my portal to the radix substratum. I wander through this new but very old world where art is inspired and religions are spawned. It is not the realm of wordy civilized religions, but of the old raw power that precedes and will outlive them. It is the world of nature worship, of homage to the spirit that inhabits ground, sky, and water -- and the eyes of a young and seeing child. Radix vision brings me into the realm of those who find God in nature and on mountain tops. Among them I find sun worshippers and night worshippers, pantheists and animists, and here and there a handful of unregenerate and imaginative psychoanalysts, along with a few meditative and thoughtful priests.

The world of radix vision is non-rational but not irrational. Images and dreams from the unconscious have their own logic. It is not the logic of words but of feelings and forms. Call it id-logic. The forms have both literal and symbolic meanings and some carry biological knowledge of the species. Call it id-knowledge. Id-knowledge existed before word knowledge. It remains with us but submerged in the culture as it is in most individual human minds. When it emerges here and there it excites terror and provokes rage. The id-knowledge, like the awe, hate, and fear it so often inspires, is little understood.

The conscious manifestations of id-knowledge that come to us in dreams and portents and in Radix Vision are suppressed and driven into the subconscious. The cultural manifestations, like outcroppings of natural animistic and pantheistic religious expressions, are suppressed and driven into a subculture. In the subconscious and the subculture, hidden from light, the id-knowledge is compounded with superstition, distorted, and mystified. Sometimes its expressions are hideous as a nightmare. These spawn myths of devils and hell. Sometimes its expressions are as beautiful as the radix vision image of a flower or a child. These spawn myths of angels and heaven.

Word knowledge is failing the world. Stripped from the organic quality and potency of the id it becomes mechanical, lifeless, and eventually anti-life. The new level and kind of knowledge, rooted in understanding the life force, threatens to emerge, but for the present is hidden by mysticism and hocus-pocus. The path ahead is not easy. Careers are ruined, lives destroyed, and good people are driven from the protective walls of respectability and must live "outside the pale" because they are on the path of id-knowledge. Its new truth threatens small souls. Wilhelm Reich was forced to destroy his own writings and hounded to his death in prison in this country in our time because he saw too much. We still burn witches and crucify prophets, not because of their flagrant and inevitable errors, but because they push us toward powerful truths we are not ready to face.

Self and Soul

Consciousness as each one of us knows it is particular, private, ours alone. However, as separate as we are, we remain connected to the universal at our centers. I have said that at one time I believed that the individual attracted and gathered the life force from the surrounding universe through skin and muscle sheath, to somehow incorporate it into the self. Now I think that the self arises entirely from its internal source, that the radix charge that comes in from around us in the environment does not become part of the self. The charge that is our own arises internally, from the void within, and is the life force from which the individual self comes into being. It is fed from the one common source, the universal, the substratum, the unity from which each individual self originates. The unity which is the substratum gives birth to the diversity of individual selves in the familiar physical universe of space, energy, and matter within which we each one live and move and have our separate being.

In the individual's radix pulsation he is poised between unity and diversity. In the outstroke of each cycle, the direction is from the center toward the world; in the instroke it is from the world back into the center. The movement is to and from his center, and gives rise to his mind, his body and the experiences and expressions of his individual self. The soul in my view is the center and the origin of the self, that from which the self is created. Through it the individual's life force moves out toward the external world in its diversity and back into the substratum in its unity. In our unity we are all one and the same being. Going back out from the center toward the external universe, each is his individual self, and can form relations externally with other selves. Going back in and through our center into the substratum there is no other, only that unity in which all individual branches of the life force merge.

There is a danger in using the term "soul" as I have for the core aspect of the self, because the term is laden with religious meanings, shadings and significance that may preempt its meaning in the minds of many. I have found no other term appropriate to my meaning, however. I don't see that the term is owned by connotations given to the term by particular religious groups and their writings, but I do wish to make my own use of the term clear and distinct.

I believe that the entire physical world has been and is being created from the underlying cosmic ocean of being which I call the radix substratum. Some would call this substratum "God." Living organisms each differentiate from the substratum around a structure – its growing body. The body contains a center connecting to the substratum. The body is fed its creative force, its life force, through this connection.

The individual grows within the constraints of the pattern imposed by its genetic inheritance as it individuates and expands its structure. The individual center with its connection to the substratum gathers the force, the radix, through its inner connection on the instroke of each cycle of pulsation, then feeds it out to its periphery, its body, that grows and develops as a result. In time it moves and acts in the familiar world.

The physical structure of the individual in all its complex subtlety is the basis of the self as I understand it. The center of the self, with its connection outward to the body and inward to the universal substratum, is what I call the soul. The self as I understand it is rooted in and expresses the individual physical structure. It is born with it, grows and matures with it, and dies with it. Thus the self is mortal. While the self is alive, the soul connects it to its root in the cosmic, the radix substratum, what some call God. When the body dies the self perishes and the connection of the self to the substratum perishes with it.

In other words, I personally do not believe that characteristics of the self, the individual personality, survive death. My form, my structure, is temporary and mortal. Death ends my existence as an individual, and my self and soul re-merge with the universal substratum from which I was created. But the content, the "material" of the universe endures, and the material which comprises my own structure endures as well. I partake in the consciousness as a whole. As I age and grow closer to my own death, my feeling about it is that I will be coming home after a period of separation that is my life.

A sand sculptor at an ocean beach took advantage of low tide to form three piglets in the wet sand at short distances apart going up from the sea. The piglets conversed for an hour or two about existence and immortality, when they noticed that the tide was coming in again and the waves were washing ever closer. The closest piglet to the water spoke: "I am piglet Larry, and I am immortal." But a moment or two later, a wave washed up over Larry, and when the wave receded, he had disappeared. Still, the next piglet up the beach was not willing to abandon her newfound faith in individual immortality. She said determinedly, "I am piglet Mary, and I know I am immortal." But very soon the waves reached to and over piglet Mary, and as they retreated back to the sea, Mary had disappeared as completely as had Larry before her.

The last piglet, Barry, took in the disappearances of his siblings, and thought about what it meant. Soon a very large wave, the largest yet, moved strongly up toward him. Before it reached him, Barry said, "I am in the form of piglet Barry, and I am created of sand, which is immortal."

The largest wave then washed far up the beach and over Barry. When the water returned toward the sea, the sand was still there.

Chapter Notes

[1] I had originally supposed the body core was more highly charged than the periphery, but the relative absence of discharge and awareness at the core made me look more deeply. If there were high charge at the core, how could charge flow out from it, to discharge in the periphery? Such an outward flow would violate the "lower toward higher" direction of flow of radix processes.

[2] This section borrows heavily from my series of articles, *Meditations of a Pain Blocker*, appearing in **The Radix Journal**, Vols. II, Nos. 2&3, 1980 and III, No. 1, 1982. Most have been reprinted as part of THE RADIX: VOL. I, RADIX PERSONAL GROWTH WORK, 1992, Vancouver, WA: K/R Publications.

[3] The slack jaw, tongue and lips, signals the cessation of inner speech and the tense muscles of speech that go with it. The mentally deficient are often slack-jawed because they are unable to think in words. Intelligent people may never be able to relax their jaws and speech apparatus because the inner speech never stops.

Chapter 10

SUPERIMPOSITION AND MATING

Imagine a human couple drawn toward each other by love or lust. "Spiraling" around each other for a few weeks they come to know each other better, and their attraction has grown. Considerations are satisfied, and they have found a way to be together at a place and time where sexual consummation of their relationship is possible.

They approach. Their eyes meet. They touch, they kiss, they caress, they explore each other with their hands. Their bodies and hearts respond. They begin to undress themselves and each other, and handle each other's bodies as new parts are exposed to them for the first time.

He already has an erection, she is becoming aroused and lubricated. Both of their hearts are pounding. They finish undressing. He leads her to the bed, lies her down gently, handles, kisses and caresses her naked body. She opens her body and mind to the intimate touch and handling. Both bodies are taut with excitement.

He lifts her legs apart, climbs between them, begins slowly to enter her, gently. He puts one hand under her buttocks, the other under her head, holding her tight and in a position that lets their eyes meet as he enters her the rest of the way. Seeing each other as they mate increases their pleasure. He slowly begins regular thrusting movements, helping her body to move in rhythm with his in the coital dance.

Their breathing synchronizes with the rhythm of their pelvic movements. As their respiration deepens, the rhythm intensifies and the movements and breathing become more automatic. Their hearts pound as orgasm approaches. On the brink he holds back a little to see if she is about to orgasm too. She is, with little involuntary cries, and he watches her enraptured face. He moves into his own orgasm. He feels as if he explodes into her, and he cries out as his orgasm brings him more intense pleasure than he can bear.

Their breathing relaxes, becomes slower and easier afterward, and their bodies are soft where they had been taut a moment ago. Their hearts slow down, their chests give in to full exhalation. The two look at each other, and feel loving and grateful. When sex is good life is good!

Pairs, couples, mate in many ways. Between consenting human adults there is no "right" and "wrong" way. The simultaneous orgasm sometimes happens, but is not a prescription for "ideal sex." Good sex is any that leaves both partners deeply satisfied.

Is sexual superimposition in a human couple to be understood in the same terms as superimposition of "orgone" streams that in cosmic space produce spiral galaxies, and as the streams of the life force from two anticyclonic high pressure weather systems in the earth's atmosphere produce cyclonic storms and weather? Reich's model and my own say: "yes, they are."

Through the immensity of astronomical space is scattered unevenly all of the "stuff" that makes up the observable physical universe. Among the uneven clumps of galaxies, free energy, gasses, dark matter and intergalactic dust lie great regions of emptiness. These cosmic voids are the regions of lowest radix charge in the universe. Through them radix charge enters the universe. This is the initial step in the cosmic creative process. The gradients of radix charge are very low in and near these empty regions. Radix charge from the substratum oozes from them infinitesimally slowly at first, over eons of time, moving gradually out toward the more charged active regions in the distance, always from centers of low charge, the sources, toward the higher charge, following the organizing principle of lower to higher charge. The movement of a bit of charge from lower toward high charge is not action at a distance, i.e., toward a distant life-charged area of space. The movement of each bit of radix charge flows in accord with the local charge gradient in which that bit is imbedded.

All directions away from a source are not equivalent, for in some directions charged regions are closer and/or stronger and the charge gradient steeper than in others. The movement along a steeper gradient quickens. As charge at the source flows away, the source charge drops lower still; the flow away from the source grows apace, most strongly along the steepest gradients. Growing tongues of charge flow out along these gradients, moving out into the space away from the source. These tongues of cosmic dimension flow further and further in the direction away from the void at the source, from "nothing" toward "something," the higher charge in the physical universe around the void.

Sometimes two such tongues from two different cosmic sources will approach each other, each moving toward the higher charge of the other, each tongue ever growing in radix charge. Their paths will curl toward each other, spiral in until they touch, begin to flow into each other, and intermingle. The charge level escalates and the universe trembles in excitement as large-scale superimposition, a cosmic mating, begins.

New particles of matter are born along the region of contact. They are a product of billions of matings of the two tongues of charge, particles being created in formerly empty space. New thin matter is pouring into the physical universe, huge dark clouds of primary matter born of radix discharge. The first and simplest material element is hydrogen. Clouds of particles appear and draw together into compressing masses. A star is born, then another, many others, thousands, millions, hundreds of millions of stars, revealing the shape of the intertwining tongues of radix charge that flow together to form that wonder of the heavens, the spiral galaxy. The huge cosmic mating is pouring new matter from the two vast empty voids together to form a new galaxy.

Each new particle of the galaxy arises from two tongues of radix charge coming from two "parents," radix sources thousands of light years apart, that have encountered each other in the lonely reaches of deep space. The sources have come together in cosmic union, produced issue in the form of billions of billions of particles, which are attracted to each other gravitationally, coalesce into clumps, are compressed, heat to atomic fusion and incandescence, and radiate through the universe as stars for all to see.

And I ask, is there, as my radix theory leads me to expect, a subjective as well as an objective side to this cosmic act of creation? As the two sources of radix charge in the emptiness of deep space pour out tongues of radix charge that approach each other, intertwine, superimpose, and discharge, do the sources each experience a cosmic ecstasy in their mating?

Perhaps the same two tongues of charge will flow into other matings, form other galaxies from the tongues of flow from the two original sources. Then there will be a family, a system of galaxies.

Birth of a Cyclonic Storm

Consider a different example, superimposition in the earth's atmosphere. Synoptic (general) weather maps of the world often show two large high-pressure systems -- in the meteorologist's parlance, anti-cyclones, air masses of high pressure and mild weather with a weather front between them. Figure 17 shows the general case. Winds circle each air mass in a clockwise direction in the northern hemisphere. As an example, the semi-permanent eastern pacific anti-cyclone often centers a few hundred miles west of the coast of California. The winds west of the center carry warm moist subtropical air to the north and then to the east along the northern part of the system, toward our Pacific coast. Far to the north another anti-cyclonic air mass is often present, centering over the north Pacific, Alaska, or western Canada. Its clockwise winds bring cold air in the opposite direction on its south side, along the boundary between the two systems. It flows from east to west above the boundary. Between these two high-pressure systems is a weather front, then, the boundary separating huge air masses of different temperature, humidity, and wind direction.

Superimposition & Mating

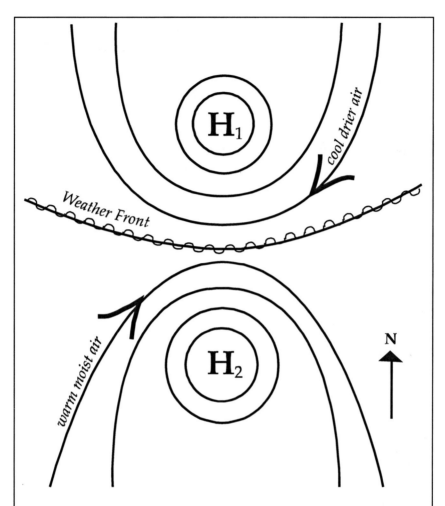

Figure 17. Two centers of low radix charge appear on weather maps as centers of high barometric pressure. They define two radix sources in the earth's atmosphere, separated by a weather front. Superimposition and mating(s) of the two sources develop from the weather front.

Weather forecasters watch this frontal boundary, because weather often develops along it, as Figure 17 shows. But the front is far out from the two radix sources, the centers of high pressure and low radix charge. Near the centers, calm or light winds and peaceful weather rule.

The high-pressure centers are radix sources in the earth's atmosphere, regions of low radix charge surrounded by higher charge in all directions. Through them radix charge is born into the atmosphere of the earth, to flow out toward the higher charge of the periphery, the boundary, including the frontal zone that stretches east to west for hundreds, even thousands of miles between the sources, and along which the two air masses touch.

Imagine yourself with me when I was a young army weather forecaster watching the development of a segment of the weather front such as Figure 17 and 18 show. Figure 18 diagrams atmospheric superimposition. It is near the Aleutian Islands southwest of Alaska. In this area, cyclogenesis, the birth of a cyclonic storm, often occurs. We notice a slight dip in the barometer, and along with it a small change in wind direction (Figure 18B). There is a slight disturbance of the regular pattern of winds flowing in opposite directions along each side of the weather front. A fascinating development has begun. The two air masses alter their direction of wind flow. They turn in and begin to interpenetrate. A tongue of the cold northern air mass alters its east-west direction at the disturbance to curl south, while a tongue of warm moist air from the southern air mass curls northward (Figure 18B and 18C) behind it. Both systems pour radix charge around and toward the center of the disturbance, which begins to rotate in a counter clockwise direction and to grow apace, as it becomes a cyclonic (low pressure) storm (Figure 18D). Clouds have appeared. The tongue from the southern air mass carries much physical energy in the form of warm, moisture-laden air. Its latent heat of condensation feeds the growth of the developing storm, much as the heat of hydrogen fusion feeds the developing stars in the spiral galaxy. The part of the front that is west of the center where the cold air from the north pushes south is the <u>cold</u> front, shown by the spikey line. The part of the front where the warm air pushes north is the <u>warm</u> front, shown by the small curves (arcs)

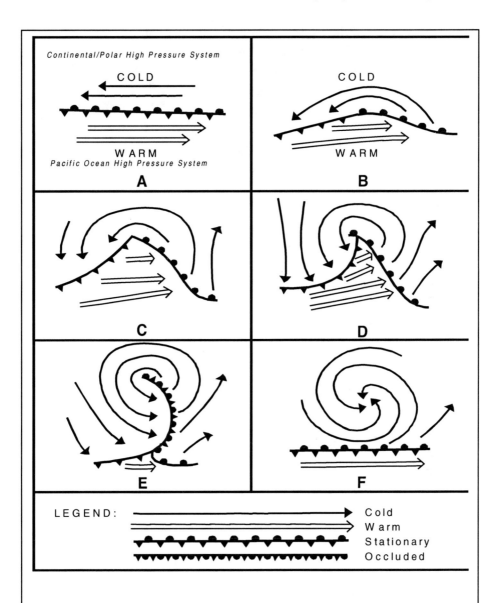

Figure 18. *Development and decline of a frontal wave type cyclone (cyclogenesis and cyclolysis) as in the Northwest Pacific.*
Arrows indicate wind flow. Concentric lines circle the developing, then subsiding, low pressure in the center of the cyclone.

rather than spikes on the frontal line. The cold front and warm front meet and inflect (make an angle) at the center of the cyclonic storm (Figure 18C), which becomes a center of low pressure. The atmospheric mating is in progress. The winds blow around this center in a counter-clockwise direction. The cold air from the east and north is heavier than the warm air from the south and west, and pushes under it. The warm air rises, and rides above the cold. The section of the front where this happens is called an occluded front. The occluded section of the front is marked by alternating spikes and arcs (Figure 18D and 18E). The tongues of the two air masses curl around each other faster, as clouds and rain develop outward from the center of the disturbance. The barometer plunges. Ever stronger winds blow around the center of the growing storm. The winds whip up the ocean. The storm expands to cover hundreds then thousands of square miles, and moves slowly west, toward our Pacific coast. Had there been a weather satellite high overhead in 1945, it would have shown the clouds growing in a beautiful spiraling pattern that looks strikingly like a spiral galaxy as diagrammed in Figure 19 and photographed in Figure 20.

And I ask, as I did about the formation of the spiral galaxy, is there a subjective side to this great atmospheric mating? Do the two anti-cyclones, the high-pressure systems that contain the two superimposing sources of the storm, experience a kind of excitement and joy in their mating and discharge?

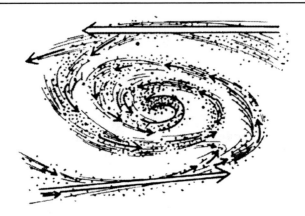

Figure 19. Two streams of the life force superimpose in the formation of a galaxy, the spawning of a cyclonic storm in the earth's atmosphere, or in the mating of male and female. Spirals may rotate in either direction, depending on relative location.

Figure 20. Photographic comparison showing similarity of cloud pattern of a spiral galaxy and cyclonic storm.

About Superimposition

Wilhelm Reich was the first to look at a photograph of a spiral galaxy and a radar map of a hurricane, which is a violent cyclonic storm, and grasp that both expressed a life force process of supreme importance. The same life force process is expressed in mating by animals at every level of the animal kingdom. He described his great act of thought in his beautiful small book COSMIC SUPERIMPOSITION half a century ago.[1] Of course he did not have satellite photographs or much knowledge of meteorology, which makes his discovery all the more remarkable. Virtually nothing has been done with his remarkable insight in that period. If my own life force discoveries presented here prove valid, it signals that we have finally caught up to Reich's insight, and can now place it in the context of a growing theory of how the cosmos is created from "nothing" through the agency of the force that Reich called *orgone* and I call the *radix*.[2]

The life force is all Reich found it to be and, as I have discovered, more. Superimposition is, from atom to galaxy, from protozoa to human being, more than Reich or then I imagined it to be. The open-minded and curious traditional scientist might like to look at sexual superimposition as a metaphor, an analogy to what happens in a spiral galaxy or a cyclonic weather system, and so miss the entire point of Reich's great insight, the door he opened to us. In superimposition, Reich spoke not of metaphor, but of a life force process of great simplicity and generality, expressing itself at every scale and level of nature. Grasping this is the essential first step to understanding what Reich's work with the life force and my own are really about.

We have everything to learn about the superimposition function, once we understand that it is real, it is there, and that we can learn from it. Reich's monumental achievement was to look at very different examples of superimposition and realize they were each the expression of the mating of two underlying streams of "orgone," the life force, whether at the microscopic level, the level of mating animals, the level of the earth's large atmospheric streams involved in the creation of hurricanes, or the astronomically huge cosmic streams responsible for the spiral galaxy. In each case two separate streams of the life force were involved in a creative process of great power, beauty, and meaning. My contribution to Reich's discovery of superimposition has been to see that the superimposing "orgone energy" streams weren't streams of energy at all, but of the precursor to energy, which I call the radix, the stuff from which new energy is created and enters the physical world. And it was I who traced the pairs of superimposing radix streams back to their origins, the <u>sources</u>, whether these were in the voids of intergalactic space, the calm centers of anticyclonic atmospheric systems on earth, or the body cores of living animals. In each of these cases, centers of lowest charge, radix sources, are the origin, where the life force comes from, emerging to initiate the creation of the physical universe. It is the contact point of the individual with the universal. At the deepest level, all such sources are one source, for there is only one universal. At this deepest level all individuals are one being. This is, I insist, a discoverable fact of nature. Our special structures, bodies, nervous systems, memories, and unique sense of self express our individual being, rooted for each one of us in our body, but arising from our own individual source, our contact with the universal. Our individual selves are separate and mortal, but in our connection to and expression of the universal we are unified, transcendent and immortal.

  Superimposition poses a special problem in understanding the creative process as that process expresses itself through the radix, because it takes two independent sources of radix charge, two individuals coming together in the creative act. How general is this requirement that there be two? I puzzled for years over this problem, and concluded that <u>all radix discharge involves two sources</u>, that discharge is, for each of us, the mating of self and other. I have said that radix pulsation and charge is <u>duplex</u>, that charge comes in from our body periphery to initiate the instroke of each cycle of pulsation. Having gone inward to and, to some degree, through the core to touch into the universal at the end of the instroke, the flow of charge then reverses, coming back out into the body to initiate the outstroke, the discharge stroke of the pulsatory cycle. Is not radix discharge the expression of the superimposition of the incoming radix from the environment that is the "other" and the outflowing radix from the core that is "me"?

I believe that it is, that in tying radix discharge to superimposition of charges from two sources, I stumbled onto a new general truth about the ultimate character of the creative process in nature.

Chapter Notes

[1] Reich, Wilhelm, 1951, COSMIC SUPERIMPOSITION. New York: Orgone Institute Press.

[2] My own early work on the subject is described in Kelley, C.R., *Orgone Energy and Weather*, in **CORE**, Vol. 7 pp. 54-67, 1955.

Chapter 11

AUTONOMY

Freeing the feelings from patterns of tension that block them works directly with the radix feeling processes, with pleasure and pain, love and anger, trust and fear. These are blocked by the new motivational system stemming from thought and will. This new system has become able, through the radix blocking process, to override the old motivational system stemming directly from the feelings and natural impulses. In the old system, attention and action flow spontaneously from the feelings. The new system does not replace the old, but rather, blocks and rechannels it when goals of new and old systems conflict.

The new motivational system is clumsy and imperfect in many respects, yet it is enormously powerful. It is no less than a branch of the individual's life force turning back inward on itself and forming the pattern of muscle tension that is at first the muscular armor. When more evolved, muscular armor becomes the radix block. The patterns of muscle tension dam, shape, and thus control central life processes, including those producing feelings. The inward curling radix is itself a higher, more evolved life process, imposing control over more primitive life processes. With it, thinking and will have come into existence, to exercise their unique role in human motivation.

The great and tragic imperfection of this new system is that because it can do so much, create so much power for groups learning to use it, social processes force it onto masses of individuals not evolved enough to use it on their own. It is forced on them <u>unautonomously</u> from outside themselves. Most people are not yet developed enough to use the radix block selectively and appropriately, out of their own independent processes of thought and will, -- but block they have been forced to do. The result has been the muscular armor as Reich observed and described it, crippling and damaging the bodies and minds of hundreds of millions of individual human beings with its potent yet badly flawed means of control of the source of life itself. The new process is the foundation of behavior control in human society as we know it today. When we engineers of personal growth loosen the armor of unautonomously over-armored human beings, e.g., by means of Radix feeling work or by Reichian therapy, it can be a wonderful gift, freeing blocks that have been choking off vital life processes. It can save someone's life. Yet, as I have said, extensive loosening of the armor without fully understanding its true function is dangerous and irresponsible, as it can seriously damage the capacity of individuals for containment and self control in the interest of the long-range conduct of their lives.[1]

Consider now how the radix block works at its best, with the most advanced, unusually autonomous people. There have been a few such people scattered through human history. Fifteen hundred years ago one of them is said to have said:

Be a lamp unto yourself, be your own confidence;
hold to the truth within yourself, as to the only lamp.

This statement, attributed to Gautama Buddha, is a principle to guide the individual in the direction of autonomy. For individuals striving to take over the control of their own life processes from the family and the social group, the radix block becomes a friend, the means of guiding their lives toward this objective. It is no longer muscular armor as a tool of the group to weaken self-hood by pushing people to conform. Instead it is the newly evolving form of the muscular armor which is the radix block. The radix block becomes the tool through which one learns to direct his or her own life force towards a self made stronger, better individuated and defined, a self developed to a new level with the capacity for self-awareness, self-understanding, self-control, and looking ahead. Such a person does not block and channel his own life processes, his own feelings, in the service of society; not for nation, religion, family, or any other group or collective. He does it in the service of the self, and what he sees to be the long-range direction of his life. That is the nature of autonomy.

The pre-autonomous armored man or woman, however, has been forced to divorce the powerful old feeling aspect of being, the Freudian "id," and force it into the subterranean underground of unconscious or semi-conscious activity. The individual is coaxed and coerced by love and by force or threat of force, to conform to group pressures and block powerful impulses toward self expression. The fruit of the tree of knowledge is swallowed but not digested as, through the armor, the rules of the group are imposed on the individual. The group requires its members to armor in order for the group to function as it does to survive, and to carry its members into the future.

The unautonomous do not know or understand that future, any more than a spider knows why it builds a web, a salmon knows why it migrates upstream, or a bird knows why it builds a nest. Unautonomous humans have been broken, first by the family and then by church and school, so that they give up the self, become "socialized" and "unselfish," and do the group's bidding. Notice well the words for what they become, -- "unselfish" and "socialized." They are deprived of sense of self and forced to conform to the group. It is not unlike the breaking of a horse. The horse is broken so that it may serve the purposes of its masters, other beings. Likewise human children are broken, so that they can be made to conform to the purpose of other beings, i.e., be "socialized" to obey the rules, values, customs, and beliefs of the family, the religion, the society, the nation they are born into. It is a lengthy, arduous, often terribly painful, process. American children are broken through twelve to sixteen or more long years of daily imprisonment and indoctrination, which has the function of breaking their will, forcing them to submit, to become docile, and to take on the beliefs, right or wrong, that prevail in their group. It is called "education," and we worship it irrationally.

It is not quite as evil as I make it sound. The "breaking" process has been necessary in some form for the continuance of the groups through which society presently operates, and it is to some degree necessary, but grotesquely excessive, today. However, we are approaching the end of the collectivist stage of human evolution, and beginning the transition to something new. We need to become aware of forms which are outmoded and holding back the progress of the human race toward something new and better.

Three Stages of Purpose

Remember the previous major transition in motivation. In it, society went from the first, biological stage of human development that we share with the animals into the second, collective stage or group. I repeat that the second transition is unique to the human species and that it is symbolized by the myth of Adam and Eve eating of the forbidden fruit of the tree of knowledge, losing their innocence, becoming "like God, knowing good and evil." In consequence they were evicted from the "paradise" of the childhood of humanity into this world of choice, responsibility, and work. Here these remarkable former animals with their budding power of thought and will developed a new form of evolution, <u>social</u> evolution, which is much much faster than <u>biological</u> evolution. Remember how wrenching and difficult the transition was that the myth of the Garden of Eden represents. We were all "cast out of the Garden." Now a few thousand years later, we are entering another such transition.

A major problem with social evolution has been that the power of thought and will evolved slowly, its development governed at the start by the old biological evolutionary process. The new powers of thought and will appeared unevenly in the race, first in a very few scattered individuals here and there. They were the "first gods" of man, the original originators, creators, discoverers, inventors. They were feared and hated and, after they died, adulated because they were so powerful and gave us so much. They again and again turned their group, and eventually most of human society, upside down. Weaponry, fire, cooking, agriculture, boats, pictorial art, language, numbering, were created, discovered, invented, reshaped in the minds of rare individual human beings, to spread across the human species. People who could not have made a discovery on their own could make use of what the creators made possible for them. Thus the new discovery was learned, applied, and made use of. It impacted human society long before most of its members could grasp it, other than to use it as taught.

In this way the group stage of the evolution of purpose came to be, with collectivism as the form of government and social organization. The individual was subordinated to the group. Independence and autonomy were heavily penalized, often with death. Unbelievers, heretics, the giants of human development, those who put their own vision, thoughts and values ahead of the group's, were and are still hated, persecuted, and criminalized during their lifetime -- witness the example of Wilhelm Reich less than fifty years ago -- to become progressively revered in the years after their death. This was effectively described by Ayn Rand through the character of Howard Roark, the hero of her novel, THE FOUNTAINHEAD. In an address to a jury, Roark said,

"Thousands of years ago, the first man discovered how to make fire. He was probably burned at the stake he had taught his brothers to light. He was considered an evildoer who had dealt with a demon mankind dreaded. But thereafter men had fire to keep them warm, to cook their food, to light their caves. He had left them a gift they had not conceived and he had lifted darkness off the earth. Centuries later, the first man invented the wheel. He was probably torn on the rack he had taught his brothers to build. He was considered a transgressor who ventured into forbidden territory. But thereafter, men could travel past any horizon. He had left them a gift they had not conceived and he had opened the roads of the world.

"That man, the unsubmissive and first, stands in the opening chapter of every legend mankind has recorded about its beginning. Prometheus was chained to a rock and torn by vultures -- because he had

stolen the fire of the gods. Adam was condemned to suffer -- because he had eaten the fruit of the tree of knowledge. Whatever the legend, somewhere in the shadows of its memory mankind knew that its glory began with one and that that one paid for his courage.

"Throughout the centuries there were men who took first steps down new roads armed with nothing but their own vision. Their goals differed, but they all had this in common: that the step was first, the road new, the vision unborrowed, and the response they received -- hatred. The great creators -- the thinkers, the artists, the scientists, the inventors -- stood alone against the men of their time. Every great new thought was opposed. Every great new invention was denounced. The first motor was considered foolish. The airplane was considered impossible. The power loom was considered vicious. Anesthesia was considered sinful. But the men of unborrowed vision went ahead. They fought, they suffered and they paid. But they won.

"No creator was prompted by a desire to serve his brothers. His vision, his strength, his courage came from his own spirit. A man's spirit, however, is his self. That entity which is his consciousness. To think, to feel, to judge, to act are functions of the ego.

"The creators were not selfless. It is the whole secret of their power -- that it was self-sufficient, self-motivated, self-generated. A first cause, a fount of energy, a life force, a Prime Mover. The creator served nothing and no one. He lived for himself.

"And only by living for himself was he able to achieve the things which are the glory of mankind. Such is the nature of achievement."[2]

Societal groups took over the discoveries and inventions of creators and adapted them to the service of the group. Progress is due not only to creations of special individuals but to the group's ability to make use of what it was given. Some groups were much more hospitable to the new than others. This is especially true of changes affecting knowledge, belief, values, customs, and rules of behavior. Rules of trade, rules of property, rules of human relationship evolved unevenly within groups and societies, as did techniques for enforcing the rules.

From the outset of the group stage of purpose there has been a conflict between the group and the rare creative individuals whose discoveries jolted human progress forward. This is shown well in the quotation above. The creator is not like the others. He is a deviant who is more self-contained, less conforming, more independent of the rules. New discoveries reflect the minds of people able to go outside or see beyond what is done in the group. These people are the prophets of the third, individual stage of the evolution of purpose lying ahead of us, the stage of autonomy.

But for now the group response to deviants great enough to threaten its beliefs, values or social structure is still fear and hate, cultivated and magnified by the group. The more insecure the group is in its beliefs, values and social structure, the more vulnerable it is to change. The more irrational the group's beliefs, distorted its values and unjust its social structure, the more rigid, cruel and severe is that group's punishment of deviants. The great danger to an irrational group is the person who is sufficiently free of the group to be able to think and act independently. I have mentioned before the "guarding function" against those who "lift the veils covering the face of God." It is the autonomous mavericks who threaten to lift the veils. Notice how they fare in communist and theocratic Islamic countries and others that punish those disagreeing with government-mandated beliefs.

Groups striving to maintain and extend their power must have members who accept the group's doctrines, respect its authority, and identify with its beliefs and practices. The "true believer," in Eric Hoffer's sense of the term[3], needs the group to compensate for a self that is defective and flawed. The group actually trains its members to think that they are defective and flawed. That's what "original sin" is all about. "You were born sinful and defective by nature" says the Church. "Your only hope of salvation is to abandon your own beliefs and humbly submit to the will of God, which we represent." So surrender your mind, your independent judgment, and follow the group. "Blessed are the meek," the book says, "for they shall inherit the kingdom of heaven." The message is: be small, be a lamb, or like a little child. Be humble -- pride goeth before a fall. Believe what you're told. Self esteem is wrong and ugly. Don't presume to try to know for yourself. Your only hope is to put your faith in the Bible, the Koran, the Torah, the I Ching, or in Moses or Christ, or Mohammed, or the Pope, or Ghandi, or the Reverend Moon, or Baghwan, or a great Rabbi or Ayatollah, or Karl Marx, or the Emperor, or the President, or Fidel Castro or Adolph Hitler; somebody, <u>anybody</u> you can believe in, because it's a great sin to believe, first and foremost, in yourself and your own mind and power of judgment.

This undermining of the individual has worked to weaken selfhood and build the power of groups for thousands of years. -- Yet for most of those years it has been needed. Peoples, nations, and religions built on power, mass psychology, superstition, and the negation of the individual have ruled for thousands of years over masses of people as yet too undeveloped to take the responsibility for their own or their group's existence. In Tennyson's words, "*Theirs not to reason why, theirs but to do or die.*"

But since the beginnings of the enlightenment just a few centuries ago, a profound change has gained momentum. In Western European countries, and especially with the founding and rise of the United States, more people are accepting their own value as individuals, apart from their membership in or identification with some religion, nation, or other group or collective. They are more and more taking the responsibility for discovering and deciding <u>for themselves</u> who they are, what they believe, and what moral rules should guide their own behavior.

The human race has had independent members in its myths and throughout its history, from Adam and Eve to Michael Servetus, Giordano Bruno and Galileo, from Prometheus to Jefferson, John Stuart Mill, Ayn Rand and scores of others, most of them unknown.

In the past, autonomous creators have always been exceptions, mavericks, someone to be wondered at. They have been thought of as legendary freaks of human nature, unlike the rest of us. They have been called "geniuses" and sprinkled not too generously across human populations, but have made extraordinary contributions to progress. Now a great change is in the making. The potential exists for unprecedented numbers of "ordinary" people to achieve a high level of autonomy in their lives, and it is beginning to happen. As it does, it brings us to a period of creativity, innovation, invention and discovery unparalleled in human history. Today we are living through the last of the second stage in the evolution of purpose, the collectivist stage, as it begins to give way to the as yet unborn third, individual stage.

The Individual Stage of Purpose

We approach the end of a great stage of human development, one that has served our kind well for tens of thousands of years. It is coming to its close, and we are on the threshold of a new stage, a passage to a different world, a different motivation, a new and different form of purpose that is beginning to guide and shape human society. The group or collectivist stage is collapsing, and should wind down in the next century or two. The third stage of the way in which purpose governs human behavior, the individual stage, is almost at hand. As the group stage of purpose has rested firmly on the biological stage from which it grew, the individual stage has formed its roots in the collectivist or group stage, and is growing from it. It will prove itself as different from its predecessor as the group stage is from the biological. But first collectivism must release its grip on the species, and this it will not do without additional struggles, convulsion, bloodshed and pain.

Major passages in life, when old ways of organizing behavior give way to untested new ways, are periods of stress for individuals and for groups. Evolutionary changes in which a whole species moves through a major passage in development in a relatively short period of time are times of great stress, social disorganization, uncertainty and strife. We saw it in the transition from the biological to the group stage of purpose, symbolized by the myth of original sin. Now the human race is in the midst of such a period once again. This new transition began a few hundred years ago, starting in western history with the enlightenment.

To put it in concrete terms, we are outgrowing the times when governments, government schools and religions claim our minds and souls. We are nearly done with the centuries when our rulers or our church or educators or families impressed their values, their view of right and wrong, their customs and forms of economic and social organization forcefully and indelibly on the next generation. In each new generation there grow more and more individuals claiming the ownership of their own souls, the right to decide for themselves the profound questions of their existence and the meaning of their lives. Such individuals decide for themselves what is right and what is wrong, how to relate to each other as citizens, as co-workers, as friends, as lovers, as parents. They are deciding for themselves whether or not they believe in God. If they believe, they choose how they understand and will relate to that God. And they decide how to organize their own lives, and participate in organizing their community and their society, economically, socially, educationally, religiously, without sacrificing their independence of thought and action.

A clear example is the committed sexual/romantic relationship. In the group stage of purpose, parents decide when and who their children marry. The state licenses and the church claims to give God's authority to the union, and its agents perform and bless the marriage ceremony. As the transition towards autonomy takes place in developed countries, individuals themselves decide if, when and with whom they will form a committed sexual partnership and, if they do, whether or not they will have that relationship licensed by the state and/or celebrated in a religious ceremony. It is a momentous change, and representative of changes in progress in all phases of life in the most advanced human societies, as humankind moves through the transition from the second, group stage toward the autonomous, third stage of purpose.

For most people in the world, such individual autonomy is but a dream, if not a frightening nightmare that reeks of chaos and anarchy. We middle-class Americans are privileged to be on the cutting edge of the change towards autonomy. Even here, in our 200-plus years as a nation, the greatest the world has yet seen, we have made only a start. Autonomy of the individual means individuals each governing themselves, so long as they do not infringe the rights of others. For this to happen, people need, first, to have the right and the freedom to govern themselves, and second, to be prepared to assume, without a safety net, the dangers and responsibilities of free existence.

Entrenched groups promote dependence to perpetuate and justify their power. Even while individuals have been gaining increased autonomy in some aspects of their personal lives, they are ruled by governments that grow like a cancer to regulate, control, take power over more and more of the other areas of life. Government and established groups that use government to entrench and augment their power surround us. Government and establishments supported by government have organized society on parent-child lines, into "those who take care of" -- the parent people, -- and "those who are taken care of" -- the child people. Parent people are those who employ and manage others, own and rent out property, teach, give health care to, counsel, and above all govern and regulate, other people. Child people get jobs, are managed, are tenants, receive health care, are counseled, and above all, are governed and regulated. All of us sometimes take a parent role and sometimes a child role in society, but usually one or the other role predominates.

Parent roles carry power, privilege and responsibility. Most people clamor for them. We create child people by making most people more helpless, less able to take care of themselves. We weaken their character by providing for them rather than requiring them to provide for themselves. Parent people recruit and create child people to satisfy their parent function. Teachers need students. Social workers need welfare cases, alcoholics, and broken families. Counselors and lawyers need clients. Doctors and nurses need patients. Landlords need tenants. Banks need borrowers, police need criminals, etc. And so educators are busy extending hours per week and the years per lifetime that children "need" to be schooled. Lawyers are busy discovering new victims of "bad" corporations or individuals with deep pockets. Psychologists and psychiatrists invent new mental illnesses each year that send patients to their care. All are promoting laws to restrict entry into their occupations and professions, and so drive up their income. And politicians, bureaucrats and courts produce a never-ending stream of plans, laws, regulations, and interpretations to guide, oversee, and control larger and larger areas of our lives. We are <u>all</u> the "child people" of government bureaucrats.

These things are relatively obvious. More obscure is the widespread weakening of self-hood that is fed by this ever-extending control over the lives of others. Government promotes this most pernicious of all parent-people activities. It is pernicious because it is a direct assault on the autonomy of the mass of the population, and because its activities are backed up by force.

<u>All of these tendencies to extend dependency and control in our society are reactive efforts to stem the evolutionary movement of human beings toward individual independence, freedom, and autonomy</u> that, despite it all, is growing apace. The increasing parent-child organization of our society is a reactionary tightening of the defenses of collectivism against this growth of autonomy.

I'm told that it was Albert Camus who said:

Do not walk in front of me; I may not want to follow. Do not walk behind me; I may not want to lead. Just walk beside me and be my friend.[4]

The society of parents and children, those who insist on leading us and the willing and unwilling followers, must and will go, will disappear as autonomy grows. Autonomy develops when people take the responsibility for their own existence. We should emblazen it across our minds. <u>Autonomy develops when people take the responsibility for their own existence.</u> -- And widespread autonomy is the destiny of the human species. It is still a long ways ahead.

The Autonomous Individual

The autonomous individual relates to God or to nature or to whatever it is that he sees as highest in the universe directly, one to one, without intermediaries. There is no one, alive or dead, and no beliefs of others, whether written or spoken, no divine text or revealed text, between him and what is for him the highest. Although the universe is vast and full of wonders, and we understand only a small part of nature's mysteries, all is "natural." There are no miracles and no intervening supernatural parent, no suspensions of natural law, and no angels, devils, saints, or other miracle workers. All that is is, without exception, subject to rational study and inquiry, regardless of our current ignorance.

The autonomous individual's first source of knowledge is his own mind; his first responsibilities are:

1) <u>Reality</u>, -- to learn to know the twin realities of the external world and the self;

2) <u>Morality</u>, -- to take the responsibility to make of himself a good person, in his being and in his actions;

3) <u>Potentiality</u>, -- to live his life so as to realize the potentiality his life holds; and

4) <u>Community</u>, -- to love and support his family and others in his sphere of influence as they grow toward living their own lives by these principles.

These four principles express the direction toward which the human race is moving, and define the nature and promise of autonomy.

Autonomy and Selfishness

The autonomous person works primarily for his own goals and values, not those of the group. This is a grave and punishable character "defect" from the group standpoint, as we have seen. When the group is insecure because some members are questioning its beliefs and values, harsh punishments are especially likely for those of independent thought. And when the group experiences a real or imaginary threat from another group, e.g., over territory or power, a truly independent stance is likely to be perceived as traitorous.

Of course groups are sometimes threatened, their very existence put into peril, by other groups, or by natural disasters. Group members are expected to fall in line in any conflict, just or unjust, or in any emergency, and to subordinate their individual lives to the alleged danger to the group's existence. The group has often owed its survival to members prepared to fight for it in time of crisis. A person, autonomous or not, who believes in the group's rightness and wishes it to survive may be prepared to put his or her life on the line in conflict or crisis. Being autonomous only means that the individual makes the sacrifice out of personal choice without being forced or coerced. An autonomous life, then, can include an autonomous death.

Are there other ways or situations in which individual autonomy is subordinate to other aspects of life? I strongly believe there are, for reasons arising from the spiritual or metaphysical outlook expressed in this book as at the end of Chapter 9. I see each individual life as being rooted in the universal force of life, the radix -- or whatever one chooses to call it. I don't believe that we have individual souls that survive our death, but rather that we are each a part, an expression of the underlying unitary substratum of all existence. At the deepest level we are all the same being.

I have been given this portion of life, and it is mine to make of what I can and will. No one can with justice take that life from me or claim ownership over it by nation, religion, community or family. That is what it means to be an autonomous adult.

Even so I am embedded in a universe huge and wonderful beyond my capacity to understand. I marvel over the bit I do understand, and accept that I have a responsibility to be as much as I can be, to try to fill the potential I see in myself in the various dimensions of my existence. I strive to make myself into a good person, to love myself and others, my family, my friends, the communities to which I belong; to open my heart to wonder, my mind to knowledge, tested by my personal thought and rationality; my life to creating what I have to create, exchanging part of what I produce for what I need from others to live, and facing difficulties with courage and determination, sharing knowledge and wealth I create with my fellow men. These are for me the ingredients of a full, autonomous, and satisfying life.

Autonomy and Armor

The origin and development of the muscular armor has been central to civilization as we have known it in the group stage of purpose. Masses of human beings have become progressively more armored as civilization has advanced. But a second development has also played a central and necessary role in that advance. This is the sporadic outcroppings of autonomous creative individuals, who resisted the "socialization" process for individual pursuits, some of which resulted in extraordinary contributions to human progress. Mass man was led, through the armor, to bury and subordinate the self. The autonomous maverick resisted the subordination of self to group in at least one area of life, and was sometimes enabled to tap into the wellsprings of life more deeply than the others as a result. This deepening of the self enabled these individuals to create the discoveries and marvels of technology, science, literature, and art that are the glory and wonder of human history. These are outcroppings of autonomy in the more uniform landscape of masses of human beings marching through history.

Mass armoring (in Wilhelm Reich's sense) characterizes the masses of humanity. It destroys their self-confidence and independence, helps them control their feelings and force themselves to conform. Through it they become malleable to the purposes of the group.

But what of those who retain their sense of self enough to resist the process, some of whom become the great exceptions. Are they not also armored? They often require the greatest capacity for self-control, to contain and delay satisfaction, living their lives long range, something that the unarmored are unable to do.

Here is exactly why I coined the expression "the radix block." The radix block and Reich's muscular armor both block and channel the life force, damming feelings and other life processes. The difference between them is that <u>muscular armor is imposed to serve the group's purposes, while the more evolved radix block serves the conscious choices of an autonomous person.</u> Although they both may look the same in the body, each being composed of patterns of muscular tension that guide and control the life force, the radix block differs by being chosen by the individual affected. A price is paid in feeling and aliveness in either case. With the radix block, however, the price is voluntarily assumed. The person is not at war with him or herself, and so does not have to force, dissimulate, suffer internal conflict that saps the aliveness and joy in living. Only with the radix block is there a united front of thought and will, of individual purpose energizing the muscular blocking and channeling of the life force that allows one to block without surrendering the deeper self to the group.

If there is personal growth in awareness and the power of choice, muscular armor can become a radix block. It is what must happen to children. Even if they are destined to become autonomous, they must learn to block feelings many years before they can really understand why.

This distinction between muscular armor and radix block should guide one's personal growth process. Once a person accepts the responsibility for discovering and choosing beliefs and values and the goals and purposes that will guide his life, the pathway to autonomy opens. Some people have always seemed to know, to flow naturally into an autonomous way of life, independent in belief and spirit. Others fight and struggle over years of their lives to gain the same end, which is sovereignty over one's own soul.

Autonomy and Government

In the more advanced nations, those in which most citizens are literate and many have a grasp of the concept of human rights, a conflict is created by the birth of autonomy. In these developed nations, there is a hunger for freedom in masses of people, and an utter failure of most people to understand the nature of freedom and the responsibilities it entails. Witness the chaos that ensued in "East Bloc" nations after decades of collectivist authoritarian communist rule. To the child people of the world, "freedom" means escape from serfdom and drudgery, and to be given a larger share of the good things of life, -- food, housing, clothes, consumer goods, entertainment. To the parent people of the world it means these same things plus a share of responsibility for that part of the political and economic system that is theirs. They are the politicians, bureaucrats, police, the military, teachers, lawyers, doctors, owners and managers of property, employers, etc. Child and parent people alike are fundamentally concerned with and live their lives through other people. Child people do it because it is through parent people that their needs and wants are satisfied. Parent people do it because not only are their physical needs and wants satisfied through other people; their needs for position, power, status, authority over others are met as well.

The autonomous person also has physical and social needs to be satisfied but, unlike parent people, authority and power over other people are not their needs. More important to the autonomous person is the freedom to function in his or her own way, without the interference of child people clamoring for support and possessions, or that of parent people and their laws and regulations asserting authority over the persons and property of others. Autonomous people want to function in the world with full responsibility for themselves and their own lives, and only such responsibility for others as they freely choose to assume. Such a way of functioning is counter to collectivism and the group stage of human development. The collectivist view of society is that "everybody should be responsible for everybody," with details of responsibility to be worked out by the parent people who are to assign responsibilities so that everybody's needs can be met, everybody's, that is, except those of autonomous people, whose great need is to be left alone. The autonomous desire a different system, one in which adults are each responsible for themselves, and are given the freedom they need to satisfy (or fail to satisfy) their own needs and to take care of their own lives.

Most of the forms of human governance have developed in the group stage of the evolution of purpose, the collectivist stage, and are not appropriate to autonomous human beings. Autonomy means self-government, and autonomous people wish in so far as possible to govern themselves. Those not capable of living autonomously or who are not permitted to do so by government and rules of social organization do need outside help. The principle is that those not able to, or not left free to, take care of themselves need others to take care of them if they are to live. How to solve this problem without theft from the citizens by government is one of the central problems of the human race.

In the meantime we must suffer through this huge transition we are in between the group, collectivist stage of purpose and the individual stage that is dawning. America, more than any nation in history, has tasted the nature and rewards of freedom and opened the way to a future based on the continued evolution of the human species toward freedom and autonomy. For a few decades, we have been in a reaction pushing us backward toward collectivism. Perhaps it has about run its course, and we can move again toward freedom.

The "Teaching" of Autonomy

Purpose can be taught, but can autonomy? There is a great difference between building a capacity for self-control and independence and the development of autonomy. Autonomous people go beyond self-awareness, self-control, independence, and the balance of thinking and feeling. The autonomous person is purposive and independent, but something more.

There is a certain contradiction involved in the very idea of "teaching" autonomy. Teaching is, after all, influencing from without, while autonomy is a reliance on what develops from within. The development of that which lies within is at the core of the autonomous person and is the central process in the growth of the individual and the evolution of the race toward autonomy. Fostering, facilitating, and furthering this growth and evolution has been my conscious objective in more than thirty years of learning and teaching personal growth, just as it has been for people like Wilhelm Reich, Carl Rogers, Abraham Maslow, Nathaniel Branden, Reuven Bar-Levav and hundreds of others.

Penetrating to the heart of the process of personal growth confronts one with the mystery of autonomy, which is part and parcel of the mystery of the human soul itself. This I see as the radix source at the center of one's being, the focus of the creative process from which each of us arises.

So the deeper nature of autonomy and personal growth turns out to be rooted in religious questions. This is not to mystify them and place them beyond investigation and scientific understanding. Rather it is to identify them with ultimate questions, with the creation of the universe, of life and its meaning to each one of us, of our nature and destiny. These questions have answers that lie beyond both religion and science as we know them today, in the dangerous death struggles of the collectivist, group stage of human development. We begin now to realize the fantastic promise of the autonomous individual stage that lies ahead.

Chapter Notes

---

[1] Kelley, C.R. 1989 revised 2004, THE MAKING OF CHICKENS AND OF EAGLES. Excerpts reprinted in Kelley, C.R., 1992, THE RADIX, VOL. I: RADIX PERSONAL GROWTH. Vancouver, WA: K/R. Publications.

[2] Rand, Ayn, 1943, THE FOUNTAINHEAD. New York: Bobs-Merrill.

[3] Hoffer, Eric, 1951, THE TRUE BELIEVER. New York: Harper & Row.

[4] I'm unable to trace the origin of this quotation attributed to Camus.

Chapter 12

RADIX AND PHYSICAL SCIENCE

Reality has a three-part nature. For each individual, there is an outer realm of objective, shared physical nature, an inner subjective realm of individual personal experience, and a third underlying realm or radix substratum from which the objective and the subjective originate.

The primary property of the radix substratum is **being**. Being is before consciousness and before action. What one can say about the substratum is that it is, and that everything else, whether subjective or objective, is created from it. It is closely akin to the concept of "god in nature," a pantheistic, non-personified concept of god that can be studied as part of the natural world.

When the radix moves from the substratum into the world of physical nature, it enters through voids, places of low charge, radix **sources,** in the form of radix **charge,** creating space in the process. Space is born in this first stage of the creative process, the charge stage.

For the next stage of creation to take place the substratum differentiates, divides off. The oneness of the substratum becomes the many radix sources of the physical world. It is through these sources that space grows. They are where the expanding universe expands from. Through them radix charge enters the familiar world, and the processes of convergence and discharge can take place.

The mating of the charge from two different sources is radix **superimposition.** Consciousness develops with superimposition and radix **discharge**, each source experiencing individually the discharge of its own charge; -- for example, the individual human experiences his own charge being discharged. With discharge the universe is changed in a small way or large. Along with consciousness, new energy is born. Something new is added to the universe. The discharge stage of the creative process has taken place.

Before Radix Discharge

Again: Radix sources bring radix charge from the substratum into the universe we know. Radix charge is, I assume, a continuous variable in its degree or concentration, i.e., it has no jumps in level (discontinuities). There are many peaks and valleys of charge. There are areas or centers of low radix charge, where there is higher charge in all directions, as well as peaks of charge where there is lower charge in all directions. Since radix charge flows from lower to higher, places of lowest charge are centers or singularities from which radix charge flows out of the substratum into the universe. (I write later of peaks of high charge, where radix charge may sometimes flow back into the substratum.) I identify places of lowest charge as the sources of radix charge, **portals** to and from the substratum. Radix charge flows from them into the physical world. Sources may be short-lived and evanescent. Since living things each have their own source, these sources live as long as the living things they animate. On earth, atmospheric sources such as anti-cyclonic weather systems are short-lived compared with geographic sources on the earth's surface, while geological sources may be very long-lived. Cosmic sources in extra-galactic space may last for billions of years, voids gradually pouring radix charge and space into the observable universe.

The charge that flows from different sources is not the same. Each source has its own connection, its portal to the radix substratum. Each individual is created through its own source. The charge flowing into the physical world through each source is unique, different from all other, but the substratum that each one taps into is unitary. Individuation takes place at the portal. On one side of each portal is the unitary radix substratum, on the other, the multifaceted physical world into which charge from the substratum is flowing.

Charge flowing from one source tends to mate, superimposing with that from another of its type or order of magnitude of charge. Perhaps a much more powerful partner would swallow it; a much smaller, it would swallow.

A source may feed many superimpositions. There may be one storm or a series of storms fed by the same pair of anti-cyclones, one volcano or a string of volcanoes, one galaxy or a family of galaxies, one mating or a series of matings with the same animal partners. With each superimposition there is discharge. Radix charge is consumed by the discharge, consciousness is born or intensified through the two sources, and new energy, primary energy, emerges into the physical world. The new energy expresses the consciousness that goes into its creation, and is <u>relevant</u> to the particular creative event. Superimposition and discharge <u>mean</u> something. They are the culmination of the creative process. Radix charge enters the world at sources to form the backdrop of physical reality. Radix discharge of charge from two sources creates the content of reality. They have created and are creating the universe.

But do not forget that the cosmos is filled with radix charge. The great bulk of it is undischarged. It has entered the world through sources, to form the framework of physical nature. Through radix sources the universe is in a never-ending process of becoming. And radix charge, though not yet physical, is real, natural, and has properties that need to be understood. Understanding the pre-physical is difficult, challenging, stretching knowledge, intelligence and intuition to its limits. I know I must make mistakes as I grasp some and almost grasp other great truths at this boundary of my own understanding.

Cosmic Sources

Back to sources of radix charge! There are levels and kinds of sources. Living things carry their own source inside, the most complex sources we know. In empty deep space, sources are huge and unstructured. When a node of low radix charge develops in deep space, it begins to ooze charge out from the substratum into the physical world. Think of radix charge as space in this context. A cosmic source has been created. In the cosmic voids of intergalactic space, there is no structure to shape or impede the flow of charge, only a slight outward charge gradient from each center of lowest charge. From each such center charge oozes out from the substratum, expanding the universe. The emerging new charge follows the law of movement from "lower to higher charge," and creates a field of anti-gravity as it moves from the low charge source toward the higher charge surround. The emerging charge organizes, following the lower to higher charge principle. Growing tongues of charge form in the charge moving out from their cosmic sources. There are enormous tongues, rivers of charge, in intergalactic space before the birth of galaxies. It is the divergence of charge from a source that creates an anti-gravitational field. Gravity results from the flow of radix charge in the universe. Converging radix charge flows in towards centers of mass, i.e., galaxies, stars and planets and perhaps dark matter, creating ever stronger gravity. Diverging radix charge, moving away from sources, flows out, creating new and growing space and so expanding the universe. The expanding universe causes inter-galactic distances to grow.

The huge intergalactic sources and the flow from them are of special interest because they have little structure. They show the functioning of sources unobstructed by matter or clutter from nearby sources that would confuse or confound the cosmic flow of charge into the universe. The sources do their work, pouring more and more radix charge into the universe over the eons, new springs of creative potential, which we see as space moving from cosmic voids out from the substratum into the expanding universe of light and matter. Tongues of charge flow out along gently curved paths, gradually developing and intensifying the charge gradients along which their charge flows.

Yes, I believe radix charge *is* space, and more. But how can we know? How can we observe it? Radix charge is before matter and energy, and is transparent, invisible. My own intuitive picture comes mostly, I believe, from the hundreds of times that my young weather forecaster's fingers drew the isobars around high pressure centers on synoptic maps in World War Two weather stations. The high pressure centers such as those I drew are, I claim, the true creative sources of our weather. In intergalactic space, without the structure provided by earth and atmosphere, cosmic sources must still be quite similar to the anti-cyclone in their shape and pattern of flow.

And yes, my intuition is that the outpouring of radix charge (= space?) from cosmic sources is the cause of the expansion of the universe implied by Hubble's red shift. It produces the accelerating growth of astronomical space from cosmic sources. The flow of that charge creates gravitational fields in "empty" space.

Astronomers infer the existence of mysterious gravitational fields in deep space from the distribution, shape, brightness, spectra, and other properties of galaxies. They attribute these "gravitational" fields to <u>dark matter</u>! The apparent effects of gravity on the visible universe are so different from expectation based on Newton's law of universal gravitational attraction that astronomers have had to fill the universe with this invisible dark matter, invisible clouds of hydrogen, perhaps, that are twenty times more plentiful than visible matter. This is needed to account for what they see in terms of Newtonian gravitational attraction. They assert that dark matter is real and exerts attraction on visible matter. But is their dark matter only "bookkeeping matter?" -- There is no reason to believe that dark matter is there except that it is required to make Newton's "universal law of gravitational attraction" work in intergalactic space. Without it there would be "gravitational" fields that are not produced by matter. But that is exactly my hypothesis about the movement of radix charge from sources in intergalactic space! The flow of radix charge from lower to higher concentration I believe <u>is</u> gravity.

Creation and Cosmology

The theory of radix charge and its entry into the universe at "sources" -- places of lower radix charge than their surrounding -- grew out of my experience with radix charge and discharge in the human body and in the atmosphere. It is the beginning of my own creation myth. The biblical story of creation given in the book of Genesis is surely a myth, but so also are the creation myths of science, including the astronomers' "big bang" and "big crunch." Thoughtful individuals endeavor to develop a world view which includes a view of origins, and that fits the universe as they know it. I am one of these. From a few facts and observations a story of creation is developed based on the story-teller's knowledge and beliefs. This has been true of human cultures throughout history.

In early Western history and the developing Judeo-Christian tradition, animism gave way to mystical religion based on authority and the "revealed truth" of sacred texts, the Torah and the Christian Bible. But authority and "revealed" truth are weak foundations of knowledge and a poor basis for understanding physical reality. Science and technology developed and became able to deal more effectively with physical reality, leaving religion the areas of god and origins, mind and spirit. Human knowledge was thus split in two, as science developed its own creation myths.

The splitting of knowledge into scientific and religious branches cut religion off from its grounding in reality, in facts, in natural processes. Most religion has, as a consequence, floated in its sea of "revealed" myth and mysticism, desperately in need of the connection with objective reality that science has inherited as its legitimate domain.

This split in knowledge has been just as devastating in its effect on science, though for many intellectuals it is not as easy to see. Science also lost its connection with half of nature, the other half. Science lost real contact with questions of creation, not only of life (which science allows as a real and great mystery) but the creation of the entire physical universe. The scientist abolishes life and abolishes creation from his world in order that he may work with it "scientifically."

We cannot deny science's remarkable success in dealing with dead matter and running-down (entropic) physical processes. These

Radix & Physical Science

are the domain of science as we know it. But because science has been so successful in developing the laws of dead matter and running-down aspects of nature, it does not follow that its methods and tools are effective in dealing with the alive and with the building-up aspects of nature. This is where science falls into its own myth and delusion.

The "big bang" is a current cosmological myth of science, holding that the creation of the universe took place at a particular time billions of years ago. The myth is that all of the energy there is, the building material of the entire physical universe, was born of one small glob which exploded into the entire universe as the "mother of all explosions" at time zero, defined by a singularity in certain mathematical equations. "In the beginning God created heaven and earth," says the myth perpetuated for millennia by Judeo-Christianity. It is only slightly recast by science: "In the beginning the big-bang created the cosmos," mythologizes scientism.

These are the creation myths today of Western religion and western science, respectively. When read as poetic flights of fantasy, they are remarkably similar. They each reflect a deterministic "nothing new is now being created" belief system. Everything that is, is traced back to a birth, a beginning in time, the biblical six days, or the instantaneous big bang. After the birth, there is the newborn universe, wound up like a clock and starting to run, -- and to run down. Inexorably, the universe deteriorates toward Armageddon or to death through the increase of entropy, depending on whether one chooses the myth of religion or of science. Absent from both myths is the actual _process_ of creation.

Most people see the story of Genesis as the myth it is, but if they are caught up in the dogma of religion they may believe the myth to be literal truth. And if they are caught up in the dogma of science, they may take the myth of the big bang seriously, as if it were a scientifically factual account. But the big bang theory is only the extrapolation backwards of a universe imagined by "big bang" scientists to be running down, its postulated fixed amount of energy being spread ever more and more thinly through expansion of the universe caused by the "big bang," and being distributed ever more evenly through increasing entropy. If you imagine an expanding, running-down, slowly-dying universe, then run it backward in time in your mind, you see that energy would concentrate more and more, eventually resulting in all the energy in the universe crammed as closely as possible to a single point. One can't reduce entropy any further than that, so it has to be "birth," the very beginning, the "singularity" when the big bang took place. This, with its ever growing ad hoc supporting rationale, makes up the big-bang myth.

Where did this cosmic glob of energy that formed the universe, together with its principles of organization, i.e., the "laws of nature," come from? What was going on before the big bang? Many scientists, when they have no accepted theory or myth to apply to important questions, call the questions "meaningless." The organizing principles governing the universe were supposed by the scientist to have been in existence from the big bang that began it all. They correspond to questions concerning religion's Genesis creation myth. "Where did energy and the laws of nature that organize it come from" corresponds to "Where did God come from?" -- And "What did God do <u>before</u> creating heaven and earth" corresponds to "What happened in the universe <u>before</u> the big bang?"

Of course the skeptic is entitled to ask of radix theory, "Where does the radix source, the "substratum" come from?" It's a legitimate question, though I don't speak of ultimate beginnings or endings, only of ongoing processes. The substratum, I say, is real, natural, and understandable, and we will learn to understand it better as we learn more about the process by which the universe as we know it is coming into existence.

<u>Continuous Creation (Steady State) Theories</u>

More than fifty years ago, some cosmologists rejected the "big bang" theory of cosmology in favor of a "steady-state," "continuous creation" theory. According to the version of the theory expounded by Gold, Bondi and Hoyle[1] who were its major originators, new matter is being created in the universe all the time in the form of new hydrogen atoms coming into existence in space. They come from nowhere to balance the mean density of the universe. Otherwise the universe would be thinning out from expansion and dying a death of increasing entropy, as most scientists believe. But these steady-state theorists believe that newly created hydrogen atoms are steadily coming into existence in the universe and become organized gradually into new galaxies and stars, and so sustain the average density of the expanding universe.

The creation of new matter violates science's sacrosanct law of conservation of energy. This has limited the acceptance of continuous creation theory. These steady-state theorists try to deal with the problem of the creation of new matter by mystifying it. They say that one is not permitted to ask where the new matter comes from or by what process. It just happens because the theory requires it. Hoyle tells us:

> *There is an impulse to ask where originated material comes from. But such a question is entirely meaningless within the terms of reference of science. Why is there gravitation? Why do electric fields exist? Why is the universe? These queries are on a par with asking where newly originated matter comes from, and they are just as meaningless and unprofitable.*[2]

Thus these continuous creation steady-state cosmologists show themselves to be as hung-up as their scientistic big-bang colleagues on the central question of creation. Yes, they concede, new matter is created, but by an unknowable process. The newly created atoms are spread out in space and time so sparsely that no one could ever hope to observe or measure an atom's initial appearance. The requirement is for new matter to appear at a rate that maintains the average density of the expanding universe. This is for one new hydrogen atom to come into existence per liter of space per billion years, according to a calculation referred to by Hoyle (Note 1). Thus these steady-state cosmologists offer a theory of the ongoing continuous creation of the physical universe by a process that cannot be observed, tested, falsified, or questioned, but must be taken on faith. This is scientistic mysticism.

Yet do not underestimate the overall achievement of the Gold-Bondi-Hoyle group. They mounted a serious challenge to the world-view of a science strictly committed to the big bang and the dying, running-down universe. Their theory is in accord with the second law of thermodynamics (the law of entropy), and with Hubble's red shift evidence that the universe is expanding. We need plausible testable continuous creation theory, theory that need not be accepted on faith. The big bang theory is on its last legs.

The primary reason for the wide acceptance of the big bang theory of cosmology was that it provided a plausible explanation for the well-established expansion of the universe. The theory that the universe is expanding has grown ever more secure as data pours in from new telescopes. Hubble's red-shift evidence of correlation between the distance of remote galaxies and their velocity of recession from us has been confirmed again and again, and by a variety of evidence. The conventional wisdom in modern astronomy has been that we live in an expanding universe as a consequence of the big-bang explosion. According to accepted physical law, the rate of expansion, however, must be slowing because of gravitational forces pulling the contents of the universe back towards each other.

The big bang was a hypothetical single extreme event at the beginning of time, and the impulse expanding the universe was delivered almost all at once. Then the contents of the universe sped apart at great velocity, creating our expanding universe. Gravity slows down the expansion, creating a very small but continuing deceleration of the velocity of expansion. The effect of gravitational deceleration is cumulative, however. Given enough time, it is expected to halt and then reverse the expansion of the universe, which would then converge back into what astronomers have called "the big crunch."

Bye-bye Big Crunch

Modern astronomy has developed the tools and techniques to measure how much the velocity of expansion of the universe has been slowed down by gravity in distant galaxies near the furthermost reach of today's instruments. The observations, now confirmed by different groups of astronomers, agree on this point: <u>The distant galaxies studied have not slowed down their velocity of expansion as expected, but have instead speeded up.</u> This accelerating movement away from us of distant galaxies cannot result in a "big crunch" of all the matter in the universe coming together. Further, this accelerated outward expansion of the contents of the universe could not be the result of a big-bang explosion at the beginning of time. The accelerating expansion of the universe is an ongoing process, not a singular event that happened once when the universe began. Its explanation needs to also be in terms of an ongoing process rather than a singular event.

Bye-Bye Big Bang?

Einstein at one time had inserted into his equations for general relativity a "cosmological constant," a term that meant there was an expansive force in the universe opposing the force of gravity. Einstein later decided he had made a big mistake, and removed the term. He called the term his "greatest scientific blunder." Cosmologists today however have gone back to Einstein's "mistake" as a possible explanation for the unexpected and unexplained accelerating expansion of the universe, evidence for which is now strong.

Seizing onto Einstein's "greatest blunder" to explain the puzzling new accelerating expanding universe has a decidedly ad hoc flavor. There are other possible explanations to be considered, including steady state continuous creation models. Any theory considered must show a more satisfactory account of the expansion of the universe than the big-bang theory offers.

A large proportion of astronomers are deeply entwined in big-bang theory, which marries the complexities of general relativity with those of quantum mechanics. These astronomers operate far above my mathematical head. What is clear is that the big-bang theory is in great trouble.

Any physical model that incorporates a satisfactory explanation of the universe's accelerating expansion does something the big-bang theory cannot do. It is likely that a satisfactory model would have a single explanation for not only the newly discovered accelerating expansion of the universe, but also the familiar Hubble expansion. This would render the big-bang theory redundant. I base my present understanding of the expanding universe on this line of reasoning. And I look for the underlying expansive process in a continuous creation theory of cosmology.

Reich's Steady-State Theory

There was another continuous creation steady-state theory proposed half a century ago, an unrecognized "new age" theory. Wilhelm Reich came to believe that matter was created, not in intergalactic space, but within the galaxies, in stars and planets, including the earth's atmosphere and oceans. He held that the creation of new matter is occurring around us all the time. He reported newly emerging matter originating in some of his work with "orgone energy." He referred to it as "pre-atomic" matter, matter in the process of developing an atomic structure. Some of the last articles in his journals were devoted to the "pre-atomic chemistry" of substances that seemed to originate for the first time in his experiments. He wrote:

> The "CREATION" of the chemical constituents of the atmosphere as well as of the organisms would not appear to be a single act at the beginning of existence, but a continuous process of creation all through the times of existence -- balancing the process of decay and disintegration. This creative process corresponds to the orgonomic potential which by building up

potential balanced the merely mechanical discharge of energy, thus nullifying the law of entropy. (Reich, in **CORE**, 1955)[3]

I have observed the development in my own life force experiments of some of the "pre-atomic" matter Reich writes about, and believe that it may have been newly created. "Pre-atomic" is perhaps an unfortunate term of Reich's. I think it likely that this new matter has an atomic structure as soon as it becomes matter, and that it becomes matter in the superimposition of charge from two sources. Yet it is conceivable that Reich was right, and the atomic structure of new matter develops through a pre-atomic stage before reaching firm structured form. If so, Reich's "pre-atomic matter" could be a physical reality.

Radix Charge and the Measurement Problem[4]

Finding ways to sense and measure the level of radix charge (the potential for discharge) is a key problem in radix physics and its applications. Because radix charge develops before energy appears in the creative process, special measurement problems exist. Radix charge is <u>pre-physical</u> in the nature of things. Once this is understood, we can search for ways to deal with it. However, because we understand it so poorly, it has created serious problems for pioneers of the life force.

If Mesmer, Reichenbach or Reich had been able to develop an effective, usable instrument that allowed them to sense and to measure objectively the life force (animal magnetism, od or odic force, or orgone) the history of their experiments and discoveries would have been very different. All three came to depend on subjective observations to measure something which, according to their own descriptions of its properties, ought to have been objectively demonstrable. Had it been subject to measurement by objective means, it would have lent itself to the development of scientific instrumentation for the purpose. How could scientific knowledge of electricity and its applications have come about without reliable objective measurements of voltage, current, resistance, capacitance, inductance, and electrostatic charge?

While Mesmer, Reichenbach and Reich got around the measurement problem that the life force poses by reliance on subjective measurements and procedures, the vitalist movement in biology, confronting the same problem, "solved" it by claiming that the 'vital force" - (e.g., Driesch's entelechy or Bergson's elan vital) was not measurable in principle. Why, asks the physical scientist, should it not be measurable, subject to the principles and techniques of physical science, if it is real, natural, and has objective physical effects? Vitalism, like the work of Mesmer, Reichenbach and Reich, was discredited largely on the basis of this difficulty.

There is a valid point in the argument that the vital force is not measurable in principle. Radix theory carries the argument a step further. Radix charge is real, natural, and demonstrable I say, but not by the usual techniques of physical science, because it is not physical. It is a stage in the creative process before radix discharge and the creation of energy, the material of the physical world. Yet there are ways that the degree of radix charge can be inferred once the impossibility of direct physical measurement is understood. Appropriate ways of inferring charge require development and testing.[5]

Radix Discharge

With discharge, the radix process becomes tangible, measurable, subject to observation, experiment, control. This is because with discharge the products of the process, consciousness and energy, are present to be experienced, and to change the physical world. The first antithesis of radix algebra is thus expressed:

subjective manifestation (consciousness)

radix process

objective manifestation (energy)

The creative process takes place. Radix charge from two sources superimposes and is consumed by the process, as consciousness is experienced in some way by the two sources, and new energy, never before present, impacts the objective world. New energy enters the physical world, to join the old energy, previously created. The "old" energy is acted on and used by "mind" through the new energy at its disposal coming from the radix process.[6]

Energy

I use the term "energy" here as it is used in physics, not as it is used in new age "energy" work with the body. I claim that the life force or radix is not itself energy, not any form of energy. Energy is the basic material of the physical world. Kinetic energy, electromagnetism, mass, nuclear and chemical energy are among the forms or expressions of energy. The life force or radix is not one of these, but is instead that from which physical energy is created.

In personal growth work with the body, intense feelings reflect large radix discharge. With the discharge comes a radix gradient from the lowered charge where the discharge has just happened, toward the higher charge the attention spontaneously moves toward. It is, I believe, the flow of the radix up this ever-changing gradient that produces the accelerations in the body that underlie its expressive movements. Thus attention and feelings, the conscious part of the discharge process, and the radix process from the changed radix gradient the discharge produces, bring about the flow of the radix that causes the neural discharge that produces body movements. The movements express the conscious processes of attention and feeling as the radix discharge produces them.

The theory is that when new energy is created in the radix discharge process, it appears in two forms. New matter, whether appearing in Reichian or radix experiments or in outer space (as per "continuous creation" cosmology), is one energy output of a radix process. But the radix process also is responsible for the freedom of the human will. The will must, by its nature, have at its disposal a variable energy process. Since our bodies can move in different ways depending on feeling, thought and will, new energy generated by or under the control of feeling, thought and will is required. I have become convinced that the radix discharge process in our bodies produces accelerations that act like a variable "gravitational" field. These internal accelerations implement "decisions" made in consciousness. In higher animals these are amplified by the neural and metabolic systems.

However, the basic energy-creating process of life is best seen in the spontaneous movements of an amoeba, the extension and withdrawal of a pseudopodium, for example. Variable accelerations are directly involved in the internal movements of fluid that express the speck of consciousness involved in the tiny creature's radix process, and result in movements within and of its body. Much larger expressions of new energy are involved in plasmatic movements of fluids in the bodies of larger animals like ourselves. It happens most strongly when intense feelings are involved.[7] The variable accelerations that radix discharge produces within the body should be measurable, given the right instrumentation. Thus both of the postulated forms of new energy -- new matter and acceleration fields within that body -- are good candidates for physical experiments.

It is worth mentioning, while talking about new matter, that the steady-state cosmologists of the Gold-Bondi-Hoyle school hypothesize that new matter takes the simplest form, hydrogen atoms, which are rich in nuclear energy and which are so plentiful in the cosmos. It is somewhat plausible that the heavier elements are then created from hydrogen by fusion processes in the interiors of stars.

How different is Reich's steady-state theory, in which several different heavier elements are present in originated material itself! My intuition is that radix systems at work in our planet have evolved, and "learned" over geological history to create, through radix discharge, the more complex molecules involved in heavier elements. I previously expressed the belief that new matter is coming into existence in the earth's crust, the ocean, and the atmosphere all the time. I can't claim to understand just how, but I do think the process has more to do with Rupert Sheldrake's radical views about our universe's learned "habits of nature" than with traditional physical theory about the evolution of stars.[8]

Energy and Antithesis[9]

In Chapter 8, "The Algebra of Radix Discharge," I discuss radix antitheses in human consciousness that show themselves most clearly in feeling and emotional life. Examples are the antitheses of fear and trust, anger and joy, pain and pleasure, as they appear in the expressions of radix algebra. My primary training and experience has been in psychology, so it has been easier for me to develop antitheses in the area of consciousness than in that of energy, the physical side of nature. It is clear that the principle of antithesis operates in both fields.

Two central principles of physical nature stand out. One is of structure, of form, of stability of arrangement of materials, so that objects and configurations of objects have a tendency to persist in their form and configuration. The second principle is of motion or change, the antithesis of structure. Through this principle objects change their form, grow or decline, and move with respect to other objects. To change or destroy either the structure or the state of motion of something requires energy. But energy is also required to create and sustain structure. Thus energy appears as the root of the antithesis between structure and motion.

Nature is full of forms, processes, and states of matter that illustrate structure and motion. The formation of atoms from smaller particles and their remarkable persistence of form; the arrangement of atoms in molecules; the bonding together of unlike molecules in the formation of compounds; the bonding of both like and unlike molecules to give structure to solid matter. -- These are but a few examples of structure at the atomic level. At the opposite end of the size scale is the structure of galaxies, stars and planetary systems, organized and held together by gravity. Their stability of form reflects the principle of structure, while their fluidity and changeability reflect the antithesis, motion or movement.

Growth and decay both involve movement within a structure. It is the structure which is identifiable over time. Structures can grow, decay, or go through other changes in which parts move and change. The changes reflect the antithesis of structure, i.e., motion, change, transformation or deformation of existing structure.

New energy creates new physical structure, such as atoms or molecules of new matter, and may break down old structure. New energy also creates change in arrangement within existing structure, such as transformations of growth, in which new energy is added. In transformations of decay, however, old energy is lost, usually through radiation.

Motion and Time

Newton thought there was an absolute time in physical nature that "flowed on" independent of any observer. Einstein thought there was a relative time in physical nature that quickened or slowed as a function of each observer's velocity. The reality is that there is no time at all in physical nature, only movement, some of which is repetitive or regular, and can be measured, calibrated and scaled because of its repetitive nature,, and so structured to form the basis of the concept of measurable time.[10]

As space is a geometric abstraction until it is dealt with in terms of real properties of something that fills it (ether, radix charge...) time is only a concept. *Time does not exist in the physical world.* The physical world is always and only an ever-present timeless now, the "past" of which is over and gone and the "future" of which never arrives.

Time is only a product of our mind that helps us to understand and organize our experience of timeless physical reality. I said above that the concept of <u>space</u> -- the geometric concept -- helps us organize and think about the <u>structure</u>, i.e., the shape and arrangement of the content of the physical reality. In a similar way, the concept of <u>time</u> helps us understand <u>motion</u>, which is the change in structure of timeless physical reality. Structure and motion are the <u>properties</u> of the physical world from which the <u>concepts</u> of space and time derive in consciousness. Space and time are not properties of the physical world, then, but do help us understand that world.

Great mischief has been done by the error of treating time as if it were a property of physical reality rather than an idea, a concept, a tool of thought. This error readily leads to absurdities such as "time travel." The idea of time travel is based on memories and fantasies of past and future happenings, which are mental constructs only. Physical reality is here-and-now, forever timeless.

To <u>really</u> travel in time, e.g., to go back in time for one year, would mean to reverse <u>all</u> of the physical motions that have taken place in the universe in that year. Stop the earth and planets, and send them backward hundreds of millions of miles. Stop the earth's rotation and spin it backward from east to west 365 times. Reverse the growth of every living thing from maturity toward youth and youth toward conception. Tear down everything that was built and re-construct everything that was worn or destroyed in the year. Re-collect the light and heat radiated out into the universe. Compound all these absurdities and millions like them, to see what time travel would require were it a reality rather than a fantasy.

Time is a wonderfully useful concept as long as it is seen for what it is. It is a concept that, correctly applied, helps us understand our experience. But Newton and Einstein to the contrary, time is not a dimension or property of physical reality, nor is relativistic space-time.[11]

Like the physical world of structure and motion, consciousness (mind), also has structure and motion. From the flexible and fluid materials of consciousness we can model parts or aspects of reality. This process is our perception of the here and now. Further, from internal traces or records of the past we can create memories that are models of how something was in the past, and we create models of how it might be in the future, "traveling" mentally in time in memory and imagination. Further, because we can create new energy, we can choose to exert a force to change the real world in the direction of our image or fantasy of a desired future. This is such an important part of our lives, it is no wonder we erroneously project our mental constructions of past and future events onto timeless physical reality.

The point about time and space deserves restating. I define reality as including both subjective reality (consciousness or mind) and objective (physical) reality. Both realities come into existence together in the one creative process. Neither is prior. They are instead different ways of observing the same process, the inside-out subjective and the outside-in objective point of view. But it is physical reality that I see as timeless. Its properties are structure and motion, the basic antithetical properties of the here-and-now physical world.

The subjective reality of individual conscious experience is <u>mind</u>. Mind also has the properties of structure and motion, a partial individual mirror of objective processes, but more. From the "material" of consciousness, which I call <u>qualities</u> of experience, mind cannot only mirror objective processes, it can create subjective processes that are original. It can produce new processes of its own. It can add to, redirect, or otherwise modify objective physical reality by producing new physical energy, primary energy, uncaused, and appearing in the physical universe for the first time. And it can do other wonderful things.

Thus in subjective reality we can create "models" that not only mirror structures and motions in the physical world; by extension we can create structures and motions in consciousness that do not exist in the here-and-now physical world. Through memory, the mind creates scenes or fragments of past physical events or processes, and of possible (or impossible) future events or processes. Arranging these subjectively ordered models of prior and potential near and far future events around the anchoring point of present here-and-now physical reality brings the concept of spatial order (structures) and change in spatial order (motion) into conscious existence. Thus the twin concepts of space and time are born. They apply to the world of consciousness but not to that of physical reality, which I repeat is a timeless here-and-now.

Space and Radix Charge

Now, what is space, really? Like time, space is a concept, with no necessary relationship to physical reality. A conceptual space can just form a frame of reference for geometric thinking, and need have no relationship to physical reality at all. It can have two or four or N dimensions instead of three, be made of curved lines and planes rather than straight ones, be in various states of motion, etc. However, only a few concepts of space fit comfortably into observable physical reality. Traditionally, in daily life we use a three-dimensional Euclidian frame of reference anchored to places and directions in the real physical world.

Structure and motion are properties of objects in the real physical world. As time is a concept that helps us deal with moving objects, space is a concept that helps us deal with objects with extension, position, shape and orientation, "spatial" properties. But many "spatial" properties seem to be properties of physical objects in space rather than of the space in and of itself. A fundamental question is, does space have properties of its own, or is there something that "fills" space -- the ether of 19th century physics or the radix charge of my point of view -- that has spatial properties? Either space has real properties or it is filled with something that does, because space as we know it:

1. has extension, which is its defining property;

2. propagates light and sustains electromagnetic fields, and

3. sustains or produces gravitational and inertial forces.

I take the point of view that radix charge is responsible for all three of these properties, which are created when radix charge enters the universe. I believe that there is no "empty" space, and that space in and of itself is a geometric abstraction, a mental concept. Space manifests itself through the above properties. I concede that these ideas are badly in need of development and clarification.

I have said that the radix, in the form of radix charge, comes into the familiar world at sources, whether small sources in the bodies of living things, large ones in the atmosphere, or huge ones in extra-galactic space. All sources are places of uniquely low charge from which there is higher charge in every direction. From these sources the radix flows out into the universe, moving ever from lower to higher charge. I believe this creation and entry into the world of radix charge adds space, making the universe grow. The radix is the "stuff" that gives space its real properties. It oozes into the world at sources that swell with new space, and the universe grows larger as it does. As it moves it accelerates any matter it contains. Its origination at internal sources and its functioning within the animal body enables the individual animal to move and behave in response to feelings and, with humans, with thought and will as well.

Feelings and thoughts signal radix discharge in the body. With discharge, the gradients of charge in the body change quickly, inducing movements of the body radix. These charge gradients are, I believe, the source of variable accelerations that initiate body movements. It is the central process in "mind-body" psychosomatic interaction. The metabolism of radix charge, i.e., the charge-discharge process, produces body movement, traceable to new energy coming from radix discharge. In the simplest creatures, the plasma moves the body directly. In complex animals, protoplasmic movement is amplified by the neuromuscular system, still moving the animal body in accord with feelings via the radix discharge process.

Speculations About Space, Mass and Gravity

The concept of space can, however, provide a framework for thinking about the physical world. It can be self-consistent, Euclidian, beautiful. Plane and analytic geometry were such exciting subjects to me as a schoolboy, in an environment where classroom and text book beauty and excitement were rare.

Radix & Physical Science

But the spatial abstractions of geometry, lovely as they were, lacked aliveness and reality when applied in the real world. The real physical world is a world of earth and sky; animals and vegetation; moon, stars, galaxies of stars, and of people. People were real. They had emotions, thoughts and dreams as well as geometric locations and shapes. Real physical space had properties that connected it to life. These properties science kept hidden. I struggled to discover them.

It had something to do with the pantheistic idea of god. God-in-nature was absent in the fundamentalist Christianity of my boyhood, but was present in certain views from the East, in the Hindu prana, the Chinese and Japanese chi or ki, and the mysterious unfathomed void and "nothingness" of Buddhism. These expressed truth of some kind, but it was difficult to grasp. At some point despite the truth their philosophy carried, the Eastern religions had given up reality, as had my father's fundamentalist Christian religion. The East's unreality went into idols, icons, incense and chanting, and belief in the myths and fables of past lives and reincarnations. Thus they lost me -- and I them.

I rested a few years on the couch of agnosticism, rested with my eyes open. Where was the framework for really understanding living, here-and-now reality? It was not Christianity, not western science, not eastern religion, although each held some important fragment of truth. Then I stumbled onto the work of Wilhelm Reich. The story that this book describes began.

New properties of space came out of the radix life force concept. We can speak of "radix charge," or just the "radix." It is the start of the creative process. I've dealt with it at some level again and again in this book, but haven't dealt enough with its spatial aspect or properties. Radix charge enters physical reality from the radix substratum. The universe expands to accommodate it. It comes through the special portals I call "sources" into the world we know. It is the fuel of the creative process. It is real, but not physical -- not yet. It has certain characteristics of physicality, but lacks others. Our universe is not finished, not complete, but in an ever-continuing process of becoming. Radix charge moving into and within the universe is the first stage of creation.

Radix charge is everywhere. By definition it is undischarged. The universe teems with this undischarged pre-physical "material." There is no empty space in the observable universe, for radix charge moves into and through everything. Coming into the universe through its sources, it creates space. Tissue swells with it. The universe expands from it. I've studied it for decades, yet cannot claim to really understand it and how it relates to space.

Some small part of radix charge from one source finds an appropriate mating charge from another source, superimposes, intertwines and, through discharge, creates consciousness and energy for each, not necessarily simultaneously. Charge disappears as it does so. Discharge involves only a very small part of the total charge in the universe, yet it "sticks out," and draws nearly all our attention because it is active. It produces energy, and so it does things in and to the world. It is the most evident part of the creative process in nature.

The remainder, the undischarged radix, we barely acknowledge. Yet it fills the universe, creates gravity and inertia, transmits light. It forms the ever-present but little-noticed ground behind the part of the universe we do pay attention to. It holds fantastic secrets for those who pay enough attention to discover them. It's hard to explain because it needs new tools, language, and mathematics.[12] For the most part, they don't exist yet, but one has to start somewhere. I bubble over with ideas about it, fantasies, intuitions, speculations. I hope that some of these will grow, will become part of the physics of tomorrow.

Radix Convergence and Matter

Matter is created from superimposition and discharge of two radix streams, but then? As I see it, matter is a process, an extremely stable process, sustained by radix charge flowing into it. Radix charge exists before energy is produced in the creative process, i.e., before superimposition and radix discharge. Matter is produced by radix discharge, and is a form of energy. Once produced, matter is an ongoing process, fed, I suggest, by radix charge. Radix charge flows convergently up the gradient of charge from outer space, which corresponds to the gravitational gradient, reaching planets, stars, clouds of interstellar gasses, and other concentrations of matter in the universe.

Although radix charge does not discharge to form energy in the absence of a mating charge and superimposition, it greatly influences matter. It converges gravitationally to form "highly concentrated space," and plays some role not yet clear to me on processes taking place in atomic and subatomic matter. What happens to the highly concentrated radix charge as it approaches its ultimate gravitational convergence in mass particles? I don't think it can be "used up" except in discharge. I said to myself, "There are <u>sources</u>, ports of entry at centers of low charge where radix charge enters the familiar world from the substratum. Are there also ports of exit back into the substratum for unmated concentrations of radix charge that converge gravitationally through space and into matter?" Such ports of exit could be places where space (unmated radix charge) and matter are annihilated and pour <u>out</u> of the physical universe, back to the radix substratum.

The geometry of space, with its continuously but unevenly distributed radix charge, is governed by the law of flow from lower toward higher charge. It dictates the existence of centers of lowest charge, from which there is an outward flow in all directions, viz, radix sources. Similar reasoning dictates that there are centers of convergence, toward which the radix flows from all directions. The convergence centers I have paid the most attention to are those involving charge flowing together from two different sources, to superimpose and discharge. This is the creative process of superimposition from which energy and consciousness emerge. But radix convergence centers that are not associated with superimposition and discharge, centers of <u>unmated</u> high charge, I have not discussed. Are the astronomers' "black holes" examples of huge centers of convergence, swallowing radix charge itself with their supergravity? Are there smaller centers of radix convergence that play a role in subatomic physics, tiny centers of convergence that contract inward into themselves, carrying their bit of superconverging radix charge back inward to the substratum? If gravity is produced by the convergent flow of radix toward and into mass, aren't the gravitational fields of stars and planets enormous inward flowing oceans of space, of radix charge? What happens, then, in the area toward which these oceans of radix charge converge?

I speculate that when there are two tongues of radix charge converging into a young galaxy or star or planet, the inpouring radix charge has radix discharge to use up much of the charge by converting it into new energy. When there is convergence in a tongue of charge that is unmated, the situation is different.

The flow of charge from one or both sources of a superimposing system may become weak or absent. The converging unmated or weakly mated radix charge can grow and intensify without the relief valve of discharge. Do such high charge radix systems create anomalies in development of stars – supermassive stars? Black holes, through which radix charge might pour back into the substratum?

Or to carry this line of thinking further still, as stars and galaxies get old, does superimposition and discharge weaken, and the star or galaxy develop a central black hole, absorbing all the matter and energy in its neighborhood into "death" with it? The new x-ray astronomy tells us now that black holes are far more numerous than has been supposed. Are these many black holes the graves of stars and galaxies that have returned through black holes to the radix substratum from which they were born? And have they often left x-ray markers of their positions?

The "Weird" Science of the Life Force

There is a reciprocal relationship between theory and applications in physical science. When scientific theory is expanded, areas of practical application may appear. The frontiers of knowledge grow, and we become able to do new things, create new technologies, build new or better devices, or make other applications of the new knowledge.[13]

Very often the direction is the other way. New devices, inventions or techniques develop in the absence of any established explanatory theory, prove themselves useful, and spawn growth of scientific explanation and understanding. Intellectuals, enchanted with theory and explanation, give far too much credit for human progress to science and too little to invention and engineering, which frequently precede and give rise to scientific theory that only later develops enough to explain a successful device, technique, or experiment. In the borderland science that has grown up with pioneer discoveries dealing with the life force the problem is especially acute.

I became interested and deeply involved in Reich's "weird science," as some of my friends called it, during the last years of his life. This was the 1950's. I had been a weather forecaster in the Army Air Force for three years, and had something to contribute to Reich's experiments with his "cloudbuster," a device he claimed destroyed clouds and could be used to bring rain, and otherwise influence the weather. See a photo of my own Reichian cloudbuster in Appendix A following this chapter, where I also summarize some cloud destruction and rainmaking experiments.

I first visited Reich in his observatory in Maine in 1951. He was excited that I was an experienced weather forecaster, and took me down outside to demonstrate his cloudbuster. He began to teach me how he used it then and on subsequent trips to "Orgonon." Reich's cloudbuster does destroy clouds and can be used to bring rain. Reich published my first major article on the subject in 1955 in his journal **CORE,** and I reprinted it as an Appendix in A NEW

METHOD OF WEATHER CONTROL, my small book on the subject, in 1961.[14]

There is little in modern western science to explain Reich's cloudbuster and other devices and procedures, nor those that are used in acupuncture and feng shui, for example, although more and more people are now familiar with the last two and acknowledge that they work.[15]

Acupuncture is the branch of Chinese medicine that uses special needles and a theory of meridians (channels) in the body that channel the flow of the life force. The flow can be altered by the insertion of acupuncture needles into a patient's body by a properly trained professional so as to provide anesthesia for surgery or other painful procedures, or to treat and promote healing of many diseases.

Feng shui is a Chinese art and practice of arrangement of indoor and outdoor environments in accord with a theory of the nature and flow of the life force in each environment. The adept in feng shui endeavor to manipulate this flow through architectural design and arrangement of living space. Some make use of a compass to align structures in the earth's magnetic field. Mirrors, furnishings, doors, windows, passages and pathways within and around buildings and natural formations of hills, dales, landscape and trees are considered.

There is a correspondence between Reich's devices, acupuncture and its manipulation of the internal environment, and feng shui and its manipulation of the external environment. All endeavor to work with, and adjust, the concentrations and flow of the life force or *chi* in their respective domains.

Western scientists such as Mesmer, Reichenbach and Reich who have independently stumbled onto a life force concept of their own have been moved in a direction similar to their Chinese predecessors, if their work is viewed in a broad enough perspective.[16] Consider the work of Mesmer in 18th century Europe and of Reichenbach in the 19th century. Mesmer, a physician, believed that he worked with a previously unknown natural force he called *animal magnetism*, which was present in external nature as well as in animal bodies. He believed he could concentrate this force in a container or "bacquet" containing water, iron filings, and other materials. He used the bacquet in his work, which he considered to be a new approach to healing. This device had many features similar to Reich's "orgone accumulator." Mesmer worked in groups that often had a lot of noisy emotional discharge. It reminds the modern reader of Radix feeling work. Traditional scientists trying to explain (and explain away) his results, which were often spectacular, attributed his successes to suggestion and group hypnotism. Indeed, the word "mesmerize" was born from their "explanations."

Something similar but less dramatic can be said about the work of Germany's Baron Karl (aka Charles) von Reichenbach in the century following Mesmer. Reichenbach was not a physician but an organic chemist of some distinction, one who developed substances such as paraffin and creosote, which have been widely used around the globe ever since. Reichenbach became interested in what he regarded as his personal discovery and previously unknown natural force which he called the *odyl*, or *odic force*, or just the OD. Reichenbach thought that the odyl was a basic physical force that could explain magnetism and other natural phenomena. He conducted hundreds of experiments to study and demonstrate the odic force. His work was rejected by the scientific community. Since his death in 1869 it has developed a world-wide following, especially among people interested in "new age" science and its applications.

Acupuncture and feng shui from the East and Mesmer and Reichenbach's work in the West I see as the background of the modern "weird" science work of Reich and his concept of, and experiments with, orgone energy. This is, at least, where my own experience with the borderline science of the life force was born. I began to develop my own work with the physics and engineering aspects of the life force and devices designed to apply it. Years later, after developing my bodywork practice, I was able to see the strong analogy between the two disciplines, both being outgrowths of the work of Reich.

Radix Body Work and Rainmaking: A Comparison

We live in a world where knowledge and practice in a field or area like Radix personal growth work seems to most people to be something entirely different from the knowledge and practice of Reichian cloudbusting and weather modification. Imagine seeing me in a typical scene doing an individual session of Radix body work as described in Chapter 5. I've first studied my careful records of recent sessions with this student. Now I kneel beside a mat on which he lies. He is stiff, blocked and remote. I suggest to him a sequence of exercises that help him to contact his blocked feelings, and to soften his barriers to their expression. During our "50-minute-hour" together the feelings often develop, intensify, and overflow in a spontaneous discharge of anger, fear, crying, or pleasurable emotion, -- whatever he brings to the session, guided but not controlled by the student's history. Afterward there is relief and relaxation and, beyond that, a greater acceptance of his own feelings.

Alternatively, picture me on a small grassy knoll with a movable assemblage of hollow parallel metal tubes, a Reichian cloudbuster, which I direct, like I am pointing a large telescope. I have already studied weather reports and maps and observed and probed the local atmosphere directly. (I have built and equipped a complete weather station for my weather work.)

Now I point the cloudbuster first to one section of sky, then another, lingering longer here, more briefly there. I feel out, mobilize and free the atmosphere where it is stuck. It is much like when I free a stuck jaw or pelvis. After a few minutes I swing up and stay 15-20 minutes on a carefully chosen setting near the zenith. While I work the sky changes, the wind shifts and comes now from the direction my cloudbuster points. A new pattern of clouds begins to form. A different weather process has developed. It is attuned to the here-and-now existing weather situation, but guided by my long-range plan. I put the equipment away. The weather operation "intervention," planned for days or weeks, is over. Its effects, its "radix discharge," are only beginning. Significant weather operations take much longer than destroying a cloud or two or than doing sessions of Radix body work. Rain begins the next morning. In two days there is unpredicted large-scale rain in the whole region, thousands of square miles, which I have every reason to believe would not have occurred without my intervention.

I am doing much the same thing in both of these applications. Radix work is with the life force, the radix processes in a living universe. I work with the pulsation, charge, superimposition and discharge of radix systems, their precursors and their blocks. Skill in working with radix processes can be developed and used in the context of enhancing the personal growth of students in a Kelley/Radix personal growth practice. It can also be developed and used similarly in the context of radix atmospheric research and, as more and more is learned, of modifying atmospheric and climatic processes, perhaps relieving drought, and reversing the growth of dor (unmated high radix charge) and the expansion of deserts that is taking place in a region of this planet. The difficulty is that we don't know enough, not nearly enough, about the radix dynamics in either application.

Working with the life force in both of these areas cuts across the average individual's preference for dealing with either "people"-- subjective feelings, thoughts and perceptions -- or "things" -- objective reality. "People" appear less foreign to personal growth and mental health oriented students than does "the weather," perhaps because their own minds can relate directly to others' minds, perhaps because they can more easily form a model of that person based on their own identity. And they can ask a person "how does this feel?" and get a response. Their own self- concept bears little apparent relation to "the weather," and they have no verbal feedback available from the weather.

By contrast, engineering and physical science oriented people tend to prefer to deal with physical processes, which may seem more easily understandable, less contaminated by the feelings, emotions and thoughts of other people, and less likely to stir up their own. Either character tendency without a measure of balance of the opposite element is a handicap in radix work, making it difficult for a student to see how the same processes operate in such apparently different realms. It is freeing for those of either persuasion to expand their point of view, as they both need to do if they are to work most effectively over time with radix processes.

Reichian Science Today

Reich's disciples number thousands, and are out trying to do work guided by Reich's theories all over the world. They have proved over and over again over more than half a century that Reich's devices "work." His cloudbuster, correctly used, can destroy clouds and even modify weather on a large scale. I've done it, and written a book about it. His orgone accumulator also "works." See the Appendix on the subject. It is a truly remarkable device. Reichian body-oriented personal growth and psychotherapy techniques are hugely effective in freeing blocked feelings, and can make changes in a person's character that are life-altering. Nonetheless, Reich's theories, and his understanding of how his devices <u>and</u> his body-oriented procedures work, are incomplete. They incorporate large errors that <u>must</u> be corrected for the field to advance. <u>These things, students need to understand, are true of the work of virtually every truly revolutionary "genius" in human history.</u> Huge creative minds make huge mistakes. These must be corrected for progress in the work they are trying to do to continue. This error correction process is dangerous, as it can serve as an excuse for those made anxious by the creator's work to destroy his great new discoveries because they seriously threaten established positions and life styles.

I continued research with Reich's devices and my attempts to understand Reich's work scientifically in the years after his death. That was the incubation period leading eventually to this book. I have not, on these pages, done justice to the physical science and engineering aspects of Reich's work, nor to my own. To address these and a few other "far-out" aspects of the physics of the life force that I have done or was involved in some way, I have written the Appendix that follows this Chapter. These topics are given attention:

- Cloudbusting and Rainmaking
- Convergent Radix Forms and Devices: Pyramids, Cones, Funnels, Tubes and Spheres
- The Radix Charge of Living Spaces: DOR, and the Life Force Becoming Toxic Around You
- DOR in Spain: The Growing Sahara
- DOR, Desert, and Unmated Radix Charge: Orgonon and Connecticut
- Reich's Orgone Accumulator (ORAC) and the Orgone Accumulator Paradox
- Sheldrake and Morphic Resonance: Life Force and the Mystery of Form in Biology
- Landmarks in the Evolution of the Life Force Concept

Maybe one of these decades I will weave them all together into a book or books that the subject deserves. I am in my eighties, however, and suspect I may be leaving that fascinating enjoyable task to my successors.

✳✳✳✳✳✳✳✳✳✳✳✳✳✳✳✳✳✳✳✳

Chapter Notes

---

[1] Hoyle, F., 1957, FRONTIERS OF ASTRONOMY. New York: Mentor Books.
[2] *Ibid.*

[3] Reich, W., 1948, THE CANCER BIOPATHY, (THE DISCOVERY OF THE ORGONE, VOL. II). New York: Orgone Institute Press, Inc.

_____, 1951, COSMIC SUPERIMPOSITON. New York: Orgone Institute Press. Reissued by Farrar, Straus & Giroux 1973.

_____, 1955, "MELANOR, ORITE, BROWNITE AND ORENE." **CORE**, Vol. 7, Nos. 1-2, pp. 29-31.

_____, 1951, *The Oranur Experiment*, First Report 1947-51. Rangeley, Maine: Orgone Institute Press. Reprinted in part in Reich, W., 1961, SELECTED WRITINGS. New York: Noonday Press 1961.

[4] Kelley, C.R., 1980, *Radix Physics: Radix Processes, Radix Systems and the Problem of Measurement.* From **The Radix Journal**, Vol. II Nos. 1 & 2. In THE RADIX: VOLUME TWO: THE SCIENCE OF RADIX PROCESSES, 1992.

[5] Radix charge can perhaps be registered in other indirect ways. Reich and Reichenbach used the subjective response of observers able to see manifestations of the charge of the life force that others do not see. Many people feel a high radix charge or charge gradient at the pit of their stomach, e.g., before a storm. This is a comparable subjective observation of radix charge.

The myriad of radix pulsation and discharge processes in the cells of the body are affected by the level and external gradient of charge. The pulsation of small cells is fast compared with that of the larger organs, or of the whole body. What subjects become aware of is not radix charge per se, but its effect on the number and frequency of small fast pulsation and discharge processes resulting from overall differences in charge level. High external charge reduces the incoming gradient of charge and slows or inhibits the charge-discharge cycle of all these small pulsations. This slowing down is what we sense. It is the discharge phase of the pulsation that is perceptible. The level of charge is inferred from its effect on the multitude of discharges of individual pulsating cells.

This suggests a direction of research. Perhaps a culture of yeast or bacteria could be used as an instrument to measure charge indirectly, through its rate of growth. Or maybe a particular cell or cell group with a high pulsation rate could be clocked to indicate the ambient radix charge level. At any rate these are possible ways of "measuring" somethng that can't be measured directly, radix charge level.

⁶ For example, feelings and thoughts trigger physical action by the neuromuscular system to produce body movements. The body movements employ existing metabolic fuel to amplify neural messages. Newly created energy, primary energy, is required only at the neural discharge level. We know new energy is involved there because different physical outcomes may occur.

⁷ Intense feelings reflect large radix discharges, and leave behind low charge areas where the charge was high prior to discharge. The drop in charge creates a gradient of charge and a flow from the low charge in the area of discharge up the steepest gradient toward higher charge, which marks the center of attention. Radix charge flows from the center of discharge toward the center of attention, which is always discharging, changing the gradient of charge and thus modifying the flow of attention.

⁸ Sheldrake, R., 1981 and 1985, A NEW SCIENCE OF LIFE: THE HYPOTHESIS OF FORMATIVE CAUSATION. London: Blond.

_____, 1988, THE PRESENCE OF THE PAST. New York: Random House. First Vintage Books Edition, 1989.

Sheldrake developed the concept that the laws of nature we take for granted as "given" and eternally present are not eternal at all, but were (and are still being) gradually learned by "nature" in the course of both physical and biological evolution. Sheldrake speaks of "morphogenic causation" in the development and replication of new forms and sequences of development that comprise new "habits of nature." It's a startling and thought-provoking set of ideas. I question his ideas about time, which are at variance with my own, and the supposed freedom of morphogenic causal processes from the constraints of time, i.e., Sheldrake's "presence of the past." That seems to me to introduce a mystical element in his otherwise excellent work on the "problem of form." See Kelley, C.R., *Sheldrake and Morphic Resonance* in the Appendix.

⁹ The original material on the antithesis of structure and motion appeared in: Kelley, C.R., 1952, *Causality and Freedom*, **Orgone Energy Bulletin**, Vol. IV No. 1.

¹⁰ Kelley, C.R., 1980, *Radix Physics: Space, Time and the Derivative Shift*. In **The Radix Journal** Vol. 11 Nos. 3&4. And in the compilation: THE RADIX VOL. II: THE SCIENCE OF RADIX PROCESSES, 1992, p.33. Vancouver, WA: K/R Publications.

¹¹ Structure and motion, the properties of the real world from which the concept of space and time derive, are, I have said, radix antitheses. Motion is change of

structure; structure is the freezing of motion. They are not <u>psychosomatic</u> antitheses such as were the focus of the prior chapter on radix algebra, as they have no evident conscious dimension. The concept of time is built on observed regularities in motion in the physical world. From the revolution of the earth around the sun, the moon around the earth, or the rotation of the earth on its axis, to the period of a quartz oscillator or an atomic clock, the concept of time rests on regular, harmonic or otherwise measurable motion(s) in the timeless physical world.

[12] **Radix Algebra**, as described in Chapter 8, is one such new tool.

[13] See especially these articles, which have to do with radix physical applications: Kelley, C.R., 1979, *The Radix Charge of Living Places*, in **The Radix Journal** Vol. 1 No. 4;
_____, 1983, *Radix Devices*, in **The Radix Journal**, Vol. III No. 2. Both articles are reprinted in the compilation: THE RADIX VOL. II: THE SCIENCE OF RADIX PROCESSES, 1992. Most extensive of my work is the early small book, Kelley, C.R., 1961, A NEW METHOD OF WEATHER CONTROL. Vancouver, WA: K/R Publications.

[14] Kelley, C.R., 1955, *Orgone Energy and Weather*, in **CORE**;
1961, A NEW METHOD OF WEATHER CONTROL. Technical Report 60-1. Also published in German, EINE NEUE METHODE DER WETTERKONTROLLE. Vancouver, WA: K/R Publications.

[15] Mann, Felix, 1963, ACUPUNCTURE, THE ANCIENT ART OF HEALING AND HOW IT WORKS SCIENTIFICALLY. New York: Random House. Reprinted by Vintage Books.

Lin, Henry B., 2000, THE ART AND SCIENCE OF FENG SHUI. St. Paul, Minn.: Llewellyn Publications.

[16] Published scientific work describing western approaches to the life force that are consistent with those in this book include original books of Mesmer, Reichenbach, Reich and myself and periodicals such as **The Orgone Energy Bulletin, CORE, The Journal of Orgonomy, The Creative Process, Energy and Character,** and the **Radix Journal.** (See the Bibliography.) Readers are advised to stay with original sources such as these as much as possible. Secondary sources dealing with the life force are often misleading.

APPENDICES

A. CLOUDBUSTING AND RAINMAKING

B. CONVERGENT RADIX FORMS AND DEVICES:
   Pyramids, Cones, Funnels, Tubes and Spheres

C. THE RADIX CHARGE OF LIVING SPACES

D. DOR IN SPAIN

E. DOR, DESERT, AND UNMATED RADIX CHARGE

F. REICH'S ORGONE ACCUMULATOR (ORAC) *and the Orgone Accumulator Paradox*

G. SHELDRAKE AND MORPHIC RESONANCE

H. LANDMARKS IN THE EVOLUTION OF THE CONCEPT OF THE LIFE FORCE

The "too-muchness" of work with the life force overwhelms me at this point. My book is written, yet there are multiple volumes unsaid. There are many paths that should be followed. I have tramped for long distances along several, and have made exciting discoveries. Yet again and again I've had to stop before reaching a proper stopping point.

Treat these Appendices as paths attempted. As you read, ask yourself if you might wish to pick up the trail and continue along one of them.

I've not endeavored to integrate these Appendices into the book itself by indexing them with the whole. Most of the Appendices are units in themselves, and most include references enough to carry one forward along a trail I was following.

The paths lead to fascinating and significant adventures.

Enjoy them!

CRK

APPENDIX A

CLOUDBUSTING AND RAINMAKING

Figure A-1. Reichian cloudbuster here being used for a weather modification operation from a high building (seven stories) in Stamford, Connecticut.

Cloud Destruction

Figure A-1 is one of the Reichian cloudbusters I have built and used for experimental cloudbusting operations in Connecticut in the years following Reich's imprisonment and death in 1957. The first of the operations was designed for controlled destruction of fair-weather cumulus clouds, as compared to matched control clouds, selected from the same cloud pool.

Figure A-2 shows before and after pictures of one experimental operation. A line-up of suitable cumulus clouds south of Stamford, Connecticut across Long Island Sound, above the north shore of New York's Long Island. The black "X" made of black wire and fastened along with the camera on the cloudbuster shows the precise direction of the cloudbuster during the operation. Additional photos of this and other cloud destruction operations can be found in the book, A NEW METHOD OF WEATHER CONTROL.[1]

Figure A-2. A "before and after" picture of an experimental cloud destruction operation. The "X" shows the target of the cloudbuster at the outset. The lower picture is the same scene 10 minutes later. Control clouds are on either side.

Hundreds of cloud destruction operations have been done successfully by experimenters around the world since Reich built his first cloudbuster more than half a century ago, such as by Richard Blasband, James DeMeo, Trevor Constable, etc.

---

[1] Kelley, C.R., 1961. A NEW METHOD OF WEATHER CONTROL. Technical Report 0-1. Also published in German, "Eine Neue Methode der Wetterkontrolle." Vancouver, WA: K/R Publications

APPENDIX A

Rainmaking

Using Reich's cloudbuster to create controlled rainfall and other weather is far more difficult and complex. However, in five experimental rain-making operations I carried out in the fifties and sixties, unpredicted precipitation occurred within 36 hours in every case. These are my only rain-making operations, so the results cannot be attributed to the omission of negative instances.

The operations were each timed to begin when rain was unpredicted, unexpected and unlikely. A conservative estimate of the average probability of rain within 36 hours in the five cases is .25. This is to say that with the conditions that prevailed at the start of these operations, the chances against rain within 36 hours are estimated to be, on the average, three to one, had these operations not taken place or had the apparatus been ineffective. From this estimate it can be further calculated that if the apparatus were ineffective, the odds against rain occurring within 36 hours on all of the five operations are more than a thousand to one ($p = .25^5 < .001$). It is extremely unlikely that unpredicted rain would have occurred on these five occasions unless the apparatus did work. Here is a summary of one of those operations.

I began at 11:00 am in Stamford, Connecticut on Sunday, August 21, 1960. The Connecticut weather was typical for August -- fair, hot, humid, smoggy, with a dark haze in all quadrants. It had been this way for two days.

The barometer had been steady for three days within the range of 29.75 to 29.85. There were no weather fronts at all in the eastern part of the country. The temperature was 80 degrees, humidity 65 percent, winds light and variable with a few gusts, visibility three miles in the smog. The forecast was for "continued fair, warm and humid, little temperature change, fair tonight." There was a high, very thin overcast, and a few fair-weather cumulus in the northwest quadrant. The previous day had shown the same picture, including the thin overcast. It was oppressive, muggy August weather, with no relief in sight. It was good timing for a rain-making operation.

At 11:20 am I began, directing the apparatus for twenty to forty second periods at different points in the dark haze and in the high overcast. The air would typically clear in the points in a direct line with the apparatus, "punching holes" in the clouds and haze. This was Reich's procedure for "loosening" the atmosphere, and I had found it useful. At 11:30 a.m. I set the antenna at 80 degrees elevation and 310 degrees azimuth to draw for rain. The pipes were thus directed northwest at a high angle, only 10 degrees from the zenith, which I believed was the appropriate draw under these conditions.

At 11:40 a fresh breeze arose, ten to fifteen m.p.h., blowing from the southwest. 1 could see that the cumulus in the northwest quadrant below my draw were beginning to grow. By 11:50 there were many cumulus congestus, thicker than the cumulus humulus of fair weather. They were moving to the southeast, toward me, along the direction of my draw. The surface wind remained from the southwest. I wondered if my operation had produced the different winds aloft that were moving the clouds toward me. At 11:55 I noted that the high thin cloud layer was taking on a granular appearance. The cumulus clouds, however, were now shrinking. There was, in the west, a growing bank of blue haze, very different from the blackish, smoggy haze it replaced.

At 12:10 pm cumulus clouds were building again, but slowly. The haze was still heavy in the lower atmosphere, but the sky overhead was lighter and more mobile. The high thin granular clouds were also getting thicker. By 12:20 the lower cumulus were building more rapidly, and had spread into the two adjacent quadrants of the sky, being absent only in the southeast. This widening of the cloud pattern reflected the total movement of the wind aloft toward the apparatus from the northwest. The clouds had all been located in the northwest at the start, and there was already a lot of development of new clouds in the area. The wind blew stronger.

At 12:30 the cumulus clouds were again shrinking in size. They were going through an oscillatory build-up, reaching a peak every ten to fifteen minutes, then shrinking again, then growing to reach a new peak. And at 12:30 I observed a dramatic wind sheer at my location. The clouds approached me from 310 degrees, the direction from which I was drawing then, when they got directly overhead, veered suddenly toward the northeast, moving in the direction of the surface wind. It also appeared to me that the clouds angled down as they approached me, before changing direction, but I could not be sure of that. Winds often seem to be affected by drawing with Reich's apparatus. The wind sheer on this operation was as vivid and clear as any I have seen. As the clouds came at me from the northwest and whipped off to the northeast just as they reached me, I was struck overwhelmingly with the power of the instrument in front of me. It was a different sky than was present one hour before. The rigid quality in the atmosphere had broken up; the winds and clouds, freed from the rigidity, could move and grow. A powerful "orgone" stream from the northwest was flowing into the sky over Connecticut toward Stamford, triggered by this arrangement of pipes in front of me. And I was at the hub of the process. The wind sheer was happening exactly where I was standing.

The sky overhead was becoming a much lighter blue, and the light blue area was expanding. By 12:35 the cumulus clouds were again growing. I continued the draw for rain until 1:15 pm, for a total of one hour and forty-five minutes, and then put away my equipment. The sky at that time was more than 50 percent covered by cumulus clouds. The oscillation in their size had continued, though it was less after I stopped. The weather stayed warm and humid, but was less oppressive. The breeze felt fresher.

In the evening in Westport, ten miles from the event, long stringy clouds appeared in the west, oriented northwest-southeast, and appearing to converge on 310 degrees, the direction of the draw. A solid tongue of middle level clouds was visible from the south. The barometer now was 29.72 and gradually and steadily falling. I wrote in my notes that I thought it would rain by morning.

At 4:00 am I was awakened by rain, with protracted growling thunder. The rain was continuous, varying in intensity from light to moderate. The rain stopped in Westport at 7:10 am. In Stamford at 8:00 am, the sky showed broken clouds, heavier than in Westport, but the rain had ended. The barometer had held steadily through the night, declining slightly to 29.70 from the previous afternoon's 29.72. The storm had brought half an inch of unpredicted rain in Stamford and in New York City, 35 miles to the west, with lesser amounts from Pennsylvania to Massachusetts.

My rain-making operation was an unqualified success.

****

Chuck Kelley

APPENDIX B

CONVERGENT RADIX FORMS AND DEVICES:
Pyramids, Cones, Funnels, Tubes and Spheres

Most convergent life force forms and devices operate in terms of the principle discovered by Reich of the flow of the life force in the direction from lower to higher potential. Convergent forms involve geometric shapes that reduce their cross section in one direction. The pyramid and cone are examples, as is the funnel and, less obviously, the cylinder and "bowl," a section of a sphere. I have not done enough work with convergent shapes to feel competent in their use, but I would like to mention a few thoughts about them.

My "idyllic" property for radix experiments in Westport proved a disaster because it was a natural bowl, which with the addition of cloudbusters attracted an enormous dor overcharge, held in the bowl-shape and the unfortunate clay soil. – (See Appendices C and E.)

The early builders of great pyramids and cathedrals must surely have had intuition, if not actual knowledge, about the power or "Feng Shui" of convergent forms. The bowl shape inverted and formed architecturally as a dome of a cathedral or auditorium builds a radix charge on the inside of its concave surface, drawing its occupants' attention upward, as do spires, steeples, and the inner walls of pyramids.

Remember that the most powerful well-tested "weird" science of the life force convergent devices is Reich's "cloudbuster," the assemblage of parallel metal tubes described in Appendix A.

****

Chuck Kelley

APPENDIX C

THE RADIX CHARGE OF LIVING PLACES*

The radix charge of an area varies widely not only from time to time with the weather but from place to place on the earth's surface. Under given weather conditions it varies from country to country, and from one area to another. It varies even from neighborhood to neighborhood, and adjacent homes or buildings can have very different radix charge properties.

Geographic and atmospheric features affect the radix charge. Valleys, dells and other concavities tend to draw in, accumulate, and hold radix charge from the atmosphere. Their atmosphere is "heavier." Houses built in a valley or dell will have a tendency to accumulate radix charge. If other factors encourage the accumulation, such as poor drainage, clay subsoil, metal and masonry construction, poor "Feng Shui" and other factors, chronic radix overcharge of the house can occur. (Feng Shui, like acupuncture, contains large elements of truth about the life force, the chi mixed with its mysticism and myth.) If overcharged, the house will then be unpleasant and unhealthy to live in. The inhabitants will be often sick, and their capacity for creative work impaired. A whole neighborhood can be "contaminated," producing high incidence of illness-prone inhabitants because it is an area of chronic radix overcharge. I'm convinced that high-cancer towns or neighborhoods -- some are many times the national average – are frequently due to this. Radix overcharge is a severe problem in certain urban areas, where it contributes to the development of smog. In this case the production of overcharge is in large part technological, though I believe natural geographic and atmospheric features always play a role.

---

* From *The Radix Journal*, Vol. I No. 4, summer 1979. Copyright © the Radix Institute, assigned 1987 to Charles R. Kelley.

Overcharged regions of a city are sensed as subtly unpleasant by many people. This affects their property value. Such areas tend to become economically depressed, and are often the sites of commercial development and of high density low-cost housing. Trees and other vegetation which metabolize radix charge disappear, replaced by concrete, steel and masonry. A high density of automobiles, electrical machinery, fluorescent lights and television drive the radix charge to higher levels.

Those living and working in such areas suffer from the chronically overcharged environment. Their own pulsation must intensify to drive their charge level higher to counteract the tendency for their charge to be drawn away by the overcharged surroundings, and their periphery must contract for the same reason. Individuals with weak or damaged radix systems cannot sustain the increased strain and suffer failing health. Others live with their higher level of charge, tension and contraction. I believe it likely that their life span is reduced, their likelihood of eventually suffering diseases of stress or hypertension increased. However, some seem to adapt to the excessive charge successfully, and may even live longer because of the adaptation.

Certain equipment used in radix experimental work drives the charge level of the environment to extremely high, sometimes dangerous-to-life levels. This problem plagued Reich's work and my own. Both of us experienced having our families become ill, buildings we lived and worked in become intolerably oppressive, trees in the vicinity die.[1] My present [2004] view of what occurs is that dor is <u>unmated</u> high charge, i.e., where the flow from lower to higher charge builds from a single source by the lower-to-higher

---

[1] See Reich, W., 1951, "The Oranur Experiment: First Report," **Orgone Energy Bulletin** Vol. 3, No.4, largely reprinted in Reich's SELECTED WRITINGS. Some of my own experiences are related in Appendix E, and more extensively in A NEW METHOD OF WEATHER CONTROL, 1961. Vancouver, WA: K/R Publications.

principle, but no mating charge leading to superimposition and discharge flows in.

Because radix charge cannot be readily measured or sensed, the charge level can rise to extreme levels without one knowing it. The situation is made worse by devices which accumulate or induce more charge, including Reich's orgone accumulator. Buildings and grounds are affected. Because the unmated charge converges toward higher charge, an overcharge, once induced, is difficult to dissipate and easily gets worse. The excessive charge inhibits normal radix metabolism. The radix systems that would absorb a normally high charge in an area (e.g., cumulous clouds, trees, vegetation, people) are not effective when the charge is extremely high. A good storm passing over is enormously helpful, but seldom occurs at the time, place, and intensity needed. The excessive charge may remain for months or years, leading into drought and desert formation.

This is how I understand today the radix physics of this stagnant high-charge condition, which Reich referred to as dor (deadly orgone). When a radix charge is unmated and becomes excessive, following the low-to-high principle, it is not metabolized, i.e., discharged. A qualitative change occurs. An overcharged building or area of ground develops a still, oppressive quality. The myriads of tiny superimpositions that give movement, pulsation, sparkle to the surroundings disappear, the charges that produce them having been lost. The unmated overcharged area has swallowed them. The variegation in charge is absent, the distribution of charge more homogenous. The Reichian cultural geographer and scientist James DeMeo writes extensively of his study of these topics in his book SAHARASIA.[1] His point of view differs somewhat from my own, but is related.

The body radix metabolism is affected by an overcharged environment. The millions of cellular level discharge processes are

---

[1] DeMeo, James, 1998, SAHARASIA. Greensprings, OR: Orgone Biophysical Research Lab.

inhibited. Unmated charge therefore accumulates in the body and is not properly metabolized there. Normal relaxed activities and human relations are replaced by either hyperactivity or paralysis induced by the high charge. Creative work suffers, as eventually must the health. Such is the effect of Reich's *dor*.

In the long run, the most important way to handle the unmated radix overcharge is to avoid the places and circumstances that manifest it. These include urban blighted areas, "smog," absence of vegetation and trees, with climates moving toward deserts, masonry and metal buildings, tightly enclosed poorly ventilated rooms, fluorescent lights, TV, radiation sources, overcrowding. Continuing exposure to unmated high radix charge associated with these factors degrades the quality of life, and is eventually life threatening.

To keep the quality of one's life from suffering due to the effects of continuing dor overcharge, a long-range life plan that takes one to live and work in a healthy radix environment is called for. Ideally one would move to a wooded hillside, lakeside, or beach location. Convex rather than concave land configuration is called for (hill rather than dale). Look for well-drained sandy rather than clay sub soil, a wooden house with an open plan, non-metallic insulation and other materials, incandescent lights, and good ventilation all are helpful. Radiant heat may allow better ventilation than tight enclosures with recirculating forced air.

When one lives in or near a city, certain areas are much better than others. <u>Other things equal</u>, in flat regions of the temperate zone the best area to live in is west and north of cities, toward the prevailing winds. The dor overcharge and its by-products (smog, pollution) will move downwind, east and south. Southeast of the city is therefore usually the poorest choice. Geographic and climatic features will modify this.

Those forced to live in overcharged areas can take steps to reduce the effects. Some buildings are much better than others. High rise buildings are often better than apartments and offices near street level, especially if there are high terraces and patios, or at least windows that open. Fluorescent lights and TV are bad in an overcharged area.

Personal life style is crucial. Sexual and emotional discharge are desirable. Many people react to overcharge by becoming immobilized, and the paralysis of overcharge is best dealt with by body-oriented personal growth work if it is available. Regular exercise, and either regular swimming, use of a hot pool, or long soaking baths are very helpful. Water can absorb unmated overcharge in the body. An excellent temporary antidote to being overcharged is to sink into a bath tub of body temperature water into which two cups of sea salt and one of soda have been dissolved. Head and hair should be soaked along with the body for 10-15 minutes (not longer). After rinsing the salt water off, one should pour or sponge a diluted vinegar solution over hair and body to restore the normal acid condition of the skin. When the overcharge is especially bad, as when the weather is smoggy and oppressive, this bath can be done daily. It is surprising how much better this simple expedient makes one feel when suffering from unmated overcharge, Reich's dor.

****

Chuck Kelley

APPENDIX D

DOR IN SPAIN*

by

Adam Margoshes

> **Introduction**
>
> LIFE FORCE: *The Creative Process in Man and Nature* is a very personal book. A central rule in its writing it has been that I write from my own experience, offering my insights, my theories, my opinions, and my own original errors, of which there are no doubt quite a few. At least they are not second hand. Now at this book's eleventh hour I'm including someone else's article in my book, and I need to explain myself.
>
> Adam Margoshes was a close personal friend in my years as a Reichian in New York. He was one of the most intelligent and perceptive men I've ever known, and we impacted each other's lives deeply. He had a profound understanding of Reich's work, and wrote about it beautifully, as you're about to discover. He died too young due to a medical blunder, and I find myself copyright owner of his article, which I published in 1961 in Volume One of my Reichian periodical *The Creative Process*. Only in recent years did I come to understand that *dor*, Reich's "deadly orgone," was an expression of the build-up of <u>unmated</u> radix charge. In 1961 I'd have called it "orgone charge."
>
> If Adam's article excites you, go to the work of James DeMeo and his Orgone Biophysical Research Laboratory (see Bibliography) and his monumental work, SAHARASIA. DeMeo is a cultural geographer and Reichian scientist of impeccable credentials. He has studied *dor* and desertification more deeply than <u>anybody</u>.
>
> Chuck Kelley

Perhaps the largest and longest-lasting single event on the planet earth in historic times has been the expansion of the Sahara

---

* Copyright © 1961 Charles R. Kelley

LIFE FORCE

Desert. According to the archeological evidence, it may well have destroyed the earliest human civilization, producing an emigration to Europe that resulted in the culture of the Altamira and Lascauz caves. Since recorded history began, its center has been the Mediterranean Sea, and part of that history -- perhaps a larger part than has until now been imagined -- has been determined by the slow, but steady and unmistakable jump of the Sahara across that body of water, drying the rich lands of Italy, Spain, and Southern France and the big islands to the South. Nowhere is this cosmic process more dramatically evident than in Spain, especially perhaps in the Southernmost province of Andalusia. I have been here, in Almunecar. Andalusia, on the Mediterranean coast, for a month now, observing and studying that process to the best of my ability.

My scientific qualifications for this task are not the highest. I know little geology and botany, and less meteorology. I have read books in these fields, but I have forgotten most of what I read. But I have read -- and remembered -- Reich, and am inspired by the way he often ignored what he had learned from books and slowly learned to trust his own unaided senses, especially the first, orgonotic sense. In recent years I have learned to trust my own feelings more, and to have confidence in my eyes. One result of this change is that my eyesight has improved. Another is that I can now venture to write about what I have seen, and what I think about it, though I am fairly ignorant of the relevant scientific disciplines.

Andalusia presents many of the aspects of a desert. It is dry, barren over large stretches, and full of cactus. The people, too, have a certain stiff dignity, a kind of characterological dryness and distance. Many of the old people -- there seem to be a proportionately greater number of very young and very old than elsewhere -- have mask-like, leathery faces. There is something unbending in the Spaniard's behavior.

Seeing these facts (not first observed by me; see any book on Spain; for example, Washington Irving's excellent <u>Tales of the Alhambra)</u> I started to look around for dor effects. As I understand

Reich's theory of desert-formation and desert-growth, a desert consists essentially of a field of dor on the earth's surface, and the desert grows as the dor-field eats away at the healthy life around it. It seems to me that most of Spain is now overlapped by the Sahara dor-field.

Often there are large, grayish-black clouds hovering in the sky, but no rain. The sea is sometimes unusually still, and the surf then has a low, moaning ring that seems to me to carry an ominous overtone; this happens even on some brightly sunny days. The surface of the water then looks like a gray sheet covering over the rippling motion of a fluid underneath. Also, it seems to me there is a dead calm in the air sometimes, and it becomes hard to breathe. At these times people move slowly, stiffly. The outlines of buildings. trees, rocks and mountains seem sharp, as though etched by a very hard, very thin, very black line. People and animals are touchy, prickly. argumentative -- and vomittey.

I'm not sure all these impressions are objective. I haven't that much confidence in my senses and my orgonotic touch with nature -- not yet. I'm afraid that some of these observations may have been "suggested" by my reading of Reich. I see no way of getting around this objection other than admitting openly that it may be partly right and so casting some legitimate doubt on every thing I say. But the fact remains that I made these observations and, despite doubts and hesitations, I believe in them.

There is a great difference between this dor-field and the great desert in the American Southwest that Reich studied and described in his last book, CONTACT WITH SPACE. There, as I have seen for myself, dor is triumphant. Here, it is resisted. And this resistance, which has been going on for centuries, is evident in every area of the region's life and landscape and weather.

Cactus, introduced fifty or seventy years ago from America, has spread widely -- but unlike its riotous overgrowth in its original home, here it is confined to certain sequestered areas, notably roadsides and particularly barren, rocky spots. Another significant difference is that in America the white population, if not the Indians

LIFE FORCE

and Mexicans, regards cactus as an enemy and nothing more; it is either ignored or fought. Here it is actually cultivated, or at least cared for when found in its wild state, because the Spaniards, like the Italians, relish the fruit of the cactus -- prickly pear, which under its prickles is moist and delicious. But the big difference is that cactus doesn't drive out the other, primary forms of vegetation; it lives side by side with them. The olive, the fig, the almond, the orange, the lemon, the custard apple, and the chestnut <u>refuse to be driven out</u>.

This refusal of healthy life to give in to the encroachments of dor seems to characterize all of Spain. I have seen no trees suffering from dor-sickness, and even no blackening rocks. It is possible I missed them, of course; but I've looked carefully, though I haven't made a systematic search. Everywhere the desert seems to put its withering finger on the country, but the country shivers a bit and then shakes it off. Dor clouds form; the wind dies down; the sea grows quiet and ominous; people sicken and stiffen; but all this lasts, at most, a day. Then it rains, softly; the atmosphere is lit up by a rainbow; the sunset is exceptionally colorful and beautiful; the breeze quickens; the sea begins to sound plangently again; people move more briskly; they laugh with one another, and warm feelings flow between them. I have seen these alternations occur within a day's time on several occasions now.

I think these observations fit in with what other travelers have reported about the look and feel of Spain, its land, its people, its animals. And I think it has been this way for hundreds of years. The Moors, for example, coming from the Sahara itself, where they had done little of historic interest other than fight and conquer, came here and built fantastically lovely buildings, such as the Mosque at Cordova -- now; with a few uglifying embellishments, converted into a Cathedral -- and preeminently, the Alhambra. This edifice is all grace, lightness, verve. The stone is alive with a dancing life. Nothing could be less "dorey." In this connection, it's interesting that one of the outstanding features of the Alhambra is the flowing water, here shooting up in splendid fountains, there running in marble channels into calm pools swarming with goldfish; everywhere there are baths. It is almost as if instinctively the Moors knew that there was something beneficent in the very presence of water, especially running water, in this climate.

What is the great difference between Arizona and Andalusia? What is it about this land that stands up to dor, fights back, and, in great measure, succeeds in holding it at bay? I don't know. But I believe something is here, something brave and lovely. I believe this quality, whatever it is, exists on all the shores of the Mediterranean, that there is something life-giving about this Sea, where the water is bluer than elsewhere and even the sky is a deeper shade of azure. I believe that this quality is responsible for the fact that it was on these shores that the first civilization was born; and very near here where man first painted pictures, where he first built in stone, where he first sailed in boats far from land, where he first killed from a distance with the space-conquering weapon of the bow-and-arrow. Man's creative powers have been stirred here -- in Egypt, Israel, Phoenicia, Greece, Rome, Provence, Spain, as nowhere else -- and I believe it is because here, somehow, there is a great concentration of the terrestrial creative process. Perhaps it was some disturbance of this process that first created the nucleus of a dor-field to the South, a nucleus that grew into the Sahara and is still growing. This disturbance may have had something to do with the original fall of man, his descent into neurosis -- perhaps the location of the Garden of Eden, as well as the other elements of the myth, point to an important truth. In any event, it may well have been the moment when dor was first created on this earth -- a creation that I feel man must have played the principal part in.

I feel that there is a deep inner connection between the planetary center of the creative process in the Mediterranean and the planetary center of "natural" destruction, so close, in the Sahara. If the secret of that connection were discovered, perhaps the origin of deserts would become clearer, and perhaps a way would be found to destroy the desert -- a possible first step toward destroying the desert within. I believe that the best place for such research is where

LIFE FORCE

the two fields intersect, and where the creative field shows unusual strength, here in Spain.

* * * * * * * * * * * * * *

APPENDIX E

DOR, DESERT, AND UNMATED RADIX CHARGE

Of all the "weird" aspects of science opened up to me by the pioneer work of Wilhelm Reich, *dor* was the strangest and "furthest out" from mainstream science. Reich first spoke of it as "deadly orgone." It soon got shortened to dor. It is more than 50 years since Reich first spoke of, and I began to learn about, dor. It is still a profound mystery. In writing about it I have stayed close to my personal experience and have not ventured far into the theories and reports of Reich, and since Reich of James DeMeo, who has gone further into the subject than any living person I know. Reich and DeMeo have each written prolifically on dor, desert, and related subjects (such as climate and culture).[1] Any serious student of the subject should study their original work with care.

I never set out to study dor, but found the subject thrust on me as a result of my experiences with dor using Reich cloudbusters, which I built for my own research purposes once I learned how. But let me back up to the beginning.

I first met Reich on a visit to Orgonon late in the summer of 1951. He had written about the beginnings of his work with the cloudbuster in his journal, **The Orgone Energy Bulletin**, and especially his small book sized report, THE ORANUR EXPERIMENT, in which he endeavored to neutralize small radioactive sources by placing them in Orgone accumulators. A vast dangerous-to-life reaction occurred, incomprehensible in terms of traditional science. His experimental animals died, the staff was

---

[1] Reich, W., 1951, *The Oranur Experiment*, First Report 1947-51. Rangeley, Maine: The Wilhelm Reich Foundation.
De Meo, J., 1998, SAHARASIA. Greensprings, OR: Orgone Biophysical Research Lab.

made ill, and most of them moved away as the entire area around Orgonon was affected. The intense radiation slowly subsided, though its effects lingered for years.

I arrived for my first meeting with Reich more than a year after the oranur experiment and its initial powerful effects, having no idea that some effects still lingered. We didn't speak about it. Reich was too busy telling about the weather control work he was doing, showing me his cloudbuster and how he used it. Because of my years of experience as a wartime army weather forecaster, and because I was basically friendly to him and his work, he hoped that I would contribute to the new field of discovery about the weather. Nothing as yet had been said about dor. Back up in his observatory after we spent an hour or so with his cloudbuster out on the hilltop grounds, we were sitting and talking about his rainmaking experience.

Sitting comfortably in the light attractive upstairs room of Reich's observatory, I suddenly was struck with strange physical sensations. I jumped to my feet abruptly, announcing as I did, "There's something wrong in this room. I've got to get out of here!" I started toward the stairs we had just come up. Reich instead took me in the opposite direction, to a door opening onto an outdoor balcony, circling part of the outside upper floor. I grabbed the wall, unsteady on my feet, panting and afraid. I had nearly fainted. I slowly regained my composure.

"I don't know what that was; I never had anything like that happen to me before," I told Reich.

"I know exactly what that was," Reich said. "Take your time. We'll talk about it in a little while."

The outdoor air revived me. I didn't want to go back inside. We sat out on the balcony. Reich then began to tell me about the traumatic environment triggered by the oranur experiment on the property at Orgonon. When the experimental animals died and the staff, including Reich's daughter Eva, became seriously ill from the oranur experiment, people left Orgonon. The total amounts of radioactive material brought in was small, and yet the effects were huge, thousands of times anything that could be a direct result of radioactivity of the materials per se. The radiation measuring equipment -- Reich had purchased more than one instrument -- appeared to "go crazy," indicating bursts of radiation so high that if they were interpreted traditionally everyone in the vicinity had received lethal levels of exposure and should be dying as a result.

But the radiation did not behave normally, the lead containers that the radioactive materials came in made the radiation measurements rise, and taking the materials out of their containers reduced the abnormally high radiation measurments associated with oranur. Remember, Reich had hoped his orgone devices --especially the orgone energy accumulators --would neutralize radioactivity. Instead they triggered abnormally higher measured levels of radiation. Reich finally removed all known radioactive sources from the buildings and grounds, and began living with the after-effects, especially the dor that came after the oranur effects. Now, from the vantage point of time, I believe my experience in Reich's observatory is best understood as some kind of mixture of the effect of oranur and dor, oranur effects being more drastic. Dor has tended to be slower acting and more insidious, as this account may show.

I did not know it, but Reich himself had three times experienced loss of consciousness in his observatory in the months before my visit. This, I believe, is why he felt he understood what was happening to me. I never had another episode of near unconsciousness like that one at Orgonon, although I was exposed to long continued high levels of dor in the course of my research with Reich's devices, the cloudbuster and the orgone accumulator.

After Reich's oranur experiment the environment at and around Orgonon underwent change. People's health continued to be badly affected, presumably by dor. Then other effects of dor over time showed themselves. Trees began dying in large numbers in peculiar fashion, always slowly, from the top down. Leaves and branches turned black from their tops, and gradually died a "black death," as the dying process continued down and toward the trunk of the tree. The effect was independent of the species of the tree, but was closely related to the distance of the trees from Reich's orgone energy equipment, i.e., his cloudbusters, orgone accumulators, and associated gear. Dying trees gradually fanned out from his observatory and laboratory areas.

Then a second strange effect occurred. The rocks that comprised the walls of Reich's observatory began turning black. Hardly noticeable at first, the blackness of the rocks increased, as did the dying of the trees. As months went by the blackening of the rocks spread and intensified. The most heavily affected rocks turned from rock gray or brown to dead black, as black as charcoal. The black surfaces did not rub off, but were a part of the rock's structure. A warmth radiated from the black surfaces. Sick animals and people, dying trees, blackening rocks—this was the pattern of progressive dor infestation in Reich's Orgonon in the 1950's.

The United States government's legal attack on Reich and his work was progressing in these same years, culminating in Reich's imprisonment and death in 1957.[1]

After Reich's death I continued my plans to study his theories and to experiment with his devices. The Reichian movement was in disarray, accomplishing little over the years following Reich's death. I involved myself in weather experiments and neo-Reichian personal growth theory. I soon had findings to report, but there was no appropriate journal to publish them in. I therefore founded my own journal to publish and write up my work and that of other interested contributors.

---

[1] See Greenfield, Jerome, 1974, WILHELM REICH VS THE USA, W.W. Norton & Co., and Kelley, C.R., 1961, "The Ending of Wilhelm Reich's Researches," Technical Report available through Kelley/Radix Publications, Vancouver, WA.

APPENDIX E

After Reich's death I purchased a property in Westport Connecticut to live on with my then wife and our baby, and to do my work with the life force, mostly with Reich cloudbusters and orgone accumulators. I published **The Creative Process** from Westport, and worked at my job as a senior scientist (soon to become Chief Scientist) at a technical research and consulting firm. That position had to support the family and my research and publications on the life force, all financed from my own pocket, with only an occasional contribution from others.

The Westport property seemed ideal for my purposes. It had a lovely wooded setting with a stream running through, widening to form a pond, then narrowing again where the stream continued. The small house was well separated from the two car garage, which would serve as my laboratory. Between house, garage, and toward the pond was an open flat area on which I installed my largest cloudbuster, which had to be grounded into the pond when being operated. It seemed a near idyllic arrangement with my severely limited budget.

Almost as soon as we had moved in I set up the cloudbuster, dissolved a few cumulus clouds, and freed a section of sky that appeared still and immobilized by dor. The apparatus seemed to work perfectly. A problem was the rather high horizon, created by the bowl shape of the land leading down to the pond, and the trees surrounding the property. I would have preferred to be on a hilltop or rise, looking down on the surrounding terrain, but that would have created problems in grounding the cloudbuster into running water, as I wished to do. Streams and ponds were low, hills and rises high. I didn't know enough then to decide, and had chosen the running stream. Today I would choose to work atop a rise or a building top, and bring the water for grounding the device to the cloudbuster and away.

In Westport there was a slow insidious build-up of the radix charge level of the property, the house, the grounds, eventually the neighborhood. The pets, two cats and a dog, got sickly and started shedding their coats out of season. The baby, so healthy when we

265

moved there, became restless, unhappy, and not well. My wife shared the baby's malaise. I was often tense, especially after operating the cloudbuster, but stayed healthy and well. But then I was away from home in Westport at least half of the time on my demanding job, plus I made frequent out-of-state business trips.

The slow insidious build-up of charge continued. Were the changes real or partly imaginary? How serious were they really? We took lots of baths, which Reich had recommended and which seemed to help. I noticed little things. The pets seemed more and more sickly as did my wife and daughter, it seemed, but I couldn't be sure. My daughter was a father's delight and we played many happy hours together. My wife was nervous and unhappy, but got relief from working heavily in her garden. When would I face the realization that something was terribly wrong?

I think it happened when the trees began to die at the tops. The ones most affected were the closest to the cloudbuster. I first noticed it in the fall, but then as leaves fell in the autumn it masked the beginning-to-die process. It was a terrible winter for us. Our pretty little house kept us warm and safe, but it no longer felt welcoming as it should have. My wife couldn't sleep, the baby didn't want to be alone, the New England winter was severe. Just keeping the snow from the driveway and walk seemed an onerous task. Joy seemed to have departed from our lives.

When spring came at last, one fact jumped out at me. The trees were dying, massively, from their tops down, and as a function of their distance from the cloudbuster's position. Tree species did not matter. They turned black from the top, and their "black death" spread down and in. (See Figure E-1) The big fine double-trunked tree between garage and house, the closest tree to the cloudbuster, was at least half dead. As we progressed into summer, one of the two trunks collapsed and fell. It weighed hundreds of pounds, and could have killed anyone it hit. I had to have the whole tree removed. But we were ringed by trees dying at the top.

APPENDIX E

Figure E-1. *Affected trees near the Reich weather control apparatus in the author's yard in Connecticut. The first and third photographs show the crowns of a mature and a young maple tree, respectively. The second photograph is a view up through the branches of three different species of trees, maple, elm, and what I believe may be a beech tree.*

During the bad winter our house was especially oppressive and "dory" when the furnace came on. I had tried to reduce the charge level by placing a small cloudbuster in the basement pointed at the furnace, and grounded into a container of water that I changed regularly. I can't say whether this did anything for the oppressivness of the house, but it did make the basement room much worse. As spring progressed into summer, the rocks in the rock wall of the basement were turning black. They came to look exactly like the rocks in Reich's observatory which turned black during the years that Reich was fighting dor at Orgonon. (See Figure E-2)

LIFE FORCE

Figure E-2: Two photographs of a section of the basement wall of the author's home in Westport Conn. A small Reichian cloudbuster drew toward the area in the lower left part of the upper left photo. The bottom photograph is of a relatively unaffected section of the same wall. -- Go to Reich's **Orgone Energy Bulletin** Vol 5 pp. 42 & 45 to see very similar pictures of the rock wall in Reich's observatory after his oranur experiment.

I dismantled my cloudbuster and other equipment and moved it to another location, atop a six floor building in Stamford, Connecticut. I continued my experiments from the Stamford location, which never suffered a dor build-up. The Westport property very slowly and gradually recovered. Four years later the dying trees had recovered all of their lost foliage.

Desert and the Nature of Dor

The article on "Dor in Spain" in the Appendix just prior to this one moves us to a more advanced stage in the study of dor. Reich's Orgonon and my property in Connecticut were each lush, green, well watered wooded areas, widely separated from each other. Each was made subject to having trees die and rock turn black as a result of what we thought of as "dor infestation." Both areas became unfriendly to living animals and plants. The blackening rocks leave me as mystified now as they did 50 years ago, though they must tie into the mystery in some way.

Dor goes with a drying out of the atmosphere and dying of trees. Blackness seemed to descend on the trees from above and move down and into them by a process as yet not known or understood by science. Dor gradually killed the trees. The dor process as it occurred in Reich's Orgonon and at my property in Connecticut several years later and hundreds of miles south of Orgonon was the result of the use of the special equipment developed by Reich to manipulate the life force. This equipment was the Reich cloudbuster and the orgone accumulator. Continuing use of the equipment in the same way would have denuded the areas of trees, both in and around Orgonon, and in Connecticut, in and around the Kelley property in Westport. The direction of change from lush woodland toward barren land compressed in a few short years what was happening slowly over the centuries in the deserts of Africa and Asia, through what many Reichian and neo-Reichian scientists see as a planet-wide development of the same process, the development and spread of dor.

Many fine minds have been working on the problem of dor and desert, but progress is slow at best. We don't know what dor is, where it really comes from, or why it seems to be producing huge progressive changes in the climate of this planet. I do have a new theory of dor processes, based on cosmological and atmospheric theories described in this book.

Cosmology, Unmated Radix Charge, and Dor

I've traced pretty fully the cosmic roots of galaxies and stars in cosmic sources, huge empty voids in spaces. Some voids become <u>sources</u> of radix charge, because they are completely surrounded by higher charge. The lower-to-higher movement of charge results in an oozing outward of charge from their center, resulting in continued reduction of the charge at the center. Charge can only be replenished from the low-charged center, which I theorize taps into another dimension, what I see as the radix substratum, underlying all existence. Thus radix charge is born from these sources into our expanding universe. The universe is expanding, I believe, because the newly born radix charge is made up of space, or is functionally identical with space. It is from the sources within the voids that space is created and from which the universe expands.

Two rivers of charge oozing out from separate sources of radix charge are required for superimposition, which is the mating of independent sources. Cosmic superimposition is the culmination of the creative process and the birth of energy and matter in galaxies and then stars. The coming together of rivers of radix charge each diverging from two separate sources, becomes the coming together, the converging that feeds into the cosmic mating that creates a galaxy. Through such matings the universe is born. But not all flows of charge from a void -- a cosmic source -- are destined to be mated with another from a different source. The universe is vast, and filled with radix charge in motion. I believe it can and does also "pile up," pool, build into centers where it is <u>not</u> mated. In these centers there is no meeting with charge from another source, no superimposition, only a build up of charge, spreading around a center, following the law of movement, from lower toward higher charge. When there are two sources of charge to draw from which superimpose and mate, there is discharge and the "using up" of charge through its conversion into matter and energy, creating a check on the growth

APPENDIX E

of charge. With unmated charge centers there is no such check. I see them building into large loose systems. A critical point in their development must occur when the initial divergent movement away from their source thins or dilutes the spreading charge just enough to compensate for the rate of creation of charge through the source and its distance. That would, I believe, result in a possibly important point of stability in the charge level. But I'll have to follow that point up another time.

I want to go now to our atmosphere, the atmosphere of planet earth. In large and expanding areas of this planet some unknown life force process Reich called dor is causing people and animals to get sick, rocks to turn black, trees to die. Over time it is causing lush green land to become arid, and so is expanding the boundaries of deserts. What is dor? Where does it "come from" and how?

Reich speculated that it was perhaps associated with UFO's, which he reported seeing several times in his cloudbuster operations. I watched out alertly, even eagerly, for UFO's in my own cloudbusting operations, and saw none. I believe Reich to have been mistaken, fooled by certain visual illusions I became familiar with in my studies of visual perception.

My current theory of dor is that it is an effect of a build up of excess unmated radix charge in certain regions of the earth's atmosphere. The result has been less superimposition and mating in these regions, hence less cyclonic activity, fewer and less intense storms and weather, less rainfall, and hence more aridity, and thus the growth of desert.

In principle the problem should be amenable to correction through informed and effective use of Reichian cloudbusting equipment, though we are a long way from knowing how. The solution requires extensive drawing from particular areas of outer space towards us to bring in appropriate mating charge from another source to produce superimposition and cyclonic storm activity. In reality it requires much research, error-prone experiments, many hazards, known and unknown. By its nature the work must be done on a global scale, or at least with a global understanding of what is being done, which is likely to have serious political implications.

I believe that it will be done in the next forty years. It could be done sooner.

****

Chuck Kelley
June 26, 2004

APPENDIX F

REICH'S ORGONE ACCUMULATOR (ORAC)
and the Orgone Accumulator Paradox

A connective radix device involves bringing together materials having different radix charge levels, to take advantage of the lower-to-higher flow that will result at their boundary. Reich's famous ORAC (orgone accumulator) is, I believe, a connective radix device. Figure F-1 is a photograph of an ORAC, allegedly built under Reich's supervision, for experimental use with human beings.

The Orgone Accumulator

Figure F-1. *Original Reich orgone accumulator.*
In use the door is closed.

I have built, or had built to my specifications, many dozens of ORACs, those enclosures of metal covered and usually bonded with dialectric material that Reich built and used. I have worked with them, done experiments, lived with them in my house, sat in them for endless hours. I know that they "work." They have a real effect, sometimes slight, sometimes powerful. They have an expansive, generally positive, pleasant effect on people who sit in them and use them properly, and an often distressing negative effect on rooms they are kept in. The question is, how do they work? Reich theorized that the layering of the walls was responsible. He theorized that the outer dialectric material absorbed the charge, passed it to the metal, which absorbed it then gave it off into the enclosure on the interior of the accumulator, where the charge accumulated. Yet Reich was not comfortable with his "accumulation" explanation. *"It's too mechanistic,"* he told me in 1951; *"there's something different involved."* I have an entirely different explanation of the ORAC than did Reich, and may now understand it better than did my teacher.

Building an effective ORAC involves conflicting requirements. First, one wants a device that works, that produces the positive effect the ORAC can have on what is placed inside it. Second, one wants to minimize the build-up of radix charge of the environment around the ORAC, which grows when the device is functioning as it should. A room or building can become oppressive and unhealthy with an ORAC in it.

Reich's principles of ORAC construction are simple. It is an enclosure built of walls of insulating material lined with sheet metal or metal screen. Two or more such enclosures that fit, one inside the other, form a stronger unit, and ORACs were referred to by Reich as one-fold, two-fold, three-fold, etc. Reich used up to twenty-fold ORACs in his work, while his standard for human use was three-fold.

Some materials are no doubt better than others. I recommend staying with iron and coated iron metal layers such as galvanized sheet iron or screen which is coated with zinc. This is because the electro-conductive, magnetic, or perhaps unknown properties of iron are essential, and the zinc inhibits rust. Other metals may in time be used, because we may learn that another

APPENDIX F

property or properties are really the important ones. In the same way, I advise using material that is a good electrical insulator such as fiberglass, rubber, most fabric, most plastic. It may be that the layer of electrical conductor next to non-conductor is the essential property of ORAC layers, so that the best materials are like the best materials of an electrical capacitor – thin alternate layers of a highly conductive material like copper, and a material with a high dialectric constant (very good insulator) like mylar.

Reich's own instructions for making a three-fold ORAC are reprinted in Greenfield, 1974.[1] The unit is a box, 4½ feet high, 2½ feet deep and 2 feet wide, sized to hold a seated human occupant. It is made of a top, bottom, three sides, a door, and a bench seat. These are formed of seven panels, each made of three alternate layers of metal and non-metal, held in a wood frame. The panels screw together to form the completed unit. The seven three-layer panels for box and seat are 1¼" thick. Screw holes are drilled around the edges to assemble top, bottom and side panels. Hinges support the door, wood strips on the sides support the bench on which the user sits. Four final screw holes hold hook and eye fasteners so that the door can be fastened closed from inside or out, or be fastened open when desired. It is as heavy to move as a solid heavy standing wardrobe. When disassembled into separate panels, it can be stacked or packed for storage or transport. It came to take me about 30 minutes to assemble mine or take it apart.

An ORAC should not be used in confined spaces, because overcharge in that space develops readily. When possible, keep it in a dry outdoor shed or open garage or carport, or on an apartment roof etc. In warm climates it can be outdoors with a rainproof cover. Never let the ORAC get wet, as this reduces its effectiveness.

---

[1] Greenfield, J., 1974, "Plans and Instructions for Building and Use of an Orgone Energy Accumulator, as Issued by the Wilhelm Reich Foundation During Reich's Lifetime." Appendix 10 of WILHELM REICH VS. THE U.S.A. New York: W.W. Norton.

LIFE FORCE

<u>To use the accumulator</u> to build your own radix charge, undress (clothes absorb charge) and sit in it on a towel quietly for 20 minutes. Use it morning and night for an on-going program. Stay present in your body during the period. This means that to the extent that you are able, stay in the "here-and-now," or create pleasant sensory memories or scenes, or sing. Follow your breathing in and out, let it relax and deepen, as you relax your body. You want full but not forced breathing. Some tapes using imagery, meditation, relaxing music, "toning," singing or radix charging exercises can be useful some of the time, but resist the impulse to always occupy your mnd in the ORAC. Follow the Zen-type injunction: *"Don't just think something; be present."*

<u>Effects of the ORAC.</u> When it is built according to Reich's specifications and used properly, the device produces a subtle but profound effect on the user. The usual experience is, for me, relaxing, centering, and enlivening. I see the body as a radix source as described in Chapter 9. The ORAC seems to enhance the flow outward from the body's center of lowest charge to its periphery, and on out toward the environment. The closed ORAC in itself and by itself is also a source, and <u>decreases</u> the radix charge of the body core, from which charge flows outward, toward higher charge.

The device produces an undesirable charging effect, however, on the room that contains it, which I call a building up of unmated external radix charge, or dor. A closed room with an ORAC in it typically develops a heavy oppressive feeling.

The Orgone Accumulator Paradox

I didn't see the paradox implicit in Reich's explanation of the accumulator until after he died. It is this. The flow of the radix (orgone energy) charge is always "uphill," from low to high. The steeper the gradient, the greater the uphill flow. Thus charge flows into a galaxy, a storm, a living thing from the less charged environment. If Reich accumulators did build a charge in the way Reich said, the charge could grow, could flow in to them from the environment, charging them and their surroundings. But now, if someone sat in the highly charged "accumulator," <u>the user would charge less quickly</u>, because the low-to-high gradient of charge would be less. A higher charge around the body in the ORAC could only make it harder for the body to attract charge. To charge most effectively, the person should be in a <u>low-charge</u> environment, since the gradient from low to high would be the greatest. I claim that a lower-charged surround can in fact be found <u>inside</u> a Reich "orgone energy accumulator." The direction of flow of the charge in the accumulator is out from its empty center (or from the body center of someone using it), out through the metal walls, out into the non-metal insulating layer around it, <u>lowering</u> the radix charge in the interior. The <u>lower</u> charge provides a <u>higher</u> gradient to charge the person sitting in it. My hypothesis is, as I have said above, that the ORAC alone forms a radix source, a center of low charge. When someone sits in it the user, who is by his structure a living source, forms a source-within-a-source, increasing the total inside to outside gradient of charge in the whole user-accumulator radix system.

Going back to the Appendix on the radix charge of living spaces, an apt comparison with another low radix charge environment is outdoors after a good storm has passed, drawing off and discharging accumulated charge in an area. The air is sweeter and softer, lower in charge, promoting pulsation, movement, metabolism, as living things, with their higher charges, absorb charge freely from it. Because a low-charged surround does promote radix pulsation and charge, people may mistakenly consider the charge high. The reverse is true; their own charge rises quickly because the radix charge around them is so low, and the gradient of charge steep. Such a low-charged environment compares with that within the ORAC, where the lowered charge promotes a rise in one's internal charge in the same way and for the same reason as the outdoor air does following a storm.

It would go beyond the scope of this article to try to review the large amounts of data that have been presented on various kinds of radix devices. Much of it does not meet rigorous scientific standards, but may be interesting and thought-provoking, and some are sound scientifically. It is a difficult and demanding area for experimental research. Anyone who goes into research with radix devices seriously, intelligently and with an open mind will, in my opinion, be forced to the conclusion that they do work. Results are variable and erratic, and reproducible effects tend to be hard to demonstrate. Nevertheless the effects are sometimes extraordinary, and cannot be explained from the standpoint of traditional science. A list of a few of the many many publications dealing with the accumulator follows.

****

Chuck Kelley

References

Kelley, C.R., 1992, THE RADIX, Vol II: The Science of Radix Processes. A compilation. Kelley/Radix Publications.

_____, 1990, *Science and the Life Force,* A correspondence course. Kelley/Radix Publications.

_____, 1979-80, "Radix Physics: Radix Processes, Radix Systems and the Problem of Measurement." **The Radix Journal**, Vol. II, Nos. 1 & 2. Kelley/Radix Publications.

Kelley, C.R. A NEW METHOD OF WEATHER CONTROL. Technical Report 60-1. Vancouver, WA: Kelley/Radix Publications, 1961.

Kelley, C.R. "Orgone Energy and Weather." **CORE**, Vol. 7, No.3 & 4, December 1955.

Ritter, Paul and Jean. "Experiments with the orgone accumulator." Nottingham, England: The Ritter Press, 7 Magdala Rd., undated (pre-1962).

Sharaf, Myron. FURY ON EARTH. New York: Saint Martins Press, 1983.

Starz, Kenneth. "The Effect of the Orgone Energy Accumulator on Air Temperature." In **The Creative Process**, Vol. 2 No. 4. Vancouver, WA: K/R Publications, December 1962.

APPENDIX G

SHELDRAKE AND MORPHIC RESONANCE[1]

Biologist Rupert Sheldrake's book, THE PRESENCE OF THE PAST, further extends his theory of "morphic resonance" which he expounded a few years earlier in his book, A NEW SCIENCE OF LIFE[2]. It is a theory with profound scientific and metaphysical implications. Sheldrake's starting point is the problem of the development of "morphogenesis," as the biologist calls it. How can living cells, viewed as physico-chemical machines, grow, evolve, learn, producing their marvelous diversity, complexity, and development over time? Mechanists often "explain" it today through genetic "programming," the DNA pattern of the genes. But, as Sheldrake points out in his book:

"If the genetic program were carried in the genes, then all the cells of the body would be programmed identically, because in general they contain exactly the same genes. The cells of your arms and your legs, for example, are genetically identical. Moreover, these limbs contain exactly the same kinds of protein molecules, as well as chemically identical bone, cartilage, and so forth. Yet they have different shapes. Clearly, the genes alone cannot explain these differences. They must depend on something else: on formative influences which act differently in different organs and tissues as they develop. These influences cannot be inside the genes; they extend over entire tissues and organs."

---

[1] From *Chuck Kelley's Radix Newsletter* Number 6, September 1990.

[2] Sheldrake, R., 1988, THE PRESENCE OF THE PAST: Morphic Resonance and the Habits of Nature. New York: Random House. (Reprinted by First Vintage Books, 1989)

_____, 1981 and 1985, A NEW SCIENCE OF LIFE: The Hypothesis of Formative Causation. London: Blond & Briggs.

The current explanations strive to explain the content of living tissues, but can't explain living form, much less function, by physico-chemical theories. Yet scientists have a history of faith that the latest physico-chemical discoveries will produce the answer. As Sheldrake says, it's as if describing the pile of materials to go into it described the structure and function of a completed house. But the same building materials could build any number of different houses. Then "morphogenesis" of the houses would be how the different houses arose. (The term is unusual but not inappropriate for houses.)

Sheldrake theorizes that, as a form develops, a morphic field that represents the form grows with it. Unlike the form, which exists only in the present instant, the morphic field of the form exists through all the past time of its development, up to and including the present, and guides future development of similar forms through the process of "morphic resonance." Morphic resonance takes place, not along the dimension of space and time, but of similarity of form. The more similar past forms there are, and the more the degree of similarity of present to past, the more morphic resonance with the past. <u>The past, in Sheldrake's theory, never ceases to exist as a real and present part of nature.</u>

Thus as time passes, forms stabilize, and new ones tend to flow along paths of development that originate in the past and which guide them by morphic resonance. In this way, nature forms "habits," processes, ways of working at all levels. Through repetition these become easier, more repeatable, more standardized and more similar as they replicate and spread. Thus, says Sheldrake, the universe and all that is in it evolves, develops, reproduces, learns. This is as true of the old established world of physics, where particles, atoms, molecules evolved and replicated to produce forms of matter on one scale of size, and galaxies, stars and planets on another. Biological development -- life as we know it -- is intermediate in scale, very recent in origin, fast in evolving and confined to a small portion of the universe explored by man.

Surprising though as yet very sparse evidence exists for this extraordinary theory. It has been observed that new kinds of crystals, difficult to grow at first, become easier to grow with time, not just where they were first developed or have spread by contact, but everywhere in laboratories around the world. A new animal habit useful to the species can spread like wildfire, not only from a local center radiating out through direct contact, but also throughout a given species "all at once" with no direct contact. A new kind of problem given to a group of animals in one laboratory soon is easier and in time much easier for animals of the same species to learn in a distant laboratory in animals with no direct contact or connection of any kind with those used in the laboratory of the original experiment. Are crystals and animals alike responding to "morphic resonance?"

This fascinating book ranges knowledgeably across the sciences and natural philosophy. I found it difficult and exciting to read, as I pored over it page by page, arguing with the author in marginal notes here, agreeing with and affirming him there. He covers so much, I can't hope to deal with the many issues he raises beyond his central thesis. Here, however, are some technical reactions.

I have two major reservations about Sheldrake's central thesis, which is the actual "presence of the past" as a reality. Like most scientists, I believe that the past is "present" only in physical records, traces, or residues, from which we recreate something of the past, sometimes accurately (e.g., a compact disk of a musical performance, the DNA pattern of the cells) but often with exceedingly fallible inferences from ambiguous data (e.g., cosmological, geological, archeological, and selectively made and preserved human historical records).

One of my big questions is, if the past is directly present, why are we so dependent on physical records and traces? Why can't we just contact the past directly, learn to resonate morphically better and better with it, and obtain the information we so much want and need? Instead of every human infant having to laboriously learn such fundamental life skills as language, why can't he just know his language by morphically resonating with the millions of his species who learned it before him?

It's like psychic phenomena. -- There's lots of evidence for certain forms of them. I've had personal and scientific experience with a few. A question closely related to the prior one troubles the scientist investigating psychic phenomena. If we can communicate and act at a distance through telepathy, clairvoyance, and psychokinesis, for example, why do we have to go to such a great effort for communication and control via the physical world? Something is missing from most theories of the psychic as from Sheldrake's theory.

At this point, I believe that the past is <u>not</u> present in the way that Sheldrake theorizes, but that there is communication between minds, independent of physical transmission of data between them, via what I speak of in radix theory as the "source," the pre- physical radix substratum. I hypothesize that "psychic" communication may take place going inward rather than out. This communication through the source may well take place via Sheldrake's morphic resonance, operating strictly in the present, but across all minds, as a function of their degree of similarity. Clearly, this is consistent with certain hypotheses about psychic phenomena and not with others. I hope that people will not use Sheldrake's theory to bolster belief in time travel, past lives, or personal immortality. But telepathic communication, a collective unconscious, and morphic resonance operating in the present are compatible with radix theory. I believe they may all prove to have scientific validity.

The second major disagreement I have with Sheldrake involves the creation of form. He does not see that it would not be possible for morphogenesis to occur without the introduction of new energy. It is obvious to me that to have several possible forms that can occur from an identical assemblage of materials would require energy, as there must be different applications of physical force to assemble or grow the forms. A central aspect of radix theory is a process of origination of energy that is precisely what is needed to give morphogenetic causation the creative force it requires.

Thus I believe that a marriage of radix with an aspect of Sheldrake's morphogenic theory is exciting, and needs to develop in the context of radix scientific work. That part is morphic resonance, not of the present with the past, but of individual radix systems with others in the present. <u>Let me define radix resonance as morphic resonance operating through the radix source, according to the principle of similarity of movement or of form.</u>

I know this may not make a great deal of sense to those of you who have not taken my course of study "Science and the Life Force." For those of you who have, read Sheldrake with the above paragraph in mind. I believe it may be important for developing our understanding of new matter, Reich's orene, "primary water," and all the elements, as well as for the evolution of life and mind.

****

Chuck Kelley

APPENDIX H

LANDMARKS IN THE EVOLUTION OF THE LIFE FORCE CONCEPT

> A chronological list of major developments in the life force concept as it has been presented in this book.

PRE-REICHIAN PERIOD

- <u>Qi or chi or ki</u>
    - ~ Acupuncture and the theory of its nature and use of meridians;
    - ~ Feng Shui – applications of the chi theory to the environment;
    - ~ Reiki
    - ~ Asian martial arts, such as Aikido and T'ai Chi
    - ~ Application to personal growth

Early oriental folk medicine expressed a grasp of the nature and properties of the life force that was used in many aspects of their lives. Those who understood it endeavored to live in harmony with the natural force of life, the *chi* or *ki*. It flowed through pathways and meridians in and on the earth and in similar fashion over and through the acupuncture meridians in the body. Experts attuned to the flow of the *ki* on the earth could put their talent to work in building and architecture. This was the art of *feng shui*, a sort of acupuncture of the physical environment. The parallels were great between *feng shui* and the environment and medical acupuncture with its focus on the meridians of the body in health and disease.

- <u>Animal Magnetism</u> (Franz Anton Mesmer, 1753-1815)
    - ~ Mesmer's life force concept
    - ~ Animal magnetism treatments
    - ~ Mesmer's devices to manipulate the life force

Mesmer was the prophet of the life force in the west. He saw it as a universal fluid that filled all space, with properties in accord with our modern view. Mesmer was a physician with an interest in physics. His treatment methods were a form of body work quite similar to orgonomy and Radix 200 years later. He could have given workshops in his work at the Esalen Institute in California in the 1970's. His methods resulted in strong discharges of emotion. He even made use of physical devices in his treatments that were supposed to intensify the process. These might be compared with Reich's orgone energy devices. The treatments involved opening and intensifying the feelings until a "crisis" developed and the feelings discharged. Patients swore by his treatments, but professionals did not understand his unorthodox theory and methods, and were quick to malign his work.

- <u>Odic Force</u> (Karl von Reichenbach, 1788-1869)

If Mesmer was the first prophet of the modern western view of the life force exemplified by this book, Reichenbach was the second and equally important prophet. While Mesmer was a physician interested in physics, Reichenbach was a physical scientist of note, the organic chemist who developed substances such as paraffin and creosote. Reichenbach spent the last half of his life learning more about the strange new phenomenon he called the *odic force.* (Sometimes the term used was the *odyl* or just the *od.*) Reichenbach saw this force much as did Mesmer in the century before, and as would Reich a century later. It was a transparent weightless universal fluid permeating everything, but difficult to detect or measure. Under conditions of complete darkness certain especially sensitive subjects could see it around the poles of magnets and certain crystals, as well as around living plants and animals. Reichenbach's "sensitives" thus became his instrument for investigating and measuring the life force. This never "caught on" in the scientific community, though Reich did something very similar, using a darkroom to himself observe "orgone energy" phenomena. The widespread use of magnets and crystals, copper bracelets, etc. for supposed health benefits owes directly to Reichenbach.

- Vital Force[1] (The "vitalism" of Hans Dreisch, Henri Bergson and others in the 19th and 20th centuries)
    - ~ Vitalism is different from the life force concepts in Mesmer, Reichenbach, Reich and Kelley.
    - ~ There is a lack of a clear physical expression of the action of a life force in vitalism.

Vitalism is mostly a philosophic movement that arose in opposition to the rise of mechanistic scientistic thought with the decline of religious authority. The "vital force" of the vitalists is not a physically investigatable force but a principle expressed in the writings of vitalists. As a principle it lacked physical expression through devices or observable and falsifiable experiments and procedures.

---

[1] For reading on the issues involved in vitalism, I recommend especially:
Jonas, Hans (1966) THE PHENOMENON OF LIFE. New York: Harper and Row; and
McDougal, Wm. (1911) BODY AND MIND. London: Methuen & Co. Republished by Beacon Press, Boston, 1961.

EARLY REICHIAN DISCOVERIES

- <u>Muscular Armor</u> (Wilhelm Reich, early period 1920-33)
    - ~ Reich's discovery of the muscular armor
    - ~ Muscular armor, character armor, and the mind-body problem
    - ~ Muscular armor and evil

Reich's discovery of the muscular armor was the single most important step in the solution to the mind-body problem. The solution came out of his close observation of the body processes and emotional expression of patients in his psychoanalytic practice. Reich quickly learned that a patient's process, how he expressed himself, was more important than what he actually said. The chronic muscular tensions that made up the armor blocked threatening or otherwise unwanted emotions and thoughts. The tensions were objective and physical, the emotions and thoughts were subjective and mental or conscious, in the large sense of these words. That was the mind-body connection.

Reich became a skilled engineer of the human body, able to read character and personality from the muscular armor. He saw the armor as the mechanism of defense, a disease process, and the cause of mental disorders and disturbances. He saw it also as a social process, creating tremendously damaging patterns of disease and distortion of life processes in masses of people. He saw the armor as evil and the removal of the armor in adults and prevention of its formation in children as the primary task of the body psychology that he founded. Creating relatively armor-free individuals and groups became the objective of his work, the pathway to a more sane and humane society.

- <u>Orgone Energy</u> (Wilhelm Reich, middle period 1932-49)
    - ~ libido, bioelectricity, bioenergy, and orgone energy
    - ~ the life force: pulsation, charge and discharge in orgasm

- sex economy and the orgasm formula
- Reichian devices and instruments: the orgone energy accumulator (ORAC), orgone energy field meter

Reich wanted to believe that he had discovered the life force, his "orgone energy," but he did not make the discovery. The life force, as we know, had a long history of discoverers before Reich came on the scene. Reich's own life force concept went through years of development. Starting with Freud's libido, Reich explored bio-electric conceptions of the life force that suggested themselves to him from his bioelectric psychophysiologic studies of pleasure, anxiety, and sexuality. Ultimately he found that "bioelectric" life force concepts did not work and he progressed to calling it bioenergy, and finally, orgone energy. This leads in to his extraordinary and poorly understood late discoveries about the life force.

- <u>Orgone Energy</u> (Wilhelm Reich, late period 1951-55)
    - The Oranur experiment and its ramifications
    - DOR, oranur, Reich's modified Geiger Counter
    - Superimposition; Reich's cosmology
    - Reich's cloudbuster and weather control work
    - The creation of matter

Reich's most significant discoveries about the life force took place in the last years of his life, in the midst of extraordinary disruptions and confusions. The oranur experiment took place, in which the combination of nuclear radiation and orgone energy rendered Reich's living and working quarters uninhabitable. The vicious persecution of Reich by the Food and Drug Administration was in progress. It culminated in Reich's imprisonment and death. Reich discovered the "lower to higher" direction of movement, the "negative entropy" of the life force. His most important and exciting scientific work with the life force was unfolding. There was Reich's steady-state cosmology, explaining the production of galaxies through superimposition of two cosmic streams of the life force. There was the beginning of control over atmospheric processes through the life force (weather control). Successful preliminary experiments were made in the creation of new matter. These were the matters occupying Reich's attention during these busy years. It was the too-brief flowering of Reich's greatest work, brought to a premature end by action of the United States government.

POST-REICHIAN PERIOD

- <u>Why There Is a Muscular Armor</u> (Chuck Kelley, period 1965-74)
    - ~ Ayn Rand and the armored hero figure
    - ~ Theodule Ribot and voluntary attention
    - ~ The radix block and the positive value of muscular armor
    - ~ Dearmoring and the radix block

Finding why there was a muscular armor led to my first major discovery about the life force. Learning the positive value of armor caused me to split off from Reich and Orgonomy, and to focus on my own concept of the life force, the *radix*, from this time on, and to acknowledge the positive value of the patterns of chronic muscular tension that I had always before called the muscular armor. I would hereafter refer to them as the *radix block* when their expression was clearly positive, and I would call my own form of personal growth work "Radix."

- <u>The Radix Process as the Heart of the Creative Process in Nature</u> (Kelley, period 1970-75)
    - ~ Pulsation, charge and discharge as radix metabolism
    - ~ The creation of mind and of new energy in radix discharge

- Creation of new energy vs. negative entropy in the building of radix charge. (Radix and the "laws" of thermodynamics)

Of all my discoveries about the life force, perhaps the most important was the realization that the discharge of radix charge simultaneously created "mind" (consciousness) and energy in the universe. This was the creative process unveiled. We still have everything to learn about the nature and ramifications of this process, but the discovery and elucidation of the nature of the process is, I believe, solid, and is my central discovery.

- Centering, Source, Self, and Soul: The Radix of Individuation (Kelley, period 1990 – present)[1]
  - Radix sources as those places where radix charge enters the familiar universe in the form of space, producing the expansion of the universe.
  - Radix sources as the bases of each individual consciousness, of self or soul.
  - The geometry of the radix source, its root at its center of lowest charge, its movement outward in all directions, toward higher charge.
- Superimposition and Sources (Kelley, period 1997-2000)

The new work on sources makes it appear that the creative process may always have roots in two sources of radix charge which flow together in convergence, superimposition and discharge.

If this is true, understanding the creative process will require that we focus on this two-ness, two-parent sources, giving birth to radix streams which gather their charge, build and flow together

---

[1] This work on source and individuation is so new that the first published work on it is this book. Discussions of these points were made during the '90's, however, in our Kelley/Radix correspondence course *Science and the Life Force*. Vancouver, WA: K/R Publications.

toward superimposition. Does this mean there must always be two? Is the creative process never singular, but always at least seeded by the radix flow from a second source?

And what of our sources? If new radix charge first appears moving through an individual source from the unseen universal substratum, taking the form of space and expanding the familiar universe by its presence, does the new radix charge not only produce space, but also inertial forces, the potential for work?

- <u>Radix Algebra</u> (Kelley, period 1974-83)
    - ~ Formal description of radix processes through a new means of representation.
    - ~ Application of radix algebra to life processes, to the emotions, and to purposive human activity.

Radix algebra provides a technique for representing and organizing radix processes that goes beyond word language. Ideas correctly expressed in radix algebra describe radix processes with a precision and elegance word language cannot match.

- <u>Radix as a New Paradigm of Knowledge</u> (Kelley, period 1990-present)
    - ~ Radix as a concept of the nature of things, of the world and of the self, with profound spiritual/religious and scientific implications.
    - ~ The radix view of body, mind and spirit and their relationship.
    - ~ The radix view of creation; consciousness and the physical world arising through the radix process.
    - ~ The radix view of human evolution; the birth of morality through the dawning awareness of the self and of moral alternatives.
    - ~ Autonomy as the direction of human social evolution.

The concepts of radix are radical. If correct they will gradually usher in a revolution in science and religion, a new paradigm. In science, radix brings in the idea that the law of conservation of energy is incorrect, and that new energy is being created all the time through the radix process. In religion, radix rejects the idea of god as a superperson pulling the strings of the universe. Radix holds that there is a universal substratum of the universe, out of which the familiar world we know and see arises, and back to which it must eventually return. We call this universal ocean the "radix substratum." The process in which physical energy and mind or consciousness are simultaneously created from the substratum we call the "radix process."

In radix personal growth work, the processes by which energy and life, feeling, thought and mind, are created are observed, understood and worked with. Through experience with the human body, knowledge about the workings of the radix is learned. What is learned in working with the human body and mind has showed to have application to every level of radix process.

****

Chuck Kelley
2004

BIBLIOGRAPHY

Allison, Nancy (Ed.) 1999. THE ILLUSTRATED ENCYCLOPEDIA OF BODY-MIND DISCIPLINES. New York: Rosen Publishing Group.

Annals of the Orgone Institute. Volume 1. New York: Orgone Institute Press, 1947.

Bar-Levav, Reuven, 1995, EVERY FAMILY NEEDS A C.E.O. Detroit, MI: Fathering, Inc. Press.

_____, 1988, THINKING IN THE SHADOW OF FEELING. New York: Simon and Schuster.

_____, 1977, "The treatment of preverbal hunger and rage in a group." *International Journal of Group Psychotherapy,* Vol. 27, No. 4. New York: International Universities Press, 1977.

Bean, Orson, 1971, ME AND THE ORGONE. New York: St. Martin's Press.

Boadella, David, 1970 to present, *Energy and Character* (Ed.), Dorset, U.K.: Abbotsbury Publications.

_____, 1976, IN THE WAKE OF REICH (Ed.), London, U.K.: Coventure Ltd. Reprinted Boston, Mass: Coventure Ltd. 1991.

_____, 1973, WILHELM REICH: THE EVOLUTION OF HIS WORK. Chicago, IL: Henry Regnery Co.

Branden, Nathaniel, 1997, THE ART OF LIVING CONSCIOUSLY. New York: Simon & Schuster.

_____, 1996, TAKING RESPONSIBILITY: SELF-RELIANCE AND THE ACCOUNTABLE LIFE. New York: Simon & Schuster.

_____, 1994, THE SIX PILLARS OF SELF ESTEEM. New York: Simon & Schuster.

_____, 1973, THE DISOWNED SELF. New York: Bantam.

_____, 1971, THE PSYCHOLOGY OF SELF ESTEEM. New York: Bantam.

Darwin, C., 1872. THE EXPRESSION OF THE EMOTIONS IN MAN AND IN ANIMALS. London: John Murray. Reprinted in 1965 by the University of Chicago Press.

DeMeo, James, 1998, SAHARASIA: THE REVOLUTIONARY DISCOVERY OF A GEOGRAPHIC BASIS TO HUMAN BEHAVIOR. Greensprings, OR: Orgone Biophysical Research Lab. Website: http://id.mind.net/community/orgonelab.htm

_____, *Pulse of the Planet* (Ed.) Ashland, OR: Orgone Biophysical Research Lab.

Eysenck, H.J. and Nins, D.K.B., 1982. ASTROLOGY: SCIENCE OR SUPERSTITION. New York: Penguin Books.
Gallert, Mark C., 1962, "Dr. Littlefield on Bio-Genesis." **The Creative Process**, Vol. 7, Nos. 3 & 4. Vancouver, WA: K/R Publications.
Greenfield, J., 1974, WILHELM REICH VS. THE U.S.A. New York: W.W. Norton & Co..
Hoffer, Eric, 1951, THE TRUE BELIEVER. New York: Harper & Row.
Hoyle, F., 1957, FRONTIERS OF ASTRONOMY. New York: Mentor Books.
Janzen, R., 2001, THE RISE AND FALL OF SYNANON: A CALIFORNIA UTOPIA. Baltimore, MD: Johns Hopkins University Press.
Jonas, Hans, 1966, THE PHENOMENON OF LIFE. New York: Harper and Row.
Journal or Orgonomy. American College of Orgonomy. Princeton: New Jersey.
Kelley, C.R., 2004 2nd Edition, 1989, THE MAKING OF CHICKENS AND OF EAGLES.
_____, 1992, THE RADIX, VOL. I: RADIX PERSONAL GROWTH WORK, VOL. II: THE SCIENCE OF RADIX PROCESSES. A compilation of Kelley's writings from the sixties to the nineties.
_____, 1990, *Sheldrake and Morphic Resonance* in **Chuck Kelley's Radix Newsletter**, No. 6.
_____, 1978-1983, **The Radix Journal**, Vols. I (1-4), II ((1-4), III (1-2).
_____, 1983, *Radix Devices*, in **The Radix Journal**, Vol. III No. 2. Reprinted in THE RADIX: VOL. II, 1992.
_____, 1980 and 1982, *Meditations of a Pain Blocker*, in **The Radix Journal**, Vols. II, Nos. 2&3, and III, No. 1. Most were reprinted in THE RADIX: VOL. I, 1992.
_____, 1980, *Radix Physics: Space, Time and the Derivative Shift*. In **The Radix Journal** Vol. 11 Nos. 3&4. Reprinted in THE RADIX VOL. II, 1992, p.33.
_____, 1980, *Radix Physics: Radix Processes, Radix Systems and the Problem of Measurement*. From **The Radix Journal**, Vol. II Nos. 1 & 2. Reprinted in THE RADIX: VOL. II, 1992.
_____, 1980, *The Radix Algebra of the Feelings*, in **The Radix Journal**, Vol. II No. 1&2, and *The Radix Algebra of Purpose*, in **The Radix Journal** Vol. II Nos. 3&4. Both reprinted with the original article *Radix Algebra* in Kelley, C.R., 1992, THE RADIX VOL. II.
_____, 1979, *The Radix Charge of Living Places*, in **The Radix Journal** Vol. 1 No. 4; Reprinted in THE RADIX VOL. II, 1992.
_____, 1972, "Mechanism in Scientific Thought," an invited "New Fellow" address to the Society of Engineering Psychologists, Division 21 of the American Psychological Association Convention, Honolulu, Hawaii, September 2, 1972.
_____, 1972, *Post Primal and Genital Character: A Critique of Janov and Reich*, *Journal of Humanistic Psychology*, Vol. 12 No. 2, Fall 1972. First printed by Kelley/Radix Publications as "Primal Scream and Genital Character."

_____, 1970, revised 1974, EDUCATION IN FEELING AND PURPOSE. In THE RADIX, VOL. I, 1992.

_____, 1965, *Orgonomy Since the Death of Reich.* **The Creative Process**, the whole of Volume 5.

_____, 1960-1965, **The Creative Process** (Ed.), Vols. I-V.

_____, 1962, *What Is Orgone Energy?* **The Creative Process**, Vol. II Nos. 2&3.

_____, 1960, "The Ending of Wilhelm Reich's Researches," Interscience Research Institute Technical Report.

_____, et al, 1961, *The Origin of Armoring,* **The Creative Process**, Vol. I No. 2, p. 104.

_____, 1961. A NEW METHOD OF WEATHER CONTROL. Technical Report 60-1. Also published in German, "Eine Neue Methode der Wetterkontrolle."

_____, 1958. PSYCHOLOGICAL FACTORS IN MYOPIA, Ph.D. dissertation. New York, N.Y. The New School for Social Research.

_____, 1955, *Orgone Energy and Weather,* in CORE, Vol. 7 pp. 54-67.

_____, 1952, *Causality and Freedom: A Functional Analysis.* **Orgone Energy Bulletin,** Vol. IV No. 1.

(All of Kelley's publications are available from K/R Publications, 917 Topeka Lane, Vancouver, WA 98664)

Lin, Henry B., 2000. THE ART AND SCIENCE OF FENG SHUI. St. Paul, Minnesota: Llewellen Publications.

Mann, Felix M.B., 1962, 1973. ACUPUNCTURE: THE ANCIENT CHINESE ART OF HEALING AND HOW IT WORKS SCIENTIFICALLY. New York: Random House. Reprinted by Vintage Books.

Margoshes, Adam, 1961, *Dor in Spain.* **The Creative Process**, Vol I No. 2. Vancouver, WA: K/R Publications.

Mesmer, F.A. (1957) MEMOIR. Mount Vernon, N.Y.: The Eden Press. Translated, and with a preface by Jerome Eden. The Memoir was first published in France in 1799. Eden's translation is out of print.

Mitchell, Meredith B., 1964, *Reich's Theory of Armor,* in **The Creative Process**, Vol. III No. 2, March. Also Kelley, C. R. 1978, *Basic Concepts in Radix Feeling Work* **The Radix Journal,** Vol. I No. 1, Fall. Vancouver, WA: K/R Publications.

Orgonomic Functionalism. Rangeley, Maine: Wilhelm Reich Infant Trust Fund.

Orgonomic Functionalism. Seven volumes of six numbers each. Nottingham, England: The Ritter Press, 1954-62.

Orgonomic Medicine. One and one-half volumes (three issues total). New York: American Association for Medical Orgonomy, 1954-55.

P.O.R.E. (Public Orgonomic Research Exchange). Website: http://www.orgone.org. E-mail: pore@orgone.org.

Rand, Ayn, 1964, THE VIRTUE OF SELFISHNESS. New York: The American

Library of World Literature, Inc.
_____, 1961, FOR THE NEW INTELLECTUAL. New York: Random House.
_____, 1959, WE THE LIVING. New York: Random House, 1959.
_____, 1957, ATLAS SHRUGGED. New York: Random House.
_____, 1946, ANTHEM. Idaho: Caxton Printers.
_____, 1943, THE FOUNTAINHEAD. New York: Bobbs-Merrill.
(All of Ayn Rand's works have been reprinted as Signet books by the New American Library.)

Reich, Wilhelm, 1955. *The Source of the Human 'No'*. From the Archives of the Orgone Institute in *Orgonomic Medicine*, Vol. I, No. 2.
_____, 1955, Melanor, Orite, Brownite and Orene, in **CORE**, Vol. 7, Nos. 1-2, pp. 29-31.
_____, 1954, "OROP Desert," **C.O.R.E.** Vol. VI Nos. 1-4, pp. 1-140.
_____, 1953, THE MURDER OF CHRIST. Rangeley, Maine: Orgone Institute Press.
_____, 1952, "DOR Removal and Cloudbusting: Preliminary Communication." **Orgone Energy Bulletin.** Vol. IV No. 4, pp. 171-182, October.
_____, 1951, *The Oranur Experiment*, First published in Vol. III No. 4, **Orgone Energy Bulletin**, pp. 185-341. Rangeley, Maine: The Wilhelm Reich Foundation. Reprinted in part in Reich, W., 1961, SELECTED WRITINGS. New York: Noonday Press 1961.
_____, 1951, COSMIC SUPERIMPOSITION. New York: Orgone Institute Press. Reissued by Farrar, Straus & Giroux, 1973.
_____, 1950, *Orgonometric Equations: 1. General Form*, in **Orgone Energy Bulletin**, Vol. II No. 4, pp. 161-183; and 1951, *Complete Orgonometric Equations*, in **Orgone Energy Bulletin**, Vol. III No. 2, pp. 65-71.
_____, 1949, CHARACTER ANALYSIS (3rd enlarged edition). New York: Orgone Institute Press.
_____, 1949, ETHER GOD AND DEVIL. New York: Orgone Institute Press. Reprinted by Farrar, Straus & Giroux, 1973.
_____, 1948, THE CANCER BIOPATHY (VOL. 2 of THE DISCOVERY OF THE ORGONE). New York: Orgone Institute Press.
_____, 1946, THE MASS PSYCHOLOGY OF FASCISM (Third, revised and enlarged edition). New York: Orgone Institute Press.
_____, 1945, THE SEXUAL REVOLUTION. New York: Orgone Institute Press.
_____, 1942-55, **Annals of the Orgone Institute, International Journal of Sex-Economy and Orgone Research, Orgone Energy Bulletin**, and **Core**. Available on microfilm from Rangeley, Maine: Wilhelm Reich Museum..

Reichenbach, Karl Von, 1851, PHYSICO-PHYSIOLOGICAL RESEARCHES. London: Hippolyte Bailliere.
Ribot, T.A., 1890 in French, THE PSYCHOLOGY OF ATTENTION. Republished in English by Marcell Rodd, New York, 1946.

Ritter, Paul and Jean, undated (pre-1962), "Experiments with the orgone accumulator." Nottingham, England: The Ritter Press, 7 Magdala Rd.,
Schroedinger, E., 1945, WHAT IS LIFE. New York: The Macmillan Co.
Shapiro, Mark. *Mesmer, Reich and the Living Process, The Creative Process*, Vol. IV No. 2, June 1965, pp. 64-71. Vancouver, WA: K/R Publications.
Sharaf, Myron, 1983, FURY ON EARTH. New York: St. Martin's Press/Marek.
Sheldrake, R., 1988, THE PRESENCE OF THE PAST: MORPHIC RESONANCE AND THE HABITS OF NATURE. New York: Random House. (Reprinted by First Vintage Books, 1989)
_____, 1981 and 1985, A NEW SCIENCE OF LIFE: THE HYPOTHESIS OF FORMATIVE CAUSATION. London: Blond & Briggs.
Starz, Kenneth, 1963-65, *The Researches of Karl (Charles) Von Reichenbach*, in *The Creative Process*, Part 1. Vol. III No. 1, August 1963, Part 2, Vol. III No. 2, March 1964, Part 3, Vol. IV No. 2, June 1965.
_____, 1962, "The Effect of the Orgone Energy Accumulator on Air Temperature." In *The Creative Process*, Vol. 2 No. 4. Vancouver, WA: K/R Publications.
Szasz, Thomas S, 1985, CEREMONIAL CHEMISTRY. Holmes Beach, FLA: Learning Publications, Inc.
_____, 1961, THE MYTH OF MENTAL ILLNESS. New York: Hoeber-Harper.
Wallnöfer, Heinrich and Von Rottauscher, Anna. (1965) CHINESE FOLK MEDICINE AND ACUPUNCTURE. New York: Bell Publishing Co.

INDEX

acupuncture, *4, 44, 230*
Adam and Eve, *12, 29, 60, 186, 190*
antithesis, *133, 219*
balance
   of charge and discharge, *120*
   of feeling and purpose, *86, 87*
Bar-Levav, Reuven, *88*
Bates, William H., *31, 55, 62*
Bergson, Henri, *5, 216*
big bang, *12, 29, 208*
big crunch, *208, 212*
Branden, Nathaniel, *88*
Bruno, Giordano, *16, 190*
chi, *xi, 4, 34, 225*
child people, *193*
cloudbuster, *44, 229*
co-confidant work, *103*
collectivism, *200*
Corbett, Margaret D., *55, 123*
cosmic voids, *172*
cosmology, *12, 34, 210*
creation myths, *209*
cyclogenesis, *176*
dark matter, *207*
dependency, *101*
diseases, *72*
DOR, *235*
DOR (deadly orgone), *251*
Driesch, Hans, *5, 216*
Einstein, Albert, *213, 220*
energy, *217*
entropy, *116, 127, 128, 209, 215*
evolution
   of anticipation, *145*
   of knowledge, *xi*

   of purpose, *187*
   social vs. biological, *186*
Federal Food and Drug Administration, *44*
Feldenkrais, Moshe, *123*
Feng Shui, *4, 44, 230*
Freedom of the will, *25, 43, 128*
Freud, Sigmund, *5, 29, 32*
fundamentalism, *19*
galaxy, *173*
Galileo, *16, 190*
genital character, *35*
God, *210*
Gold, Bondi and Hoyle, *211*
government, *15, 16, 20, 72, 187, 189, 193*
gravity, *206*
guarding function, *19, 44, 45, 189*
Hoffer, Eric, *189*
instroke, *119, 137, 148, 157*
integration, *108*
Jesus, *25*
Jonas, Hans, *11, 130*
Littlefield, Dr. Charles, *5*
MacDougall, William, *5*
mating, *203*
   atmospheric, *178*
   by animals, *180*
   human, *172*
memories, *109*
Mesmer, Franz Anton, *4, 129, 215, 230*
Michael Servetus, *190*
Newton, Sir Isaac, *138, 207, 220*
orgasm formula, *114*

Orgone Accumulator, 235
Orgone Therapy, 31, 38
original sin, 189
outstroke, 119, 122, 137, 148
parent people, 193
perception
    and Radix vision, 161
    and sensations, 141
    visual, 32, 74
portal, 204
prana, 4
protect mode, 144
psychosomatic identity, 133
radix source, 139, 153, 158, 201
radix substratum, 139, 158, 167, 203
Radix Vision, 161
Rainmaking, 232, 235
Rand, Ayn, 51, 62, 187
Reich, Wilhelm
    and 'chickens', 71
    and 'energy', *xi*
    and cosmology, 129
    and id-knowledge, 166
    and mysticism and mechanism, 23
    and orgone energy, 5
    and pre-atomic matter, 214
    and superimposition, 180
    and 'too muchness', 2
    his legacy, 29
    Infant Trust Fund, 37
Reichenbach, Karl von, 5, 129, 215, 230
Ribot, Theodule, 55
Sheldrake, Rupert, 218
soul, xi, 1, 14, 18, 22, 167
spiral galaxy, 178
superimposition
    of radix charges, 68
Synanon, 88
technology, 26
time
    as a concept, 220
venture mode, 144
violence, 19, 20, 41, 73, 90
vision, 62
    'radix vision', 161
    and feeling, 74
    improvement, 55, 123
    long-range, 74
voluntary attention, 56
weather, 174, 229
weird science, 231
White, George Starr, 5

B-1
- Lift
- Shower

A - floor I
Admission